# Family Violence and Men of Color

## Healing the Wounded Male Spirit

**SECOND EDITION**

# Family Violence and Men of Color

*Healing the Wounded
Male Spirit*

SECOND EDITION

RICARDO CARRILLO, PhD

JERRY TELLO, MS

EDITORS

SPRINGER PUBLISHING COMPANY

New York

**Ricardo Carrillo, PhD,** maintains a private practice in Visalia and Fresno, California, as a clinical forensic psychologist. He is currently conducting policy research for the California Endowment on disparities in Latino Mental Health. He is the Director of Training and Technical Assistance for the National Compadres Network, Inc. He is the executive director of Primer Paso Institute, Inc., a Latino behavioral health organization serving rural communities in the areas of substance abuse, mental health, and domestic violence.

He has served as Director of Latino Mental Health for Kaweah Delta Health Care District and is most recognized as an expert witness and international consultant in the areas of family therapy, domestic violence, cross-cultural psychology, forensic psychology, and cultural competence. He has provided leadership in the areas of program development with domestic violence offenders, Latino mental health, and chemical dependency populations. He has 15 years of recovery and stems from several generations of addicts.

Dr. Carrillo enjoys the performing and culinary arts. He is the father of Regina and Reynaldo, and grandfather to David Valenzuela Preciado and Micah Daniel Preciado. He is the co-founder of the Latino Men's Circle, which is dedicated to living as noble men, and is an advisory board member of the National Latino Compadres network and the National Latino Fatherhood Institute.

**Jerry Tello, MS,** comes from a family of Mexican and Texan roots and was raised in south central Los Angeles. He is co-founder of the National Compadres Network, founding member of ALIANZA, the National Latino Alliance to Eliminate Domestic Violence, and the Director of the National Latino Fatherhood and Family Institute. He is an internationally recognized expert in the areas of family strengthening, community mobilization, and culturally based violence prevention/intervention issues. He has extensive experience in the treatment of victims and perpetrators of abuse and in addictive behaviors, with a specialization in working with multi-ethnic populations.

Mr. Tello is the author of various curricula including a Male "Rites of Passage," a Young Fatherhood Curriculum, a bilingual Family Strengthening curriculum, and a bilingual Fatherhood Literacy Curriculum, and he has served as a principal consultant for Scholastic Books on an International Bilingual Literacy curriculum. In addition, Mr. Tello has authored a series of children's books and co-edited the first edition of this book. He has appeared in *Time*, *Newsweek*, and various Hispanic magazines, and in April 1996, Mr. Tello received the Presidential Crime Victims Service award, which was presented to him by President Bill Clinton and Attorney General Janet Reno. In June 1997 he received the Ambassador of Peace award from Rotary International.

Mr. Tello is presently the Director of the Sacred Circles Healing Center in Whittier, California, and is a member of the Sacred Circles performance group, a group dedicated to family/community peace and healing. He is also the proud father of three children: Marcos, Renee, and Emilio.

Springer Publishing Company, LLC
11 West 42nd Street
New York, NY 10036
www.springerpub.com

*Acquisitions Editor: Jennifer Perillo*
*Production Manager: Kelly Applegate*
*Cover design: Mimi Flow*
*Composition: Publication Services, Inc.*

0 9 10 11/5 4 3 2 1

**Library of Congress Cataloging-in-Publication Data**

Family violence and men of color: healing the wounded male spirit / Ricardo Carrillo, Jerry Tello, [editors].
    p. cm.
Includes index.
ISBN 978-0-8261-1178-4 (hardcover)
1. Family violence—United States—Cross-cultural studies.  2. Abusive men—United States—Cross-cultural studies.  3. African American men—Psychology.
4. African American men—Attitudes.  I. Carrillo, Ricardo.  II. Tello, Jerry.
HV6626.52.F35 2008
362.84'96073—dc22

2008017848

Printed in the United States of America by Bang Printing

# Dedication

To my mother, Guadalupe Chavez, the first survivor of domestic violence; mi compañera, Stella Botello; mis hijos, Regina Carrillo Preciado and Reynaldo Antonio Carrillo; my grandchildren, David Valenzuela Preciado and Micha Daniel Preciado; my brother, Arturo Carrillo, who showed me the true meaning of *Canalismo* (or "I got your back, bro"); to all the men, women, children, grandchildren, and elders who have given us the language, consejos (counsel), and huizo (wisdom) to help men and their families heal from domestic violence, substance abuse, and intergenerational trauma. To the communities around the world that have shared their view of family violence and their particular approaches to healing their communities. To the healers within and around us all, we are grateful for your blessings, lessons, love, and cariño.

Ometeolt, Ricardo Antonio Enrique Carrillo Chavez Santiesteban

To the ancestors, elders, and wisdom carriers for preserving the teachings and medicine that allow us to heal and find balance in our lives.

To CALMECAC, the Circulo de Hombres, and Sacred Circles for their wisdom, ceremony, guidance, and support.

To all those who have come to me seeking counsel and healing, I give thanks to them for their trust and teachings.

To Maestro Jose Montoya, Maestra Adelina Padilla, Ricardo Carrillo, Susanna Armijo, Citlali Arvizu, Atil and Reena, ALIANZA Board members, the brothers and sisters at NLFFI, and all those Joven Noble, Cara y Corazon maestros for the leadership, guidance, and dedication, to this work.

To my children, Emilio, Renee, and Marcos; to Gloria, George, Veronica, John, Bobby, and the rest of the familia; to my Dad, Jorge Tello; and finally . . .

I truly dedicate this to my MOM, Maria de Jesus "Jessie" Olague Ramos for all the sacrifice and her example of unconditional love and survival.

With humbleness and gratitude to all the above and everyone who has touched my life I dedicate this work.

Con Dios, Tlazocamati, Jerry Tello

# Contents

# Contributors

**Etiony Aldarondo** is Associate Dean for Research and Director of the Center for Educational and Community Well-Being in the School of Education at the University of Miami. He is an experienced clinician, researcher, teacher, researcher, and social justice advocate. A recipient of various recognitions for academic excellence, he aims through his scholarship to promote both individual healing and social transformation. His publications include *Advancing Social Justice Through Clinical Practice* (Lawrence Erlbaum Associates) and *Programs for Men Who Batter: Intervention and Prevention Strategies in a Diverse Society* (Civic Research Institute with Fernando Mederos, EdD). Dr. Aldarondo currently serves on the boards of directors for the Council on Contemporary Families, the Melissa Institute for Violence Prevention and Treatment, and the National Latino Alliance for the Elimination of Domestic Violence.

**Michelle Castro-Fernandez** has a Master's degree in Mental Health Counseling and is completing a doctorate in counseling psychology at the University of Miami. Her research and clinical interests are in wellness promotion in ethnic minority children and families.

**Ulester Douglas, MSW,** is Director of Training for Men Stopping Violence. He is also a Certified Imago Relationship Therapist and has specialized training in working with individuals, families, and communities affected by violence. He provides consultation, training, and presentations to organizations, corporations, and governmental groups. He has authored and co-authored articles and curricula on family violence and other issues. Douglas has also been honored a number of times for his work to end violence against women. Among those honors are awards from Lifetime Television for Women and the National Network to End Domestic Violence (NNEDV) in 2003 and the National Black Herstory Task Force Comrade Award in 2004.

**Bonnie Duran, DrPH,** is an Associate Professor in the Department of Health Services, University of Washington School of Public Health and Community Medicine, and is also a Director at the Indigenous Wellness Research Institute. Her research is focused on alcohol, drug, and mental disorder services and prevention and social determinants such as historical trauma, violence, and cultural and spiritual protective factors. Bonnie has worked in public health practice, research, and education for over 30 years.

**Eduardo Duran, PhD,** has worked and continues to work as a clinician, administrator, researcher, and theoretician in Indian country. He has developed and implemented a rural Indian mental health clinic in central California as well as an urban clinic in

Oakland and one in Albuquerque, New Mexico. He has written several articles in the area of mental health theory as well as the recent book *Native American Postcolonial Psychology*, which he co-authored with his wife, Bonnie. Most of the theoretical underpinnings of Duran's work have to do with the legitimization of non-Western epistemologies as valid methods of clinical and research activity. Presently he is Senior Principal Investigator on a research project that is evaluating some of his theoretical work. Duran is also the director of Behavioral Services at First Nations Community Healthsource in Albuquerque. He lives in Colfax, California.

**Daryl Gregory, BA,** is from New Zealand. His tribal affiliations are Waikato and Hauraki. He is the founder and current Managing Director of He Waka Tapu, an indigenous (Māori) health and social service agency in Christchurch. He has extensive experience in working with Māori men and their families around relationship violence, sexual abuse, and alcohol and other drugs. His approach to these issues is focused on the healing of families through inviting men to look at traditional cultural practices that uplift the *mana* (prestige) of men, women, and children. Gregory has been married to Rosemary for 22 years, and they have a 14-year-old son, Miharo.

**Sulaiman Nuriddin, MEd,** is Men's Education Program Manager. He began working with Men Stopping Violence in 1987 after completing the year-long internship program. He currently oversees educational interventions for MSV. He is also a Certified Imago Educator. Nuriddin works intensively with the DeKalb County court system, intervening with men who have been arrested for domestic violence. He coinstructs ongoing classes for men and has been instrumental in planning effective interventions with men of color who batter. He has conducted training for such organizations as the National Council of Churches, the U.S. Department of Justice, the Atlanta Police Department, the Institute on Domestic Violence in the African-American Community, and the National Organization of Black Law Enforcement Executives. He also has led trainings at Clark Atlanta University, and Morehouse and Spelman Colleges.

**Phyllis Alesia Perry, BA,** is Communications Coordinator for Men Stopping Violence. She is responsible for producing written materials for a variety of purposes, including education, marketing, and information dissemination. She co-authored the curriculum "Men at Work: Building Safe Communities." Perry has worked as a writer and editor for more than 25 years, most of that time as a print journalist. She has also written two novels: *Stigmata* (1998) and *A Sunday in June* (2004), and has been anthologized in *Step Into a World: A Global Anthology of New Black Literature* (2001); *Shaking the Tree: A Collection of New Fiction and Memoir by Black Women* (2004); and *The Remembered Gate: Memoirs by Alabama Writers* (2002).

**Benjamin R. Tong, PhD,** is a Professor of Clinical Psychology with the PsyD Program at the California Institute of Integral Studies, San Francisco; Faculty Emeritus of the Asian American Studies Department, San Francisco State University; Executive Director at the Institute for Cross-Cultural Research, San Francisco; psychotherapist and mind/body health consultant in private practice; Director and Head Instructor at the School of Taoist Internal Arts. Among other pursuits, he is currently conducting group therapy/healing retreats for adult survivors of clergy sexual abuse. Further information can be found at his Web site, http://drbenjaminrtong.com.

**Lee Mun Wah** is a 49-year-old Chinese American community therapist practicing in Berkeley, California. For the past 10 years he has been the founder and facilitator of an Asian Men's Group and a Multicultural Men's Group dealing with racism, intimate anger, and the development of community leadership. He is a poet, filmmaker (*Stolen Ground* and *Color of Fear),* and director of Stir Fry Productions, which deals with the dynamics of developing a multicultural community in social agencies, businesses, and schools.

**Oliver J. Williams, PhD,** is Executive Director of the Institute on Domestic Violence in the African American Community and a Professor in the School of Social Work at the University of Minnesota in St. Paul. He is also the Director of the Safe Return Initiative, which addresses the issues of prisoner reentry and domestic violence. He has worked in the field of domestic violence for more than 29 years. Dr. Williams has worked in battered women's shelters, developed curricula for batterers' intervention programs, and facilitated counseling groups in these programs. He has provided training across the United States and abroad on research and service delivery surrounding partner abuse. Dr. Williams's extensive research and publications in scholarly journals and books have centered on creating service delivery strategies to reduce violent behavior. Dr. Williams received a bachelor's degree in social work from Michigan State University; a master's in social work from Western Michigan University; and a master's in public health and a PhD in social work, both from the University of Pittsburgh.

**Pamela Woodis (Apache), MA,** is a therapist/coordinator at First Nations Community Healthsource in Albuquerque. She received her master's degree from the University of New Mexico and her undergraduate degree from Fort Lewis College in Durango, Colorado. She is a member of the Jicarilla Apache tribe and has worked with the tribe as a counselor. Pam spent her early years living with the Dine' in Shiprock, New Mexico, and her present work is serving urban Indian families and children who include Indians from many tribes.

**Wilbur Woodis, MA,** Dine' (Navajo) Mud Clan (Hasht'ishnii) and born into the Zuni Clan (Naasht'ézhí Dine'é), was the fourth-born of seven sisters and four brothers and was raised in Shiprock, located in Northwest New Mexico in the four corners area on the Navajo Reservation. He is married and has two children. His favorite pastime is reading books on the psychology and psychological treatment of the American Indians. He earned a master of arts degree in counseling and family studies at the University of New Mexico, and received the Outstanding Achievement Award, College of Education.

Wilbur is currently employed with the Office of Clinical and Preventive Services (OCPS) within the Division of Behavioral Health of the Indian Health Service Headquarters East. He has many roles at this national office, located just outside the Washington, DC, metropolitan area. He currently assists with the collaboration, coordination, and management of behavioral health information systems and prevention and treatment improvement activities, and works in partnership with other federal agencies in partnering to address American Indian/Alaska Native behavioral health issues. He was recently detailed to SAMHSA's CSAP for approximately two years, two days per week. He is most interested in culturally appropriate and sensitive behavioral health prevention, intervention, and treatment outcomes and benefits.

Mr. Woodis has also been project officer or active consultant on many national initiatives covering such topics as domestic violence, suicide, wellness, Headstart, men, gathering of Native Americans, postcolonial psychology, fetal alcohol syndrome, treatment drug courts, community health, and other behavioral health–related topics. He also has co-authored articles for publications.

Mr. Woodis has an extensive background in providing direct clinical services among this nation's indigenous tribal people. One of his goals is to learn what he can at the national level and return to his first love, which is providing counseling and help services to grassroots native healers and practitioners. He would someday like to write about interventions that involve the use of native healers in combating behavioral health and social illnesses.

He is always willing to help as best he can, and wants to travel around the world with his family as appropriate.

**Maria J. Zarza, PhD,** obtained her doctoral degree in psychology at the University of Madrid (2001). Dr. Zarza's pre-doctoral experience was earned at Rutgers, The New Jersey State University, and Womanspace, a nonprofit organization dedicated to support victims of intimate partner violence and sexual abuse. Dr. Zarza's doctoral dissertation was on treatment and prevention of domestic violence and the study of family violence risk factors such as substance abuse, co-occurring disorders, and trauma. Dr. Zarza has extensive experience providing development/program evaluation; organizational development; and education, prevention, and intervention services to improve minority women's health. Dr. Zarza has extensive knowledge as a practitioner, educator, and evaluator of minority women's health issues related to domestic violence, substance abuse, HIV/AIDS/STDs, and mental health. Program evaluation and capacity building experience include projects funded by the United Nations Office on Drugs and Crime, SAMHSA, and the Department of Health and Human Services. Dr. Zarza has received awards and recognition for her services to victims of abuse and for research with minorities. She is a Research Scientist Member of the National Hispanic Science Network on Drug Abuse, funded by NIDA, and a reviewer for a scientific journal. Dr. Zarza worked at the University of California, Los Angeles, with other colleagues on a capacity-building project funded by the United Nations Office on Drugs and Crime (UNODC) to provide training and capacity building on substance abuse treatment to 20 resource centers worldwide. She is currently in Spain working on research and implementing clinical programs on substance abuse and intimate partner violence and is collaborating with the United Nations in capacity building for substance abuse treatment centers.

# Acknowledgments

Acknowledgement/Permiso

We begin by giving thanks to the Creator for another day of life, another day of lessons, and another day to be able to serve.

We look to the WEST, the direction of the female spirit, where all life begins . . . those who are the givers of life, they lend us their breath, they give us their blood and their rhythm, our heartbeat in order that we could begin this journey. Our mothers, grandmothers, sisters, daughters, partners, friends, comadres . . . we give thanks and ask for their blessing, pray for their healing, and acknowledge their medicine.

En lak etch, el otro yo, the mirroring direction of the women, the EAST . . . the direction of the male spirit, the reflective spirit that creates life. Our fathers, grandfathers, brothers, sons, partners, friends, compadres . . . those who need these teachings to find balance, those who offer these teachings to promote healing and harmony . . . we give thanks for their blessing, pray for their healing, and acknowledge their medicine.

The direction of the SOUTH, that of the children, which resides between the West and the East . . . recognizing that whatever is created in relationship between the women and the men falls to their young spirits. The babies, those who are crawling, walking, talking, searching, learning; the adolescents who are imitating us and now questioning the lessons. Those in whom our wounds break generational cycles and who become our hope for the future. To the children we ask forgiveness, pray for healing, and dedicate this work.

And to the direction of the NORTH, where the elders sit. The ancestors and ancient ones carry the memories of who we really are when we are in balance . . . the medicine traditions and customs that guide us and offer us a way to heal . . . the carriers of all wisdom, the slow walkers, storytellers, medicine keepers, vision seekers . . . of them we ask for permission to offer this book, in hopes that it will further carry on their teachings.

As we look ABOVE, we give thanks to the sky elements of grandfather sun, grandmother moon, our wind creatures, and the elements that sustain our life . . . BELOW we give thanks to mother earth and sister ocean, who holds us, heals us, and feeds us on a daily basis. We give thanks finally to the seventh cardinal direction in the CENTER, where we all come together as one. The interconnected place where all people of all roots, all races come together . . . the center, heart filled with love, honor, and respect for all our relations, because if one of us hurts, we all hurt, but if one of us heals, we all heal.

To all our relations, in a very humble way, we ask for permission to offer these teachings and share these reflections as one element in the journey for all of us to be able to live in peace and harmony with ourselves and each other.

Aho, Con Dios, All Our Relations

# Introduction

*Family Violence and Men of Color* was conceived because the family violence literature was absent of color, and the question continues to arise: To what extent does culture contribute to domestic violence? What contributes to the violence in men of color specifically? We have found that race matters—historical roots of colonization have contributed significantly to the learning of violence as an accepted form of power, control, and learned oppression. Men of color continue to be ignored and institutionally discriminated against, and more barriers exist for the successful engagement and retention of men of color in treatment and prevention efforts. It is not enough to send men of color to traditional batterer intervention programs, jails, or institutions. It is necessary to address the social, political, psychological, and anthropological institutional factors that constitute the culture of domestic violence, and to change the culture itself—the culture from which those men stem, the culture that is designed to assist them in change, and the cultures that contribute to the use of violence as socially acceptable.

Our first endeavor was not complete. We did not have a theoretical or application chapter for each major community of color. In this second edition we have accomplished that goal. The research chapter, written by Etiony Aldorondo and Michelle Castro-Fernandez, views domestic violence from an international perspective, addresses the successes and failures of current methodologies for research and treatment of batterers, and ends with a cry for social justice.

Each and every one of the contributors has a special relationship to their respective communities: poets, musicians, actors/actresses, researchers, clinicians, theoreticians, and filmmakers. This is an attempt to bring the best to the reader. Domestic violence does cut across communities and is an equal opportunist; however, culturally competent approaches have taken time and effort to develop, and we showcase them here.

The Latino section has a rock-solid foundation in the pre-Columbian theory of childhood development, the impact of colonialization in the Americas, and the integration of Cara y Corazon (Face & Heart) for teaching about balance, rhythm, and harmony by Jerry Tello. The application section is an integrated model for co-occurring conditions of substance abuse and trauma, as well as for the cessation of domestic and community violence. The national Compadres model, El Hombre Noble Buscando Su Palabra (the noble man searching for his word), advocates for men to stand up against violence and mentor youth to prevent it.

The African American section is powerful, based on theory and practice principles as advocated by Oliver Williams. It takes a very political and social justice–oriented viewpoint on how ineffective criminal justice approaches have been for African American men, as discussed by the Atlanta, Georgia, group, Men Stopping Violence, represented by Ulester Douglas, Sulaiman Nuriddin, and Phyllis Alesia Perry. This chapter also traces the effects of slavery and freedom on domestic violence in the African American community.

The Native American section, spearheaded by Eduardo Duran, Bonnie Duran, Wilbur Woodis, and Pamela Woodis, views domestic violence from a postcolonial position. The applications chapter is new and comes from New Zealand. Daryl Gregory posits the Māori perspective of rebuilding a nation with the entire community involved, as in the building of the sacred canoe, preparing for the journey of life. The metaphor of traveling long distances and planning what type of life one will lead is the foundation for healing from violent colonialization.

Finally, the Asian American section, mentored by scholar Benjamin Tong, gives us his view of the philosophies of oppression, migration, adaptation difficulties, racist oppression, and repressive heritage that contribute to domestic violence in the Asian community. Filmmaker Lee Mun Wah, through the lenses of his own experience, gives us practical clinical interventions that are as useful for all treatment providers today as they were then.

We embark on this journey, as Daryl Gregory states:

> He Waka Tapu, literally translated, means "a sacred vessel." *Whānau* (families) are invited to come on a journey of exploration, to discover new pathways, and to reach for horizons that have only been a far-off dream. The *wero*, or challenge, laid before men and their *whānau* is to consider what our *tūpuna* (ancestors) had to do in preparing to cross the vast Pacific Ocean, *Te Moana nui a Kiwa*, and reach Aotearoa safely, equipped to begin a new life.

We invite participants to consider that the *waka* that will carry them and their *tamariki* (children) into the future is the *whānau*. To ensure that they will reach that far-off horizon, to ensure that the dreams and visions of *tūpuna* for their *mokopuna* (grandchildren) are realized, *whānau* must ensure that the *waka* they build are seaworthy enough to face the challenges that lie before them."

We invite you to join us in our journey to help men heal, to stand up against the learned oppression in their respective four directions, pray to the ancestors for guidance, and finally to ask forgiveness for the pain we have caused the women, children, elders, and ourselves.

# Intimate Partner Violence and Recidivism Following Interventions with Men Who Batter: Cultural and Empirical Considerations

## 1

ETIONY ALDARONDO AND
MICHELLE C. FERNANDEZ

This book as a whole considers the dynamic nature of the relationship between culturally based clinical practices and the promotion of healing and change in men who batter their intimate partners, highlighting the often neglected oppressive social structures and cultural needs that link intimate relationships and violence against women. In this chapter we attempt to provide a context within which this relationship can be appreciated, reviewing research on the incidence and prevalence of intimate partner violence (IPV) by men against their female partners and evaluating the efficacy of interventions with men who batter.

When it comes to the relationship between culture and IPV, the news from practitioners and scientist is mixed. The good news, as the authors of this book herald, is that cultural practices and ways of being hold out a legitimate promise for generating non-violent and healthy relationships. The bad news is that IPV is not confined to specific cultures, countries, or ethnic groups. Moreover, there is considerable lack of clarity about how best to intervene to protect women, promote family well-being, and redirect the men into pathways of healing and change. In addressing some of these issues, we are less interested here in articulating a comprehensive cultural framework for domestic violence than in examining it as a phenomenon reflective of the complex issues faced by providers of service to men of color who batter their intimate female partners and for whose resolution we all share some responsibility.

We have divided this chapter in three main sections. In the first, we present international and national statistics on the incidence and prevalence of IPV against women by men. In the second section we present an assessment of the literature on interventions with men who batter. We conclude the chapter by discussing the role of culture in IPV, how culture-based strategies and models can enhance the efficacy of existing intervention programs for men who batter, and the various roles that practitioners working with men of color who batter must assume if they are to heal the men and redress the social inequities fueling their violence.

## DEFINITIONS

Intimate partner violence includes physical violence, psychological or emotional violence, sexual violence, and stalking by a current or former partner or spouse. It may include behaviors such as intimidation, harassment and persecution, verbal aggression, denial of access to resources, sexual coercion and assault, or physical assault and torture. Intimate partner violence occurs in both heterosexual and same-sex relationships and is arguably the dominant context in which violence against women takes place in our society.

Before we go ahead, two caveats should be mentioned. First, the IPV literature to date has focused primarily on "presumably" heterosexual men's physical violence toward their female partners. We put the term "presumably" within quotation marks because, even while a growing number of researchers are now focusing on domestic violence in same-gender relationships (Cameron, 2003; McClennen, 2005), most researchers and service agencies do not collect sexual orientation data from men and their partners. Second, although other manifestations of IPV such as sexual and psychological violence are emerging as important areas of study, the integration of these works with the literature on physical violence in intimate relationships remains a work in progress (Tolan, Gorman-Smith, & Henry, 2006). Thus, the information we share here favors studies on physical violence by men against their female partners. By no means do we wish to perpetuate the myth that IPV is exclusively a heterosexual phenomenon or that other forms of IPV do not have devastating effects on victims.

# PREVALENCE OF PHYSICAL VIOLENCE BY MEN AGAINST THEIR FEMALE PARTNERS

## Intimate Partner Physical Violence by Men Against Women Across the World

Intimate partner violence typically occurs under a veil of secrecy that makes it difficult to develop accurate estimates of its prevalence. This situation is true in the United States and arguably more so in countries with little or no history of promoting and protecting equal rights for women and men. In order to evaluate the extent and seriousness of IPV, researchers and government officials turn to national surveys, community samples, and official records. In the past 15 years at least one survey on IPV has been conducted in 71 countries. Moreover, we now have national IPV survey data for more than 40 countries. These data provide abundant evidence that violence against women by their male partners is a common and devastating reality for large numbers of women around the world.

The main sources of information on the incidence and prevalence of violence against women by their male partners across the world are the WHO Multi-Country Study on Women's Health and Domestic Violence Against Women (World Health Organization [WHO], 2005), the in-depth study on all forms of violence against women presented in 2006 to the General Assembly by the United Nations Secretary General's Office (United Nations [UN], 2006), and the report by the Economic Commission for Latin America and the Caribbean on gender violence against women in Latin American and the Caribbean (ECLAC, 2007). The UN and ECLAC reports summarize knowledge on domestic violence at the national, regional, and community level. These reports include information obtained through different formats and methods by government agencies, community groups, and non-government research organizations. The WHO study, on the other hand, was designed to generate reliable and comparable information on domestic violence across countries.

Table 1.1 shows the incidence and lifetime prevalence rates of physical violence against women by their male partners in 45 countries for which national estimates were found. The data show that between 8% and 67% of women around the world are physically assaulted by their intimate male partners at some point in their lives. More than half of the countries report lifetime IPV prevalence rates of at least 20%. In all but four countries (Albania, Canada, France, and Germany), 10% or more

Table 1.1

## INCIDENCE AND LIFETIME PREVALENCE RATES OF PHYSICAL VIOLENCE AGAINST WOMEN BY THEIR MALE PARTNERS ACROSS THE WORLD

| COUNTRY BY CONTINENT OR REGION | YEAR OF STUDY | SAMPLE SIZE | 1-YEAR INCIDENCE OF PHYSICAL VIOLENCE AGAINST WOMEN BY THEIR INTIMATE MALE PARTNERS | LIFETIME PREVALENCE OF PHYSICAL VIOLENCE AGAINST WOMEN BY THEIR INTIMATE MALE PARTNERS |
|---|---|---|---|---|
| **AFRICA** | | | | |
| Egypt | 1995–1996 | 7,123 | 13 | 34 |
| Malawi | 2005 | 3,546 | NR | 30 |
| South Africa | 1998 | 10,190 | 6 | 13 |
| Zambia | 2001–2002 | 3,792 | 27 | 49 |
| **ASIA, PACIFIC ISLANDS AND AUSTRALIA** | | | | |
| Australia | 2002–2003 | 6,438 | 3 | 31 |
| Bangladesh | 1992 | 1,225 | 19 | 47 |
| Cambodia | 2000 | 2,403 | 15 | 18 |
| China | 1999–2000 | 1,665 | NR | 15 |
| India | 1998–1999 | 90,303 | 10 | 19 |
| Papua New Guinea | 2002 | 628 | NR | 67 |
| Philippines | 1993 | 8,481 | NR | 10 |
| Republic of Korea | 2004 | 5,916 | 13 | 21 |
| Samoa | 2000 | 1,204 | 18 | 41 |
| **CARIBBEAN** | | | | |
| Barbados | 1990 | 264 | NR | 30 |
| Dominican Republic | 2002 | 6,807 | 11 | 22 |
| Haiti | 2000 | 2,347 | 21 | 29 |
| Puerto Rico | 1995–1996 | 4,755 | NR | 13 |
| **CENTRAL AMERICA** | | | | |
| Guatemala | 2002 | 6,595 | 9 | NR |
| Honduras | 2001 | 6,827 | 6 | 10 |
| Nicaragua | 1998 | 8,507 | 13 | 30 |
| El Salvador | 2002 | 10,689 | 6 | 20 |
| **NORTH AMERICA** | | | | |
| Canada | 1999 | 8,356 | 3 | 8 |
| Mexico | 2006 | 128,000 | NR | 43 |

Table 1.1 *(continued)*

| COUNTRY BY CONTINENT OR REGION | YEAR OF STUDY | SAMPLE SIZE | 1-YEAR INCIDENCE OF PHYSICAL VIOLENCE AGAINST WOMEN BY THEIR INTIMATE MALE PARTNERS | LIFETIME PREVALENCE OF PHYSICAL VIOLENCE AGAINST WOMEN BY THEIR INTIMATE MALE PARTNERS |
|---|---|---|---|---|
| **SOUTH AMERICA** | | | | |
| Bolivia | 2003 | | NR | 52 |
| Colombia | 2000 | 7,602 | 3 | 44 |
| Ecuador | 2000 & 2004* | | 12 | 31* |
| Paraguay | 2004 | 5,070 | 7 | 19 |
| Peru | 2000 | 17,369 | 2 | 42 |
| Uruguay | 1997 | 545 | 10 | NR |
| **EASTERN EUROPE** | | | | |
| Azerbaijan | 2001 | 5,533 | 8 | 20 |
| Georgia | 1999 | 5,694 | 2 | 5 |
| Republic of Moldova | 1997 | 4,790 | 8 | 15 |
| Romania | 1999 | 5,322 | 10 | 29 |
| Ukraine | 1999 | 5,596 | 7 | 19 |
| **NORTHERN EUROPE** | | | | |
| Finland | 1997 | 4,955 | NR | 30 |
| Lithuania | 1999 | 1,010 | NR | 23 |
| Norway | 2003 | 2,143 | 6 | 27 |
| Sweden | 2000 | 5,686 | 4 | 18 |
| United Kingdom of Great Britain and Northern Ireland | 2001 | 12,226 | 3 | 19 |
| **SOUTHERN EUROPE** | | | | |
| Albania | 2002 | 4,049 | 5 | 8 |
| **WESTERN EUROPE** | | | | |
| France | 2002 | 5,908 | 3 | 9 |
| Germany | 2003 | 10,264 | 2 | 5 |
| Netherlands | 1986 | 989 | NR | 21 |
| Switzerland | 2003 | 1,882 | NR | 10 |

NR = Rates not reported by data sources.
Data sources: ECLAC, 2007; UN, 2006; INEGI, 2007

of the women have been victimized by their male intimate partners. No region of the world assessed to date has an average lifetime physical IPV prevalence rate of less than 13%. The percentage of women physically assaulted by their male partners over a 12-month period of time ranges from a low of 2% of women in Germany to a high of 27% in Zambia.

While the foregoing data help us see domestic violence as a cultural phenomenon and a human rights issue, we must be cautious about drawing fine inferences from data obtained using diverse methodologies and definitions of IPV. The WHO Multi-Country Study was designed to overcome some of these limitations, relying on standardized assessment instruments and procedures to obtain information from 24,097 women from 15 sites in 10 countries representing diverse cultural settings (Garcia-Moreno, Jansen, Ellsberg, Heise, & Watts, 2006). The study relied on women's reports of violent acts perpetrated by male partners against them to generate prevalence estimates for intimate physical and sexual violence.

Figure 1.1 presents the lifetime prevalence of intimate partner physical violence (IPPV) by level of violence severity for all 15 sites in the WHO study. The severity of a physical violent act was defined

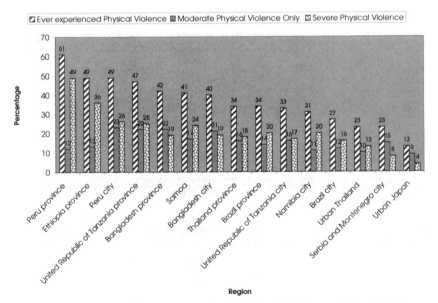

**Figure 1.1** Lifetime prevalence of intimate partner physical violence by level of violence severity in the WHO Multi-Country Study on Women's Health and Domestic Violence Against Women.

in this study as the likelihood that the act would cause physical injury. Thus, slapping, pushing, and shoving were defined as moderate physical violence, while hitting with a fist, kicking, dragging, threatening with a weapon, and using a weapon were defined as severe physical violence. The lifetime prevalence rate of intimate partner physical violence ranged from 13% of women in urban Japan to 61% in provincial Peru, with most countries falling between 23% and 49%. Only three sites (urban Thailand, Serbia-Montenegro, and urban Japan) reported prevalence rates of less than 25%, while seven reported prevalence rates of at least 40%. Note also that in 12 of the 15 sites surveyed, more women reported experiencing severe forms of violence than moderate violence.

International and cross-cultural studies of patterns of physical violence against women by male partners suggest not only that women across cultures are victimized by their male partners at very high levels but that cultural factors may account for the variable rates in the occurrence of IPV across the world. In line with the main thrust of this volume, these studies suggest that domestic violence is not inevitable and that a critical evaluation and transformation of cultural practices that promote violence against women is needed to protect women and reduce their victimization by male partners.

## Intimate Partner Physical Violence by Men Against Women in the United States

The main sources of national data on the occurrence of physical violence against women by their male partners in the United States are the National Violence Against Women Survey (NVAW) conducted in 1995 (Tjaden & Thoennes, 2000) and the National Family Violence Survey and National Family Violence Resurvey (NFVS I, NFVS II) conducted by the Family Research Laboratory in 1975 and 1985 (Straus & Gelles, 1990). These surveys used similar sampling strategies and relied on the Conflict Tactics Scale to measure acts of intimate partner physical violence. Figure 1.2 shows the incidence and lifetime prevalence rates of physical violence against women by their male partners obtained through these surveys. According to these data, approximately a quarter of the women in the United States are physically assaulted by their male partners as some point in their lives. National estimates of the annual rate of IPV indicate that somewhere between 1.3 million (Tjaden & Thoennes, 2000) and more than 8 million (Straus & Gelles, 1990) women are physically assaulted by their male partners each year.

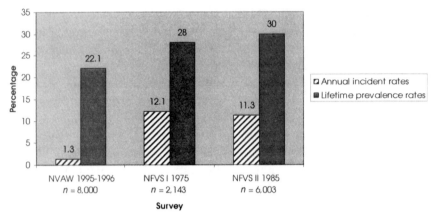

**Figure 1.2** Annual incidence and prevalence rates of physical violence against women by their male partners in the United States.

With respect to comparisons among diverse cultural groups, the data show that different American groups report significantly different rates of IPPV. Data from the NVAW (Tjaden & Thoennes, 2000) suggest that American Indian/Alaskan Native (30.7%) and Asian/Pacific Islander (12.8%) women experience the highest and lowest lifetime prevalence rates of IPPV among specific cultural groups, respectively. The lifetime prevalence rates for African American, Hispanic, and White groups were 26.3 percent, 21.3 percent, and 22.1 percent, in that order. The differences between these three groups were not statistically significant. In terms of annual incidence, data from the second NFVS shows that both African American (17.4 %) and Hispanic (17.3%) women experience significantly higher rates of IPPV than white women and women of other cultural backgrounds (Hampton & Gelles, 1994; Straus & Smith, 1990). Another national survey of IPV, including an oversample of African American and Hispanic respondents, found the annual prevalence rate in Black couples (23%) to be twice that of white couples (11.5%) and 1.3 times the rate for Hispanic couples (17.0%) (Caetano, 2001; Field & Caetano, 2004).

There are important methodological reasons to be prudent not to reach categorical conclusions about the differential rates of IPPV in diverse cultural groups on the basis of data obtained from the national surveys discussed so far. Some of these limitations include language barriers, lack of demonstrated validity of IPV measures for specific cultural groups, and reliance on telephone interviews as the main format for data collection. Moreover, all the aforementioned surveys are designed to ignore the diversity within specific cultural groups. This is particularly relevant when considering grouping together responses from ethnic groups with very different histories of colonization, religious traditions, cultural identity, and gender role expectations into pan-ethnic categories such as the Asian/Pacific Islander and Hispanic groups, and when Black people are treated as a homogenous group with little or no attention paid to regional differences within the United States as well as to and other differences between African-Americans, African-Caribbean, and Africans.

To date, the National Alcohol and Family Life Survey is the only national survey that has been designed to overcome some of these limitations with respect to the study of IPPV among Hispanics in the United States (Kaufman Kantor, Jasinski, & Aldarondo, 1994; Aldarondo, Kaufman Kantor, & Jasinski, 2002). Data from the NAFLS found annual rates of IPPV in Puerto Rican, Mexican American, Mexican, Cuban American, and white couples of 20.4%, 17.9%, 10.5%, 2.5%, and 9.9%, respectively. These findings underscore the need for culture specific research on IPPV and serve as a warning that combining data on different cultural groups is likely to conceal large differences between groups while overstating the differences between whites and other cultural groups.

## The Role of Culture of Intimate Partner Violence

Given the sources of data reviewed so far, one may assume that much is known about men who abuse their female intimate partners and the role played by culture in the violence against women. However, a perusal of the research literature reveals a tenuous understanding of violent partners and many inconsistent findings on issues of theoretical and practical importance such as sex role attitudes, alcohol use, psychopathology, and (more pertinently to the purpose of this chapter) issues related to culture and ethnicity. To be sure some of these inconsistencies are the result of methodological deficiencies such as reliance on self-selected samples, lack of appropriate control groups, and different definitions of violence and culture, that will improve as intimate partner violence research continues. However, there is reason to believe that many discontinuities in the literature are also the consequence of our failure to recognize the multiple oppressions affecting the life of men and women of color in the United States and to modify our understanding of intimate violence accordingly. As a result to date, the research literature has very little to say about the role of culture-specific dynamics and factors in the occurrence and resolution of IPV. Instead, social factors such as socioeconomic inequities, relationship factors such as high levels of conflict in intimate relationships, and individual factors such as excessive alcohol consumption by men and childhood experience of IPV, have emerged among the most consistent predictors of IPV against women in the literature (Aldarondo et al., 2002; Bennett & Goodman, 2005; Field & Caetano, 2004; Kafuman Kantor et al., 1994; UN, 2006; Van Wyk, Benson, Fox, & DeMaris, 2003).

## RECIDIVISM FOLLOWING INTERVENTIONS WITH MEN WHO BATTER

Having documented considerable variability in rates of physical violence against women by their male partners across cultures around the world and within the United States, we now turn our attention to the evaluation of interventions with men who batter their female partners. A fair assessment of effectiveness of these interventions is necessary to avoid reducing proposals for culture-based practices into ideological speculation. Knowing how well more traditional interventions work gives us a point of reference against which the effectiveness of culture-based interventions for men of color who batter their female partners, such as those proposed in this volume, could be compared. This knowledge can also help elucidate specific ways culture-based practices can improve upon existing services. If non-culture-specific interventions with men who batter are demonstrated to be effective, then the challenge for proponents of culture-specific approaches to working with men who batter is to demonstrate that these approaches are as effective or that at the very least they allow access to services for targeted groups of men for whom the existing models may not work. If non-culture-based interventions with men who batter are not effective, or if they do more harm than good, then the case remains to be made as to how culture-specific models may be better at protecting women and guiding men of color into eliminating violence from their intimate relationships.

In this section we review data from studies on the effectiveness of court orders of protection for abuse victims, pro-arrest policies, "no-drop" prosecution policies, educational programs for men who batter, and coordinated community response initiatives.[1] We present a broad view on the effectiveness of interventions for men who batter as an antidote to

---

[1.]Updated version of Aldarondo, 2002

what we consider to be a misguided preference by IPV researchers to approach interventions with men who batter as discrete medical procedures rather than as social policies and practices intended to respond to individual and social needs.

## Legal Sanctions Against Men Who Batter

To date, no single statutory code on domestic violence has been adopted through the United States. Instead, "the states have adopted widely variant statutory models that in some instances reflect strong legislative intent to protect domestic violence victims, while other states' laws perhaps reflect more compromise than fervor" (Miller, 1997, p. 2). The most commonly used legal interventions with men who batter are court order protection against domestic violence and mandated arrest and pro-arrest policies. Both types of interventions are based on the assumption that domestic violence can be stopped through legal sanctions and that legal sanctions are effective in reducing violence.

## Court Protection Orders as a Deterrent

Prior to the adoption of Pennsylvania's 1976 Protection from Abuse Act, only two states had protective order legislation specifically for domestic violence victims. Since then all fifty states, the District of Columbia, and Puerto Rico have enacted protective order laws. These laws grant the courts authority to use a wide range of injunctions against perpetrators of domestic violence, such as staying away from the abuse victim's residence or place of employment, not committing additional acts of violence, not harassing or threatening family members, and enrolling in counseling and educational programs.

Orders of shorter duration are called temporary restraining orders. Typically, on completion of a temporary order, the person requesting the order has to attend a court hearing in which the judge decides whether to issue a permanent order. This order remains active until the person who requested the order asks for it to be cancelled. Violation of a protective order is punishable by contempt of court. In most states, violation of a restraining order is now punishable by arrest and incarceration (Miller, 1997; Buzawa & Buzawa, 1996).

Several studies (Carlson, Harris, & Holden, 1999; Grau, Fagan, & Wexler, 1985; Harrell & Smith, 1996; Holt, Kernick, Lumley, Wolf, & Rivara, 2002; Klein, 1996; Macfarlane et al., 2004) have examined the

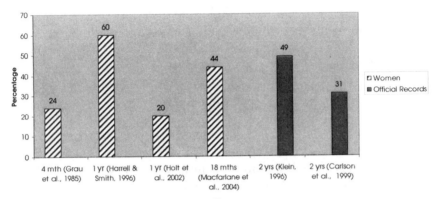

**Figure 1.3** Protective order recidivism studies.

effects of protective orders in the reoccurrence of violence. These studies rely on a combination of reports by female victims and court and criminal records. The follow-up times range from four months to two years. The rates of recidivism range from 20% to 60%. Approximately one man out of four is found to reassault his female partner within four months of the protective order. The sample size, data source, follow-up time, and recidivism rate of these studies are shown in Figure 1.3. In the ensuing two years, this figure may increase to approximately two out of five men.

In comparing men who received temporary orders and men who received permanent orders, both Harrell and Smith (1996) and Keilitz, Hannaford, and Efkeman (1997) failed to find significant differences in violence recidivism between these groups, while Carlson et al. (1999) found that a significantly lower proportion of men who received permanent orders reassaulted their partners within a year. According to Carlson et al.'s (1999) data, the deterrent effect of permanent orders was most noticeable among men with limited socioeconomic resources.

Few victim characteristics have been related to IPV recidivism by men after a protective order. Carlson et al. (1999) found that Black women and those with low socioeconomic status (SES) were more likely to report reassault than were Hispanic women and those with higher SES, respectively. Carlson et al. (1999) and Herrell and Smith (1996) found that victims who were mothers were more likely to report reabuse than women without children.

Reassault following a protective order does appear to be strongly associated with the man's history of violent and contentious behavior. Compared to men who cease or interrupt the violence, men who reabuse their partners tend to be younger (Klein, 1996), have prior criminal records

(Keilitz et al., 1997; Klein, 1996), have a history of persistent and severe violence against their female partners, and to have voiced strong objections to restraining orders at the time hearing (Harrell & Smith, 1996).

Concerning factors associated with the success of protective orders in stopping or reducing reabuse, Harrell and Smith found that arresting the abuser during the incident that led to the protective order significantly reduced the likelihood of severe violence but not other types of abuse. Carlson et al. found that arresting men before a protective order was issued significantly reduced reabuse for low-SES women. On the other hand, Klein failed to find a significant effect of arrest at the time of the protective order in the reabuse rate.

Female victims report that protective orders are helpful in documenting the abuse (Harrell & Smith, 1996) and in promoting a greater sense of security and safety in their life (Keilitz et al., 1997). Consistent with women's experiences, these studies suggest that protective orders are an effective form of violence deterrence for many men. In particular, it seems that these orders work better for men without criminal records. However, regardless of prior history of violence and crime, research shows that a very large number—30% to 40%—of men violate their restraining orders and reabuse their partners (Harrell & Smith, 1996; Klein, 1996; Keilitz et al., 1997). Although arresting men who batter their female partners appears to enhance the deterrent effect of protective orders in some cases, the data on this issue is far from conclusive.

## Arrest as a Deterrent

One of the most substantial changes in the criminal justice response to men who batter in the last three years has been the change from "arrest as a last resort" to mandatory arrest laws and pro-arrest state policies. These laws and policies either mandate or authorize police officers to arrest domestic violence offenders based solely on a probable cause determination that an offense has occurred and that the person arrested committed the offense. In this section we review both quasi-experimental and experimental studies about the effects of arrest in the behavior of men who batter.

### Quasi-Experimental Arrest Studies

Quasi-experimental designs are used to tell us how domestic violence arrest policies and procedures work within the realities of particular communities. Jaffe, Wolfe, Telford, and Austin (1986) did just this when they evaluated the experiences of female victims before and after the implementation of a domestic violence arrest policy in London, Ontario. Women whose partners had been arrested reported significantly lower levels of reassault than women whose partners were not arrested; they reported reductions of 66% of the prearrest total. Similarly another study of 270 women seeking domestic violence services in Florida, North Carolina, Ohio, and Vermont and found that those whose male partners had been arrested reported lower recidivism rates than women whose partners were not arrested (Fagan, 1996).

## Domestic Violence Arrest Experiments

Experimental designs are considered to be an improvement over quasi-experimental designs because they afford investigators better control over the effects of unspecified contextual factors and potential selection bias in the construction of groups. Seven social experiments have been conducted to test the effectiveness of arrest in reducing domestic violence.

In the early 1980s, Sherman and Berk (1984) completed the first domestic violence arrest experiment in Minneapolis, Minnesota. They found that

> [A]rrest was the most effective of three standard methods police use to reduce domestic violence. The other police methods—attempting to counsel both parties or sending the assailants away from home for several hours—were found to be considerably less effective in deterring future violence. (Sherman et al., 1992a, p. 269)

And while expressing the need for "other experiments in other settings," they stated that "the preponderance of evidence in the Minneapolis study strongly suggests that the police should use arrest in most domestic violence cases" (Sherman et al., 1992a, p. 269).

In the mid-1980s and early 1990s, the National Institute of Justice sponso six domestic violence experiments to evaluate and elaborate on the findings of the Minneapolis experiment. Collectively, these experiments came be known as the Spousal Assault Replication Program, or SARP. Unfortunately, the published reports of these experiments vary in their analytical approaches and choices of comparisons (Garner, Fagan, &

Maxwell, 1995). Not surprisingly, the authors also varied in their conclusions. Both Hirschel, Hutchison, and Dean (1992) and Dunford, Huizinga, and Elliot (1990) concluded that arrest was not more effective in reducing reabuse of victims than nonarrest practices. Berk, Campbell, Klap, and Western (1992) indicated that arrest was effective according to abuse victims' reports but not according to official records. For Sherman et al. (1991) there were short-term gains to arrest, which over time dissipated and gave way to violence escalation. Pate and Hamilton (1992) reported that arrest significantly reduced the prevalence of violence and increased the time it took for repeat offenders to reabuse their female partners.

Garner et al. (1995) reported the raw data of these experiments in order to provide a more consistent form of comparison. Figure 1.4 includes the six-month recidivism rates and outcome for the evaluations according to official police records and abuse victims' reports. Considering the evaluation of official records, the six-month recidivism rate across experiments ranged from 6.5% to 25.8% and from 14.8% to 25.2% for arrested and nonarrested men, respectively. The average reabuse rate for arrested men across experiments was 17.2%. In other words, according to official records, approximately one out of six men arrested for domestic violence reoffended within six months of the initial arrest. Closer to one out of five men (19.1%) who were not arrested reassaulted within the same time period. Only the Minneapolis experiment found statistically significant differences in the rates of reabuse among arrested and nonarrested men. Looking beyond the criteria

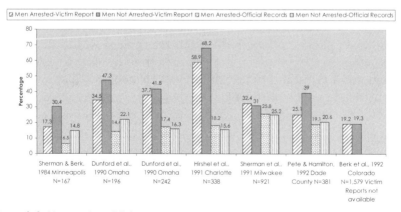

**Figure 1.4**  Six-month recidivism rates in arrest studies by source of data.

of statistical significance, the remaining experiments were evenly split between reduction and escalation of violence following arrests (Aldarondo, 2002).

With respect to violence recidivism data obtained from women's reports, Figure 1.4 shows that, in all but one of the experiments, women whose partners were arrested reported lower recidivism rates than women whose partners were not arrested. However, this difference was statistically significant only for women in the Minneapolis and Dade experiments. The rates of reabuse ranged from 17.3% to 58.9% and from 30.4% to 62.8% for arrested and nonarrested men, respectively. The average six-month recidivism rate reported by abuse victims across experiments was 34.3% and 42.1% for arrested and nonarrested men, in that order.

## Significance for Female Victims of Domestic Violence

There are no theoretical or empirical estimates on the deterrent effects of arrest in men who batter that can be used as benchmarks in the evaluation of the findings presented above. In the absence of such criteria, prudence dictates that we take into account the clinical and human significance of these findings for victims of domestic violence. According to both official records and abuse victims' reports a smaller number of men who were arrested than of nonarrested men reassaulted their partner in the ensuing six months. Specifically, women's report a reduction of almost 8% in the recidivism rate for arrested men compared with men who are not arrested. This means that without arresting men who batter, 180 additional women of the 2,245 included in Table 3.3 would have been reassaulted by their partners. Having said this, however, it is important to recognize that approximately one-third of all women whose male partner is arrested will be reassaulted within six months. Thus, although the positive effects of arrest should not be trivialized, the limitations of arrest as the primary way to change the behavior of men who batter should be obvious.

## Effect of Employment and Marital Status

Although arrest is associated with important reductions in violence recidivism, the effects of arrest are known to vary with the men's employment status (Berk et al., 1992; Sherman et al., 1992a; Pate & Hamilton, 1992) and marital status (Sherman et al., 1992b). Arrested men who are employed and married appear to be less likely to reabuse than their counterparts who are not arrested. On the other hand, among men who lack a "stake in conformity" or commitment, arrest is associated with higher rates of violence recidivism. Thus, the effectiveness of arrest in reducing domestic violence appears to be associated with the presence of informal social controls in the life of men who batter.

## Batterer Intervention Programs

Intervention programs for men who batter, commonly known as batterer intervention programs (BIPs), are now a standard sanction for the criminal justice system in cases involving domestic violence. Legitimized and supported by the courts, BIPs have proliferated at a remarkably high rate across the country (Mederos, 2002).

There is a great deal of variability among BIPs in terms of theoretical orientation, duration of program, number and structure of sessions, counselors' training experiences, sponsoring agency, referral sources, sources of funding, and ethnic composition of the men in the program. Typically, men attending a BIP are asked to join other men in orientation and psychoeducational groups led by one or more group counselors. From a pragmatic point of view, groups are an affordable form of intervention for poor or financially strapped men and are a cost-effective operation for agencies relying on a small number of trained professionals to serve a large number of men needing intervention. From a clinical point of view, groups are also presumed to reduce men's social isolation, provide a safe environment in which they can deal with potentially volatile issues and challenge fellow groups members who directly or indirectly engage in abusive behavior, and expose men to alternative, nonviolent coping models and strategies.

Many BIPs are informed both by pro-feminist values and concerns and by social learning theory principles of behavior. From a social learning perspective, violence is viewed as a pattern of behavior familiar to men in part because they have witnessed such behaviors in their families of origin. Moreover, the men's use of violence against their female partners is presumed to have a functional significance for the men and becomes a regular part of their interpersonal relationships. In accordance with feminists' ideas about the social construction of gender and power in intimate relationships, many education programs for men who batter also understand violence against women as one of several forms of controlling behaviors men use against women, which is learned during childhood and is maintained into adulthood through a myriad of cultural messages and practices that legitimize male violence against women.

This conceptualization of men's violence against women as learned, functional, and maintained by interpersonal and cultural dynamics has favored the development of highly structured educational intervention strategies focused on the cessation of violent behaviors in contrast to unstructured, growth-oriented approaches. These programs try to educate men about the causes, dynamics, and consequences of violence; teach them how to recognize and deal with anger without resorting to violence; reduce their general level of arousal through relaxation and self-control techniques; teach them to use time-out techniques to avoid emotionally arousing situations and promote rational problem solving; change views and attitudes about intimate relationships that men have used to justify their abusive behaviors, including sexist attitudes; and teach them appropriate conflict resolution skills.

Despite these multiple goals, the effectiveness of education programs for men who batter is typically judged by the reduction in the number of men who reassault their partners following program completion. However, accurate estimates of IPV recidivism are difficult to obtain. Moral reproach for violent behavior and possible negative social and legal consequences of disclosure can heighten men's tendency to underreport violence. Official records, although not affected by the men's self-report biases, have their own limitations and are thought to produce much lower recidivism figures than evaluations using partner reports (Bennett & Williams, 2001).

Unfortunately, outcome studies have shown follow-up contact with abuse victims to be problematic (e.g., Taylor, Davis, & Maxwell, 2001) and that women may underreport their abuse out of shame, fear, or repression of traumatic events (Saunders, 1996). Other reasons why unbiased estimates of recidivism are difficult to obtain include that outcome studies tend to report data only for men who complete intervention programs and are available at follow-up time; that there is a low response rate to all follow-up data gathering techniques; that respondents to follow-up assessments often compare favorably with those who do not in important risk markers for IPV such as economic resources, alcohol problems, violence in the family of origin, and severity of violence against women; and that many BIPs include men with different psychological and social needs in the same groups while excluding the most difficult or inappropriate men. For all these reasons, we think it is prudent to assume that the available data may underestimate the rate of violence recidivism following group intervention.

## Evaluations of BIPs

Evaluations of BIPs have consistently appeared in the literature since the early 1980s. Today there are close to 40 published evaluations of BIPs in professional journals, most of which assess recidivism following participation in a specific intervention program (individual outcome studies). Others compare men who complete the intervention program with either dropouts or a matched group of men (i.e., quasi-experimental studies). A third group of studies compares violence rates among men who are randomly assigned to different intervention conditions (i.e., BIP experiments).

### Individual Outcome Studies

In the typical BIP, violent behavior is assessed before and after the provision of services. Some programs also conduct follow-up assessments months and even years after termination. This information provides a rough measure of how intervention programs affect the violent behavior of their participants.

Feazell, Mayers, and Deschner's (1984) survey of 90 intervention programs for men who batter revealed that between 25% and 34% of men reabused their partners within a year. Another survey of sixteen intervention programs (Pirog-Good & Stets-Kealey, 1985) found a four-month average recidivism rate of 16%. However, as Edleson (1990) points out, neither of these studies indicates how the follow-up data were collected, who provided the information, and how the programs computed reassault.

Davis and Taylor (1999) identified 22 individual batterer intervention evaluations. Two-thirds of the follow-up assessments relied exclusively on reports given by men. Four evaluations were based on reports by men and their abuse victims. Three evaluations used only victims' reports. One evaluation presented data obtained from men and police records. The follow-up time ranged from seven weeks to three years, with two-thirds of the programs completing follow-up assessments of at least six months. Recidivism rates ranged from 7% to 47%, with an average of 26% across evaluations. Abuse victims and men who batter reported average recidivism rates of 24% and 24%, respectively. One evaluation including police records reported 15% recidivism. Considering follow-up time, the combined average recidivism rate for follow-up evaluations of up to five months was 14%, while recidivism for evaluations with follow-up time of six months was more than 32%.

According to data from individual outcome studies, most men cease or interrupt the use of violence following completion of a BIP; however, about one-third of program completers go on to reabuse their female partners. Consistent with both protective orders and arrest studies, women report considerably higher rates of reabuse than police records and men's reports.

## Quasi-Experimental Studies

In judging the effectiveness of BIPs, it is important to know not just that program completers reduce their use of violence, but also the extent to which they are more likely to do so than men who either drop out of programs or do not attend them. This is what quasi-experimental studies are designed to do.

Several quasi-experimental evaluations of BIPs based on police records have been published in professional journals (Babcock & Steiner, 1999; Chen et al., 1989; Dobash, Dobash, Cavanagh, & Lewis, 1996; Dutton, 1986; Dutton, Bodnarchuk, Kropp, & Hart, 1997; Gondolf, 1998; Waldo, 1988). Violence recidivism and outcome results from these

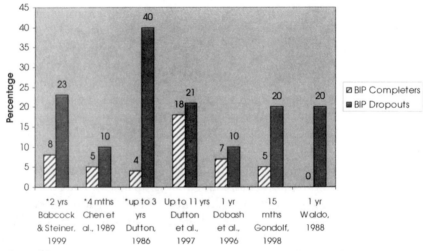

**Figure 1.5** Quasi-experiments of BIP recidivism based on police records.

studies are shown in Figure 1.5. All seven studies report lower recidivism rates among men following BIP completion than for men who did not complete a program. Three studies report this difference to be statistically significant. Recidivism rates for program completers ranged from 0 to 18%. Recidivism rates for dropouts ranged from 10% to 40%. Considering follow-up time, evaluations of up to one year's duration showed combined reabuse rates of 4% and 13% for men who completed BIPs and men who did not, respectively. The combined average recidivism rates for follow-up evaluations of more than one year was 9% and 26% for program completers and dropouts, in that order.

Recidivism data obtained from abuse victims in quasi-experimental evaluations of BIPs (Dobash et al., 1996; Edleson & Grusznski, 1988; Gondolf, 2000, 2001b, Hamberger & Hastings, 1988) are shown in Figure 1.6. Again, all six studies found that men who complete BIPs were reported to reabuse their female partners less than men who did not. In four studies, the differences between groups were statistically significant. Women whose partners completed BIPs reported recidivism rates from 26% to 41% (mean 32%). In contrast, between 40% percent and 62% (mean 46%) of women whose partners did not complete BIPs indicated that they had been reassaulted.

Quasi-experimental evaluations of intervention programs for men who batter indicate that men who complete the programs reassult their partners considerably less than those who do not. Consistent with data obtained from individual outcome studies, close to one-third of female

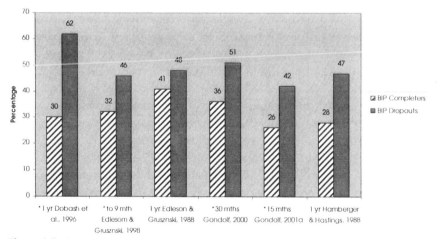

**Figure 1.6** Quasi-experiments of BIP IPV recidivism based on female victims' reports.

partners of program completers reported being reassaulted by their partners. Again, recidivism rates based on police reports were approximately one-half the rate obtained from women's reports.

Keep in mind that program completers and dropouts have both experienced the same type of legal sanctions for abusing their partners. Thus, the lower recidivism rates among program completers suggest that there is a program effect beyond the effect of legal sanctions such as protection orders and arrest. In an analysis of BIP program effect, Gondolf (2001b) argues that completing a program reduces the likelihood of reassault by 44% to 64%. To put this in perspective, treatment completion by all dropouts included in Figure 1.6 would reduce the average recidivism rate as reported by abuse victims from 46% to a minimum of 17% and a maximum of 26%. Also keep in mind that difference in recidivism rates between program completers and dropouts may be accounted for by other contextual and individual differences between these groups. Studies of attrition in BIP completers suggest that they are more likely than program dropouts to be employed, be married, have children, be more educated, perceive the program as important, and admit violence at intake (Daly & Pelowski, 2000). They also tend to be less likely than dropouts to have criminal records and substance abuse problems. Thus, like arrest, BIPs appear to be more effective with men who have a stake in conformity.

## BIP Experiments

Although the effect of pre-existing differences between program completers and dropouts in recidivism rates can be assessed through various statistical procedures, it cannot be completely eliminated. In theory, unbiased estimates of violence recidivism can be achieved only through random assignment of participants to experimental and control groups.

Four batterer intervention program experiments have been published in professional journals. The recidivism rates, data source, and direction of outcome reported in the first three experiments (Dunford, 2000; Palmer, Brown, & Barrera, 1992; Taylor et al., 2001) are presented in Figure 1.7. The most recent experiment conducted by Feder and her colleagues (Feder & Wilson, 2005) is not included here because methodological limitations make comparison with the remaining studies difficult. Evaluation of police records show one-year recidivism rates for men assigned to BIPs ranging from 4% to 18%,

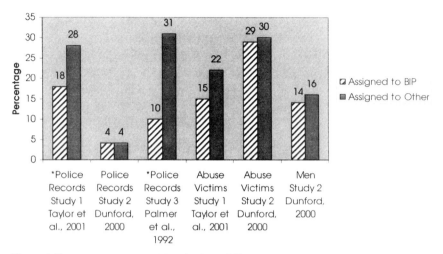

**Figure 1.7** One-year IPV recidivism in three BIP experiments.

with an average of 11% across experiments. Further, both Taylor et al. (2001) and Palmer et al. (1992) found men assigned to BIPs to have significantly lower levels of reassault in their police records than men assigned to other experimental conditions.

In terms of abuse victims' reports, both Taylor et al. (2001) and Dunford (2000) report lower levels of reassault among men assigned to BIPs than among men assigned to other experimental conditions; however, this difference was not statistically significant. Overall, BIP experiments suggest that men assigned to group programs have lower rates of reassault than men assigned to control conditions. That this is the case is somewhat surprising given that, for methodological and practical reasons, experiments calculate recidivism rates based on the number of men assigned to conditions and not on actual number of men completing programs (Gondolf, 2001a). Thus, there is evidence of a program effect even after data from program completers, dropouts, and untreated men in the same group are mixed together.

## Coordinated Community Responses

Coordinated community responses have been heralded by some as "the best hope for improving the social responses to domestic violence" (Worden, 2000, p. 246) and as "the guiding principle shaping policy for the [year] 2000 and beyond" (Ford, Reichard, Goldsmith, & Regoli, 1996,

p. 243). This type of response involves integrating the activities of multiple organizations and services such as BIPs, the criminal justice system, shelters for battered women, social service agencies, and health services into a communitywide violence intervention and prevention network. These initiatives are, by definition, shaped by the characteristics and resources of each community and are thus unique.

Although the specific form of these responses may vary across communities, all coordinated community responses assume that each part of the community network of interventions contributes something to the reduction of violence; that coordination of activities enhances the efficacy of the separate parts; and that the combined effects of coordinated community responses are greater than the individual effects of their parts. Our review of criminal justice interventions and BIPs provides evidence in support of the first of these assumptions. Evaluations of coordinated community responses are beginning to document the effects of these initiatives in other parts of the network and in violence recidivism.

Gamache, Edleson, and Schock (1988) used a multiple baseline design to evaluate the impact of three community intervention projects created by the Domestic Abuse Project (DAP) of Minneapolis. These initiatives included the participation of police, volunteer women, and men advocates to support and advise female victims and assailants, city attorneys, probation officers, judges, and BIPs. The DAP's staff maintained communication between the agencies, kept track of the cases, collected outcome evaluation data, provided community education and training, and recruited and supervised volunteer advocates. The researchers found that each community experienced significant increases in the number of arrests, successful prosecutions, and referrals to BIPs following the implementation of the community intervention projects. The authors concluded that the community responses "had a significant impact upon both the police and judicial responses to woman battering" (Gamache et al., 1988, p. 205).

Babcock and Steiner (1999) examined recidivism of domestic violence following a coordinated community response involving the courts, probation officers, and BIPs in Seattle ($n = 387$). In this system, individuals who are found guilty or receive a deferred sentence can be court-mandated to attend a BIP and are assigned a probation officer with whom they meet once a month for two years. Babcock and Steiner (1999) found significantly lower rates of rearrest during a two-year follow-up period among men who completed court-mandated intervention programs (8%) than among men who were court-ordered into the programs but who did not complete them (40%). Among the men in the programs, 14% completed treatment only after one or more bench warrants for their arrest had been issued, suggesting that court and probation involvement increases compliance with domestic violence treatment. The coordinated legal response appears to be a significant component in the intervention of domestic violence.

Tolman and Weisz (1995) evaluated the effectiveness of the pro-arrest and prosecution aspects of a coordinated community response in DuPage County, Illinois ($n = 341$). This system includes procedures for law enforcement, prosecutors, and advocates that are designed to ensure that most domestic violence cases are not dismissed. It also provides sentencing disposition guidelines for men who plead guilty or are found guilty, taking into consideration the men's history of domestic violence offenses. Following the evaluation of police reports for an 18-month period, these authors found lower rates of recidivism (25%) when the intervention prescribed by the protocol was exercised than when it was not (35%), and they concluded that this system "appears to be an effective strategy for deterring subsequent domestic violence" (p. 491).

Shepard, Falk, and Elliot (2002) evaluated the effects of an enhanced coordinated community response in Duluth, Minnesota. The "enhanced" model included methods for criminal justice practitioners and advocates to collect and share risk assessment data used to determine the level of legal sanctions recommended for men who batter. They found significantly lower 6- and 12-month recidivism rates during the second (28% and 39%) and third intervention years than during the pilot year (36% and 46%), suggesting "that improved coordination through the sharing of risk assessment information among criminal justice professionals can reduce recidivism among men who abuse their partners" (p. 568).

Murphy, Musser, and Maton (1998) examined the effects of a coordinated community response in Baltimore, Maryland ($n = 235$). Using official criminal justice data for a period of 12 to 18 months, they found that men who had been court-ordered to BIPs were 56% less likely than other men to generate a new charge. In addition, the combined effects of successful prosecution, probation monitoring, and participation in a BIP were associated with significant reductions in violence recidivism. To illustrate this point, the recidivism rates of men not successfully prosecuted, men found guilty, men also ordered to attend BIPs, and finally those men who completed BIPs were 19%, 13%, 9%, and 0%, respectively.

## CONCLUSION

This chapter reviews data from studies on the incidence and prevalence of IPV against women by male partners around the world and in the United States as well as from studies on efficacy of protective orders, arrest policies, BIPs, and coordinated community responses in this country. National and cross-cultural IPV studies tell us that the victimization of women by their male partners is a serious problem for women around the world. Women on all continents experience reprehensibly high levels of IPV. Moreover, there is considerable variation between countries in the rates of IPV, suggesting that important cultural dynamics and factors may contribute to the observed differences. Consistent with these findings, differential rates of IPV have also been found across cultural groups within the United States, with particularly high rates of IPV found in families of African American, Native American, and Hispanic descent. Having said this, however, we questioned the validity of IPV prevalence data collected under the assumption that people of color can be adequately studied as homogenous groups. To date, the research literature offers limited information about culture-specific dynamics or factors associated with IPV. Instead, there is a growing consensus that socioeconomic factors, relationship conflict, and alcohol abuse are important determinants of IPV among ethnic minority groups in the United States.

In terms of studies on recidivism following interventions with men who batter, the data show that each level of intervention is making modest and important contributions to stopping and reducing violent behavior by men against their female partners. Protective orders are an effective form of violence deterrence for more than one-half of the men. Approximately two-thirds of all men arrested for domestic violence offenses do not reassault within six months. About the same number of men (66%) who complete BIPs remain nonviolent following treatment. There is evidence that coordinated community response networks can significantly enhance the efficacy of various interventions and further reduce IPV recidivism.

On the other hand, the evidence clearly suggests that much more remains to be done to improve upon existing interventions. Protective orders, arrests, and BIPs are most inadequate in reducing reassault among men with weak social and intimate bonds. This is not surprising given that existing domestic violence interventions are not designed to deal with the many social and psychological shortcomings of this population. These men are more likely to violate protective orders, drop out of BIPs, and engage in criminal behavior outside the home. We must endeavor to improve our ability to engage men who batter in the process of change.

The data suggest that the higher the stakes are for men to conform to nonviolent social norms, the more likely they are to comply with intervention programs and to remain nonviolent following the interventions. Herein lies an area where culture-based batterer intervention programs and practitioners interested in culture-based practices could make important contributions to the field. The challenge here for proponents of culturally sensitive models and practices is to link the experiences of low-income and racially or ethnically diverse men in BIPs and the cultural competence of service providers with increased program completion rates and reduced IPV recidivism. This is particularly important, given that experts in the field agree that the majority of existing programs are not culturally competent (Aldarondo & Mederos, 2002; Carrillo & Tello, 1998; Gondolf, 2002; Williams & Becker, 1994). Initial efforts to evaluate the effects of culture sensitive interventions are now beginning to emerge and have produced mixed results (Gondolf, 2004; Perilla & Perez, 2002; Rothman, Gupta, Pavlos, Dang, & Coutinho, 2007). As we move forward with these efforts, we would do well as a field to expand our knowledge base and explore culturally sensitive models now being successfully used in the field of health promotion to enhance the quality of services, increase treatment adherence by ethnic minorities, and reduce health disparities (Tucker et al., 2007).

Another challenge for proponents of services for men of color who batter is how to devise ways to integrate their efforts effectively with coordinated community response networks. The emerging data on the effectiveness of coordinated community response initiatives suggest that when it comes to protecting women and increasing the likelihood that men with histories of IPV do not recidivate, this is a winning strategy. Moreover, the research literature makes it abundantly clear that partnership with alcohol treatment services should become the standard of practice in the field. When working with men of color who batter, however, the potential benefits of coordinated community responses need to be tempered by the reality that the U.S. criminal justice system is a multilayered, confusing and "racist system to those who come from marginalized communities" (Erwin & Vidales, 2001, p. 13). Knowing that men of color are arrested more often and charged with more serious crimes and with a greater number of crimes than their White counterparts makes it imperative for service providers to men of color who batter to enter into these coordinated community response networks as intentional agents of social control, individual healing, and social change.

The aforementioned considerations about the broader social context in which service for men of color who batter are provided brings to mind the words of the eminent community psychologist George Albee, who, while commenting on the unity of clinical practice, mental health, and social justice, wrote,

> As one steeped in the culture and values of public health, I must note the long-held public health dictum: No pathological condition has ever been eliminated by intervention with individuals one at a time. In other words no disease or disorder has ever been treated out of existence. The benefit of working with individuals damaged by the exploitative system is that we learn the nature and causes of injustice that produce that produce the toxic social stresses. Then, we must move beyond treating individuals to unified efforts to change the system. (Aldarondo, 2007, p. xvii)

With respect to working with men of color who batter, Albee would ask: What does it mean to want to promote individual healing when you know that the men you serve tend to live in communities where ethnic and minority groups are more likely to lack medical insurance, to receive lower quality of care, to have trouble paying their bills, to go without needed health care, to have poor transportation systems, to have witnessed community violence, to die younger, to live in inadequate housing, to have limited access to high-quality nutritional products, and so on than other segments of society?[2]

We agree with a growing number of domestic violence experts who propose that to heal men of color who batter, we must also intentionally aim to transform the communities in which they live (e.g., Almeida & Hudak, 2002; Sinclair, 2002; Perilla, Lavizzo, & Ibanez, 2007; Williams, 2002). We believe that the current state of the knowledge about determinants of IPV and the efficacy of interventions with men who batter presents an opportunity for providers of services to men of color to remain true to the commitments to social change and social justice that gave rise to the domestic violence field. Moreover, we believe that progress

---

[2] See Agency for Health Care Research Quality (2005); Hofrichter (2003).

can be made by expanding the roles for providers of services to men of color who batter beyond the role of healer and agent of social control to include the role of agent of social change. In this role, providers of services of men of color can use their understanding of the oppressive effects of unequal power, their honed sensitivity to process of denial and minimization, their knowledge of culture-specific practices and preferred modes of communication, their familiarity with the organization and functioning of the criminal justice system, and their understanding and connection with men of color to cross disciplinary boundaries and foster the development of culturally sensitive and competent partnerships and reform initiatives with other stakeholders in the legal, community, business, and professional systems.

Culturally sensitive, broad-based partnerships are needed to promote healing and change in men who batter. There are diverse players in the nonprofit, governmental, business, and higher education communities with commitment and expertise with social justice and social change practices. We must indentify these individuals in our communities and enlist them in our efforts to put an end to IPV. In doing so, however, we should take note of Audre Lorde's (1984) dictum: "The master's tools will never dismantle the master's house." Men of color who batter not only need to learn how to live free of violence but must also be our allies in the transformation of the toxic social conditions fueling their violence. It is through the participation of men who batter in this process that individual healing and lasting social change is most likely to take place. The words of another eminent community psychologist, Julian Rappaport (1981), now come to mind: "If the antidote for arrogance is the ecological view of man, the medicine for mediocrity is the pursuit of paradox" (p. 8). As currently conceived, the roles of the provider of services to men of color who batter are inherently paradoxical. Uncovering these paradoxes at a time when service for men who batter are under increased scrutiny is likely to give a new found sense of direction and urgency to the field.

## REFERENCES

Agency for Health Care Research Quality. (2005). *2005 national healthcare disparities report* (DHHS publication). Rockville, MD: Government Printing Office.

Albee, G. (2007). Foreword. In E. Aldarondo (Ed.), *Advancing social justice through clinical practice* (pp. xv–xvii), Mahwah, NJ: Erlbaum Associates.

Aldarondo, E. (2002). Evaluating the efficacy of interventions with men who batter. In E. Aldarondo & F. Mederos (Eds.), *Programs for men who batter: Intervention and prevention strategies in a diverse society* (pp. 3.1–3.20). New York: Civic Research Institute.

Aldarondo, E., & Mederos, F. (Eds.) (2002). *Programs for men who batter: Intervention and prevention strategies in a diverse society.* New York: Civic Research Institute.

Aldarondo, E., Kaufman Kantor, G., & Jasinski, J. L. (2002). Risk marker analysis for wife assault in Latino families. *Violence Against Women: An International and Interdisciplinary Journal, 8,* 429–454.

Almeida, R. V., & Hudak, J. (2002). The cultural context model. In E. Aldarondo and F. Mederos (Eds.), *Programs for men who batter: Intervention and prevention strategies in a diverse society* (pp. 10.1–10.48). New York: Civic Research Institute.

Babcock, J. C., & Steiner, R. (1999). The relationship between treatment, incarceration, and recidivism of battering: A program evaluation of Seattle's coordinated community response to domestic violence. *Journal of Family Psychology, 1,* 46–59.

Bennett, C. L., & Goodman, L. A. (2005). Risk factors for reabuse in intimate partner violence: A cross-disciplinary critical review. *Trauma, Violence, & Abuse, 6*(2), 141–175.

Bennett, L., & Williams, O. J. (2001). Intervention programs for men who batter. In C. M. Renzetti, J. L. Edleson, & R. K. Bergen (Eds.), *Sourcebook on violence against women.* Thousand Oaks, CA: Sage.

Berk, R. A., Campbell, A., Klap, R., & Western, B. (1992). The deterrent effects of arrest in incidents of domestic violence: A Bayesian analysis of four field experiments. *American Sociological Review, 57,* 698–708.

Buzawa, E., & Buzawa, C. (Eds.). (1996). *Do arrests and restraining orders work?* Thousand Oaks, CA: Sage.

Caetano, R. (2001). Alcohol-related intimate partner violence among White, Black and Hispanic couples in the United States. *Alcoholism: Clinical and Experimental Research, 27*(8), 1337–1339.

Cameron, P. (2003). Domestic violence among homosexual partners. *Psychological Reports, 93,* 410–416.

Carrillo, R., & Tello, J. (Eds.) (1998). *Family violence and men of color: Healing the wounded male spirit* (1st ed.). New York: Springer Publishing Co.

Carlson, M. J., Harris, S. D. & Holden, G. W (1999). Protective orders and domestic violence: Risk factors for re-abuse. *Journal of Family Violence, 14,* 205–226.

Chen, H., Bersani, S., Myers, S. C., & Denton, T. (1989). Evaluating the effectiveness of court-sponsored abuser treatment programs. *Journal of Family Violence, 4,* 309–322.

Daly, J. E., & Pelowski, S. (2000). Predictors of dropout among men who batter: A review of studies with implications for research and practice. *Violence and Victims, 15,* 137–160.

Davis, R. C., & Taylor, B. G. (1999). Does batterer treatment reduce violence? A synthesis of the literature. *Women & Criminal Justice, 10,* 69–93.

Dobash, R., Dobash, R. E., Cavanagh, K. & Lewis, R. (1996). Reeducation programs for violent men: An evaluation. *Research Findings, 46,* 309–322.

Dunford, E W. (2000). The San Diego Navy experiment: An assessment of interventions for men who assault their wives. *Journal of Consulting & Clinical Psychology, 63,* 468–476.

Dunford, E. W., Huizinga, D., & Elliot, D. S. (1990). The role of arrest in domestic assault: The Omaha experiment. *Criminology, 28,* 183–206.

Dutton, D. G. (1986). The outcome of court-mandated treatment for wife assault: A quasi-experimental evaluation. *Violence and Victims, 1,* 163–175.

Dutton, D. G., Bodnarchuk, M., Kropp, R., & Hart, S. D. (1997). Wife assault treatment and criminalrecidivism: An 11-year follow-up. *International Journal of Offender Therapy and Comparative Criminology, 41,* 9–23.

Economic Commission for Latin America and the Caribbean. (2007). *No more! The right of women to live free of violence in Latin America and the Caribbean.* (LC/L/.2808), Santiago, Chile, October.

Edleson, J. L. (1990). Judging the success of interventions with men who batter. In D. J. Besharov (Ed.), *Family violence: Research and public policy issues.* Washington, DC: AEI Press.

Edleson, J. L., & Grusznski, R. J. (1988). Treating men who batter: Four years of outcome data from the Domestic Abuse Project. *Journal of Social Service Research, 12,* 3–12.

Erwin, P. A., & Vidales, G. (2001). *Domestic violence, people of color and the criminal justice system: A case for prevention.* Domestic Violence Research for Racial Justice Project. Family Violence Prevention Fund.

Fagan, J. (1996). *The criminalization of domestic violence: Promises and perils.* Washington, DC: National Institute of Justice, U.S. Department of Justice.

Feazell, C. S., Mayers, R. S., & Deschner, J. (1984). Services for men who batter: Implications for programs and policies. *Family Relations, 33,* 217–223.

Feder, L., & Wilson, D. (2005). A meta-analytic review of court-mandated batterer intervention programs: Can courts affect abusers' behavior? *Journal of Experimental Criminology, 1,* 239–262.

Field, C. A., & Caetano, R. (2004). Ethnic differences in intimate partner violence in the U.S. general population: The role of alcohol use and socioeconomic status. *Trauma, Violence, & Abuse,* 5(4), 303–317.

Ford, D. A., Reichard, R., Goldsmith, S., & Regoli, M. J. (1996). Future directions for criminal justice policy in domestic violence. In E. Buzawa & C. Buzawa (Eds.), *Do arrests and restraining orders work?* Thousand Oaks, CA: Sage.

Gamache, D. J., Edleson, J. L., & Schock, M. D. (1988). Coordinated police, judicial, and social service response to woman battering: A multiple-baseline evaluation across three communities. In G. T. Hotaling, D. Finkelhor, J. T. Kirkpatrick, & M. Straus (Eds.), *Coping with family violence: Research and policy perspectives* (193–209). Thousand Oaks, CA: Sage.

Garcia-Moreno, C., Jansen, H. A., Ellsberg, M., Heise, L., & Watts, C. H. (2006). Prevalence of intimate partner violence: Findings from the WHO multi-country study of women's health and domestic violence. *Lancet, 368,* 1260–1269.

Garner, J., Fagan, J., & Maxwell, C. (1995). Published findings from the spouse assault replication program: A critical review. *Journal of Quantitative Criminology, 11,* 3–28.

Gondolf, E. (1998). Do batterer programs work? A 15-month follow-up of a multi-site evaluation. *Domestic Violence Report, 3,* 64–80.

Gondolf, E. W. (2000). A 30-month follow-up of court-referred batterers in four cities. *International Journal of Offender Therapy and Comparative Criminology, 44,* 111–128.

Gondolf, E. W. (2001a). Limitations of experimental evaluation of batterer intervention programs. *Trauma, Violence, & Abuse, 2,* 79–88.

Gondolf, E. W. (2001b). The program effect of batterer programs in three cities. *Violence and Victims, 16,* 693–704.

Gondolf, E. W. (2002). *Batterer intervention systems.* Thousand Oaks, CA: Sage.

Gondolf, E. W. (2004). Regional and cultural utility of conventional batterer counseling. *Violence Against Women, 10,* 880–900.

Grau, J., Fagan, J., & Wexler, S. (1985). Restraining orders for battered women: Issues of access and efficacy. In C. Schweber & C. Feinman (Eds.), *Criminal justice politics and women: The aftermath of legally mandated change.* New York: Haworth Press.

Hamberger, K., & Hastings, J. (1988). Skills training for treatment of spouse abusers: An outcome study. *Journal of Family Violence, 3,* 121–130.

Hampton, R. L., & Gelles, R. J. (1994). Violence towards black women in a nationally representative sample of black families. *Journal of Comparative Family Studies, 25*(1), 105–119.

Harrell, A., & Smith, B. (1996). Effects of restraining orders on domestic violence victims. In E. Buzawa & C. Buzawa (Eds.), *Do arrests and restraining orders work?* Thousand Oaks, CA: Sage.

Hirschel, J. D., Hutchison, I. W. III, & Dean, C. W. (1992). The failure of arrest to deter spouse abuse. *Journal of Research in Crime & Delinquency, 29,* 7–33.

Hofrichter, R. (Ed.) (2003). *Health and social justice: Politics, ideology, and inequality in the distribution of disease.* San Francisco: Jossey-Bass.

Holt, V. L., Kernick, M. A., Lurnley, T. Wolf, M. E., & Rivara, F. P. (2002). Civil protection orders and risk of subsequent police-reported violence. *Journal of the American Medical Association, 288*(5), 589–594.

INEGI (Instituto Nacional de Estadistica,Geographia e Informatica) (2007). El INEGI, Inmujeres y Unifem dan a conocer los resultados de la encuesta nacional sobre la dinamica de las relaciones en los hogares, 2006 [INEGI, Inmujer, and Unifem announce the results of the national survey on relational dynamics in the home, 2006]. Mexico City: Author. Retrieved February 1, 2008, from http://www.inegi.gob.mx/inegi/contenidos/espanol/prensa/Boletines/Boletin/Comunicados/Especiales/2007/

Jaffe, R, Wolfe, D. A., Telford, A., & Austin, G. (1986). The impact of police charges in incidents of wife abuse. *Journal of Family Violence, 1,* 37–49.

Kaufman Kantor, G., Jasinski, J. L., & Aldarondo, E. (1994). Sociocultural status and incidence of marital violence in Hispanic families. *Violence and Victims, 9,* 207–222.

Keilitz, S., Hannaford, R., & Efkeman, H. S. (1997). *Civil protection orders: The benefits and limitations for victims of domestic violence* (Grant No. 93-IJ-CX-0035). Washington, DC: National Institute of Justice.

Klein, A. R. (1996). Re-abuse in a population of court-restrained male batterers after two years: Development of a predictive model. In E. Buzawa & C. Buzawa (Eds.), *Do arrests and restraining orders work?* Thousand Oaks, CA: Sage.

Lorde, A. (1984). The master's tools will never dismantle the master's house. In A. Lorde, *Sister Outsider: Essays and Speeches* (pp. 110–113). Berkeley, CA: The Crossing Press.

McFarlane, J., Malecha, A., Gist, J., Watson, K., Batten, E., Hall, I., et al. (2004). Protection orders and intimate partner violence: An 18-month study of 150 Black, Hispanic and White women. *American Journal of Public Health, 94,* 613–618.

McClennen, J. C. (2005). Domestic violence between same-gender partners: Recent findings and future research. *Journal of Interpersonal Violence, 20,* 149–154.

Mederos, F. (2002). Changing our visions of interventions with men who batter—The evolution of programs for physically abusive men. In E. Aldarondo and F. Mederos (Eds.), *Programs for men who batter: Intervention and prevention strategies in a diverse society* (pp. 1.1–1.23). New York: Civic Research Institute.

Miller, N. (1997). *Domestic violence legislation affecting police and prosecutor responsibilities in the United States: Inferences from a 50-state review of statutory codes.* Paper presented at the Fifth International Family Violence Conference, Durham, NH.

Murphy, C. M., Musser, R. H., & Maton, K. I. (1998). Coordinated community intervention for domestic abusers: Intervention system involvement and criminal recidivism. *Journal of FamilyViolence, 13,* 263–284.

Palmer, S. E., Brown, R. A., & Barrera, M. E. (1992). Group treatment program for abusive husbands: Long-term evaluation. *American Journal of Orthopsychiatry, 62,* 276–283.

Pate, A. M., & Hamilton, E. E. (1992). Formal and informal deterrents to domestic violence: The Dade County spouse assault experiment. *American Sociological Review, 57,* 691–697.

Pennsylvania 1976 Protection from Abuse Act, R L. No. 1090, S. B. 1243 (1976).

Perilla, J. L., & Perez, F. (2002). A program for immigrant Latino men who batter within the context of a comprehensive family intervention. In E. Aldarondo and F. Mederos (Eds.), *Programs for men who batter: Intervention and prevention strategies in a diverse society* (pp. 11.1–11.31). New York: Civic Research Institute.

Perilla, J. L., Lavizzo, P., & Ibanez, G. (2007). Towards a community psychology of liberation. In E. Aldarondo (Ed.), *Advancing social justice through clinical practice* (pp. 291–312). Mahwah, NJ: Erlbaum Associates.

Pirog-Good, M., & Stets-Kealy, J. (1985). Male batters and battering prevention programs. A national survey. *Response to the Victimization of Women and Children, 8,* 8–12.

Rappaport, J. (1981). In praise of paradox: A social policy of empowerment over prevention. *American Journal of Community Psychology, 9*(1), 1–25.

Rothman, E. F., Gupta, J., Pavlos, C., Dang, Q., & Coutinho, P. (2007). Batterer intervention program enrollment and completion among immigrant men in Massachusetts. *Violence Against Women, 13,* 527.

Saunders, D. G. (1996). Feminist-cognitive-behavioral and process-psychodynamic treatments for men who batter: Interaction of abuser traits and treatment models. *Violence and Victims, 11,* 393–413.

Sherman, L. W., & R. A. Berk (1984). The specific deterrent effects of arrest for domestic assault. *American Sociological Review, 49*(2), 261–272.

Sherman, L. W., Schmidt, J. D., Rogan, D. R, Gartin, E, Cohen, E. G., Collins, D. J., et al. (1991). From initial deterrence to long-term escalation: Short custody arrest for poverty ghetto domestic violence. *Criminology, 29,* 821–850.

Sherman, L. W., Schmidt, J. D., & Rogan, D. R. (1992a). *Policing domestic violence: Experiments and dilemmas.* New York: Free Press.

Sherman, L. W., Smith, D. A., Schmidt, J. D., & Rogan, D. R. (1992b). Crime, punishment, and stake in conformity: Legal and informal control of domestic violence. *American Sociological Review, 57,* 680–690.

Shepard, M. F., Falk, D. R., & Elliott, B. A. (2002). Enhancing coordinated community responses to reduce recidivism in cases of domestic violence. *Journal of Interpersonal Violence, 17*(5), 551–569.

Sinclair, H. (2002). A community activist response to intimate partner violence. In E. Aldarondo and F. Mederos (Eds.), *Programs for men who batter: Intervention and prevention strategies in a diverse society* (pp. 5.1–5.53). New York: Civic Research Institute.

Straus, M. A., & Gelles, R. J. (1990). How violent are American families? Estimates from the National Family Violence Resurvey and other studies. In M. A. Straus and R. J. Gelles (Eds.), *Physical violence in American families* (pp. 95–112). New Brunswick, NJ: Transaction Publishers.

Straus, M. A., & Smith, C. (1990). Violence in Hispanic families in the United States. Incidence rates and structural interpretations. In M. A. Straus and R. J. Gelles (Eds.), *Physical violence in American families* (pp. 341–382). New Brunswick, NJ: Transaction Publishers.

Taylor, B. G., Davis, R. C., & Maxwell, C. D. (2001). The effects of a group batterer treatment program: A randomized experiment in Brooklyn. *Justice Quarterly, 18,* 171–201.

Tjaden, P., & Thoennes, N. (2000). *Extent, nature, and consequences of IPV: Findings from the National Violence Against Women Survey.* Washington, DC: National Institute of Justice.

Tolan, P., Gorman-Smith, D., & Henry, D. (2006). Family violence. *Annual Review of Psychology, 57,* 557–583.

Tolman, R. M., & Weisz, A. (1995). Coordinated community intervention for domestic violence: The effects of arrest and prosecution on recidivism of woman abuse perpetrators. *Crime & Delinquency, 41,* 481–495.

Tucker, C. M., Herman, K. C., Ferdinand, L. A., Bailey, T. R., Lopez, M. T., Beato, C., et al. (2007). Providing patient-centered culturally sensitive health care: A formative model. *The Counseling Psychologist, 35,* 679–705.

United Nations (2006). *In-depth study on all forms of violence against women: Report of the Secretary-General, Division for the Advancement of Women.* Retrieved from http://www.un.org/womenwatch/daw/vaw/violenceagainstwomenstudydoc.pdf

Van Wyk, J. A., Benson, M. L., Fox, G. L., & DeMaris, A. (2003). Detangling individual, partner, and community level correlates of partner violence. *Crime & Delinquency, 49*(3), 412–438.

Waldo, M. (1988). Relationship enhancement counseling groups for wife abusers. *Journal of Mental Health Counseling, 10,* 37–45.

Williams, O. J. (2002). Developing the capacity to address social context issues: Group treatment with African American men who batter. In A. Mullender & M. Cohen (Eds.), *Gender and group work.* Thousand Oaks, CA: Sage Publications.

Williams, O. J., & Becker, L. R. (1994). Partner abuse programs and cultural competence: The results of a national study. *Violence and Victims, 9*(3), 287–295.

Worden, A. E. (2000). The changing boundaries of the criminal justice system: Redefining the problem and the response to domestic violence. *Criminal Justice, 2*, 215–266.

World Health Organization (2005). *WHO Multi-Country Study on Women's Health and Domestic Violence Against Women: Summary report of initial results on prevalence, health outcomes, and women's responses.* Geneva: Author.

# 2

# El Hombre Noble Buscando Balance: The Noble Man Searching for Balance

JERRY TELLO

The ancient teachings, through storytelling, helped to guide, correct, and heal. Through them, the "rites of passage" lessons of "manhood" were conveyed and passed on from one generation to the next. This elder's lesson, which has parallels in many cultures, begins the dialogue and journey toward honorable and balanced manhood.

## THE YOUNG MAN AND LIFE'S LESSON

The *viejito* (the elder), lived way up on a hill and had been married for many years. His lifelong goal was to have a good relationship with his family, and he was able to do this. Then one day, his wife was called by the other world and left him. But before she left, she said to him, "Remember the promise."

The elder said, "What promise?"

And she answered, "Remember the promise of how we got this house and this land."

And he remembered that the way he got the enormous house and this land was that *dueño* (the owner) gave it all to them, based on one promise. The promise was that when they were ready to go to that "other place," when they were going to die, they would give it to someone who would continue on with the same *valores* (values), someone who would live in this house in a way that was harmonious, a way that would make the other happy. The *dueño* had said, "Remember, before you go, you have to give it—to someone who can carry these *valore* and make their partner happy."

The *viejito* remembered, and he realized that his time was getting short. So he called a meeting. He called everybody to the circle, and said, "I'm almost ready to leave and to go to the next world, but first I must keep a promise I made to my wife. I will give this mansion, this huge house and its ten thousand acres, away." (In those days you didn't get houses and you didn't get land unless someone gave them to you.) The *viejito* continued: "I'm going to give this house and this land to anyone who wants it, as long as he's able to tell me how you can make a harmonious life, how you can make a *mujer* (woman) happy. My life was devoted to my wife, so if you know, as an *hombre* (man), how to make a *mujer* happy, then you know how to live in harmony. Now, who among you wants to take the challenge of telling me the four things you have to do, the four values? Who wants to take the challenge of coming back and telling me these four *valores*? You must do it; however, by the time the sun sets on the seventh day. Do any of you want to take this challenge?"

Four men raised their hands and said that they would take the challenge.

And the *viejito* said, "There's one thing you should know: Anyone who takes the challenge but doesn't come back with the answers by the time the sun sets on the seventh day, that man will die, and all his generations to come will have disease and will suffer. Now, knowing that, how many of you would still like to take the challenge? Anyone? Remember, this is a huge house, ten thousand acres."

Well, something that happens to men sometimes is that we pretend we're not afraid and that we know everything.

And there was one man like that. "I'll do it!" he said. "Hey! Four values! No problem! I'll get that big house, and the land, and I'll be all set."

So this one man took the challenge. The *viejito* sent him out and said, "Now, go about the countryside and look for these values among the people, because the values are out there."

Off went the man, walking, and looking, and trying to think of the *valores*. And he was thinking, maybe one of the *valores* was to value money. But no, it couldn't be that. Could it be control? No, that couldn't be it. And the harder he thought about it, the harder it was for him to find the values.

As he was walking on this hot day, he became thirsty. He went by the river where there were some children playing in the water. He stopped to get a drink, and seeing the children, he remembered that, being children, these little ones know our spirits, they are honest, they say things we don't want them to say, they do things we don't want them to do, but they're so honest, so clear with us. And the children, seeing this man, knew that he was searching for something, and they asked, "*Señor, señor,* what's the matter? You look lost—are you looking for something?"

And the man replied, "Ah-h, what do you know? You're just little children, what do you know?"

"Well, what's the matter, sir—what's the matter? You need something?" Then one of the kids whispered, "Hey, he's the one—he's the one! He's the one looking for the *valores.*"

And one of the children spoke up, saying, "You're the one looking for the *valores*!"

Another chided, "Oh, you're going to die if you don't find 'em, huh?"

Because the children know. The children know when we're lost, and they know when something's happening to us, when we're searching. And they're honest—and open—and ready to give us their knowledge, telling us, "We'll tell you! We'll tell you!"

And our usual answer is, "Ah-h, what do you kids know?"

"Well, we know what makes us happy!" the children said to the man. "What? What?" asked the man.

"We like *cariño* (love), we like our moms and dads to hug us and kiss us. We like *cariño*—we like *cariño*! We *really* like *cariño*! It's good! Yeah, that's what we like!"

And the man answered with a sigh, "Well, thank you-thank you."

"Okay! Bye, sir—bye, sir. Hope you find everything you need by the seventh day," the children said, adding "'Cause if not, you're going to die!"

The man continued on his search, and a couple of days passed. He came to some orchards where *campesinos* (farmworkers) were harvesting fruit, working the land. Seeing the food, and being hungry, he asked one of the men, "Can I have some food?"

"You look a little bit lost and a little bit hungry; of course, you can," the worker said, and gave some fruit to the man. He asked, "*¿Que tiene, señor?* (What's the matter, sir?)"

The man replied, "Nothing, nothing. Ah-h-h, you men just work the land, what do you know?"

The worker replied, "No, no, we're close to the land, and we know what's going on. We can feel when something's not right, and you don't seem quite right."

And the man said, "But what do you know?"

Then the worker, talking to one of the others, said, "Ah-h, he's the one, he's the one," and they talked among themselves, saying, "He's the *loco* (the crazy one), the one who's looking for the *valores.*"

"I'm not crazy," the man protested, "but I *am* looking for the values. But what do you know?"

The first worker replied, "Well, we work all day long, every day, and all we want is dignity, just for people to give us valor, to value what we do. We feed the people. We work hard just for one thing: dignity. That's all we ask-all we ask. So that's a value for you."

"Ah, ¡*gracias!*" the man said. And on he went.

Soon it was the fourth day, then the fifth, and the man was getting a little nervous, starting to think that perhaps he shouldn't have taken on the challenge. He had thought it was going to be easy. As he came to the top of a hill, he saw a little house with a porch, where two *viejitos* (elders), an old couple, were sitting, drinking coffee, rocking and rocking, and talking to each other.

The man, who was getting tired, wanted a place to sleep, so he went up to the couple and asked, "Have you any place to sleep?"

The old man replied, "We always have room for people passing. Where are you going?" (And the *mujer* whispered, "He's the one, he's the one!") The *viejito*, laughing, said, "You're looking for the *valores*, eh?"

The man answered, "Yes, yes, but I don't know if I'm going to find the four *valores* soon enough."

The old man replied, "*Muy facil, es muy facil* (it's very easy)."

"So what do you mean?"

The old woman replied, "My husband and I, we've been married many years, 60 years, and the most difficult one is him!"

The old man turned to his wife, and said, "Agh, and she likes things in their place, just her way. We fought for years until we learned to respect each other, and we've been together all these years."

So the man stayed overnight with the old couple and realized he had learned a third value: respect. But it was the seventh day, and the sun was in the middle of the sky and now he was back, walking through the village and getting very nervous. As he walked on, he heard a noise somewhere off to the side: "Ps-s-st, p-s-s-t." He looked around, but he saw nothing. Then, he heard the same noise again. "Ps-s-s-t, p-s-s-t." Suddenly he saw a *mujer*, saying again,

"Ps-s-s-t, p-s-s-t." He looked. "Ps-s-s-t, p-s-s-t, come here!" As he drew closer to her, he saw that she was very ugly, with big warts. As he came even closer, he noticed how bad she smelled. Stinking!

The man asked, "¿*Que tiene*? (What do you want?)"

The woman said, "So, you're the one looking for the four *valores*, eh?"

"Yes, but (phew! phew!) what do you know?"

The woman answered, "I've got it for you—I've got the last value!" "But look at you!" he said with disgust. "You're over here, and you're all stinky and smelly, and what could you know about anything!"

She replied, "Well, I sit here all day long. I see a lot. I know a lot. I see what shouldn't happen. I know. I know the fourth value." "You don't know anything!"

"Well, it's up to you, *señor*. What's your choice? If you don't get the value from me, then what? Death. You want to die?"

"No, but you're so ugly, and I . . ."

"Well, it's up to you, *señor*. Go ahead."

"All right, all right, give me the *valor*!" he said impatiently.

"No, no, no, no, no!" the woman said solemnly. "You know nothing in this world is free. Life is a circle. I'll give to you, but you give to me."

"But what do you want?"

"If I give you the *valor*, you have to marry me."

"Marry you!" the man said. "Let's be realistic!"

"Well, it's up to you," she said. "Either you marry me—or you die. Which would you like?"

"Aw, you don't know the value anyway," he muttered.

"Yes, I do."

"Well, what is it?"

"Well, it's very easy," the woman said slowly, "It's *palabra*. It's giving your word, meaning the value of trust. Trust is such an important thing, and the reason I'm sitting here is because people have broken trust with me. Your *palabra, señor. Si no tienes palabra, no tienes nada* (if your word isn't trusted, then you have nothing)."

"Agh, that's a stupid value," he replied.

"But you have no choice. It's the last one, eh?"

As the sun began to set, the man ran to the top of the village hill, where sat the *viejito*, the elder, smiling. "Did you find them?" the old man said. "Did you find them?"

The man answered, "Well, from the children, I learned about love."
"Yes, that's one."

"And from the farmworkers, I learned about dignity."

"Yes, that's the second one."

"From the elders, I learned the value of respect. But I don't know about this last one . . ." The man hesitated.

"Well, what's the last one?"

"Well, it's. . . . it's trust, and it's about giving your word . . ." And the *viejito* says, "Yes, you got it! Where'd you learn about that value?"

"Well, there's this old, ugly woman, sitting on the—"

"No, no, I know about her! But how did you *get* it from her?" "Well, I promised I'd marry her."

"A-g-h-h-h-h, ho, ho!" the *viejito* laughed. "So then you will have to marry her, because you can't only *have* the values, you have to *live* them."

The man looked at the house, and thought, Well, it's a big house; maybe she could live on that side and I'll live on this side, eh?

So the *viejito* gave them the big house and the land.

And the *viejito* that night, because his job was done, passed to the next world.

The man and the ugly woman then had a wedding. They invited everyone, and everyone came and celebrated the marriage. After the wedding, the couple went into their house, into the bedroom. There were many bedrooms, but they were in the one room, and the man said, "Well, I'm going to go to another bedroom and sleep, and you can sleep in this bed."

"Yes, okay," replied the woman. "But before you go to sleep, give me a kiss goodnight."

"Do I have to?" he said with revulsion.

"Well, remember the *valores*," she replied, "love, dignity, respect, and . . . come on, kiss me."

"Do I really have to?"

"Yes," she said adamantly.

"Do I have to keep my eyes open?"

"No, you can close your eyes if you want," she said, "just as long as you kiss me."

So, with his eyes closed, the man, thinking that with his eyes closed he would not feel anything, kissed her.

And when he opened his eyes, the woman wasn't ugly anymore. She was beautiful!

And the man said, "Wait a minute! You're not ugly anymore! What happened?"

She replied, "It's because you're not afraid anymore. You were able to get close to what you were afraid of. And when you get close to, and hold, what you fear, it's not ugly anymore. It turns into a lesson about something of beauty. But that's not the end of it."

"What do you mean?" he said.

She replied, "You have a choice."

"What's the choice?"

"Well, I can either be beautiful in the house but ugly when we leave, or I can be ugly when we're in the house but beautiful when we're outside."

Which would you choose? Ugly when inside the house, beautiful when outside? Or beautiful inside the house, ugly when outside, where all your friends could talk about your ugly wife? If you choose beautiful inside, all your friends will talk about you and wonder how you could marry an ugly woman.

So what did this man do? What did he choose? He had learned something in his life.

Well, what he did is what wise men do, and he said to his wife, "Whatever you want." He gave up his control, he gave up the power, and he allowed the spirit of healing, and of the Creator, to guide him. He gave up trying to dictate.

And with that, she was beautiful inside the house and she was beautiful on the outside, because it didn't matter anymore.


## BACKGROUND

Many people, and even many Chicano/Latinos, do not know that there was a time when there was little violence or fighting among Chicano/Latino people. In fact, many people believe that violence is a part of our core cultural identity.

> Because neither do you understand us, nor do we understand you. And we do not know what it is that you want. You have deprived us of our good order and *way* of government, and the one with which you have replaced it we do not understand. Now all is confusion and without order and harmony. The Indians of Mexico have given themselves to fighting because you have brought it upon them. . . .

Those who are not in contact with you do not fight; they live in peace. And if during the time of our "paganism" there were fights and disputes, they were very few. And they were dealt with justly and settled quickly because there used to be no difficulties in finding out which of the parties was right, nor were there any delays and cheating as there are now. (Zurita, 1891)

In specific reference to domestic violence, this belief of inbred false perception *is* so ingrained that some think it is part of being a Chicano/Latino male to beat his wife, a part of his "*machismo.*" It is within this falsehood that the root of the problem lies, the systematic, multigenerational process of internalized oppression.

E. S. Maruse writes that oppression is the "systematic, pervasive, routine mistreatment of individuals on the basis of their membership in a particular group." It is the denial or nonrecognition of the complete humanness of others. Oppression has an order, and the cycle begins with the circulation of lies, misinformation, or half-truths about a people. This misinformation then serves as a justification for their mistreatment. The cycle continues, whereby this misinformation is woven into the fabric of society. The final stage is when the target group believes the lies are attributed to a deficit in their own culture, and they begin internalizing the oppression in actions and behavior against themselves, thus breaking their own true spirit.

This "spirit breaking" came in a variety of direct and indirect measures as a means of the Europeans' attempting to "conquer" the physical, emotional, mental, and spiritual identity of the indigenous Mexican people. This historical genocide resulted in over 50 million people being killed—men, women, and children; thousands of women and children raped; sacred writings, sacred sites, art, and precious belongings destroyed; and the distortion and disharmony of traditional values, customs, ceremonies, and spiritual teachings (Leon-Portilla, 1961). The result of this has been a deep imbalancing wound, referred to as intergenerational post-traumatic stress disorder (PTSD) (Duran & Duran, 1995).

At the same time, the wisdom of elders was so profound that the occurrence of these devastating events was actually prophesied by them, long before it came to pass, in the story of *La Llorona* (The Crying Woman) (Leon-Portilla, 1992).

The origin or root of the story is ancient and goes back to before the Europeans invaded Mexico. At this time, there were a number of prophecies, visions, or omens foretelling the arrival of the Spaniards, and one of these omens was that of *La Llorona*. The people heard a weeping woman, night after night. She passed by in the middle of the night, wailing and crying out in a loud voice, "My children, my children, where will I take you? My children." At other times, she cried, "My children, my children, where are my children?" The indigenous reference for this "crying woman" is Cihuacoati, an ancient earth goddess, whose principal role was to care for the children. During the time of the European invasion, it has been documented that one of the main preoccupations of the mothers was their fear of "losing" their children. The fear was a literal fear of losing them to death or torture by the invaders, but more importantly, the fear that the children would lose their spirit, their *destino*, or purpose in life connected to their people. The essence of knowing one's *destino* was seen as the most significant element of keeping balanced and being well rooted.

In indigenous times, there was much focus and attention devoted to the proper "rooting" or raising of all children, both male and female. An ancient document describing the way the children were taught morals in the past stated that every morning after the children's usual meager breakfast they would be taught:

How they should live,
How they should respect others,
How they were to dedicate themselves to what was good and righteous,
How they were to avoid evil,
How to flee unrighteousness with strength, and
How to refrain from perversion and greed. (Garibay Kintana, 1943, p. 97)

The teachings were the same for males and females, and as we see in the next passage, a purity of heart and a sense of spirituality were at the base of these teachings.

Even if he were poor and lowly,
even if his mother and his father
were the poorest of the poor . . .
His lineage was not considered, only his way of life mattered—the purity of his heart,
His good and humane heart . . .
His stout heart. . . .
It was said that he had God in his heart, that he was wise in the things of God. (Torquemada, 1943, I, p. 1988)

The above two accounts are directly opposite to the stereotypical view of the *"macho"* male's self-centeredness. The following account is also contrary to the stereotypical "superior" controlling attitude that is typically considered to be a prerequisite of a traditional Chicano/Latino male:

> Not with envy,
> > not with a twisted heart,
> > shall you feel superior,
> > shall you go about boasting.
> > Rather in goodness shall you make true
> > your song and your word.
> > And thus you shall be highly regarded,
> > and you shall be able to live with the others. (Olmos, n.d.)

In a slightly different way another test describes the good man's just reward:

> If you live uprightly,
> > you shall be held highly for it,
> > and people will say of you
> > what is appropriate, what is just. (Olmos, n.d.)

So we see that at the base of the culture were direct teachings to reinforce a sense of respect and interconnectedness founded on spirituality. In addition, contrary to the pervasive "Latin Lover" falsehood and the false stereotype that Latinos didn't talk directly about sexuality, in the following, a father speaks to his son about the importance of sexual moderation and preparation.

> Do not throw yourself upon women
> > Like the dog which throws itself upon food.
> > Be not like the dog
> > When he is given food or drink,
> > Giving yourself up to women before the time comes.
> > Even though you may long for women,
> > Hold back, hold back with your heart
> > Until you are a grown man, strong and robust.
> > Look at the maguey plant.
> > If it is opened before it has grown
> > And its liquid is taken out,
> > It has no substance.

It does not produce liquid, it is useless.
Before it is opened to withdraw its water,
It should be allowed to grow and attain full size
Then its sweet water is removed all in good time.
This is how you must act:
Before you know woman you must grow and be a complete man.
And then you will be ready for marriage;
You will beget children of good stature,
Healthy, agile, and comely. (*Códice Florentino*, Book VI, fol. 97, r.)

This passage states, "Before you know woman, you must grow and be a complete man." This reference directs itself to a "rite of passage" that must take place in order that a young man can be ready to enter into a complete relationship with a woman. The passage further states, "And then you will be ready for marriage" or be prepared to make a commitment to another. This aspect of commitment or *palabra* (word), then, becomes the basis for manhood in the traditional sense; your word, credibility, and essence are based on who and what you represent.

The true essence of what was expected of a man is very clearly articulated in the following passage:

The mature man
Is a heart solid as a rock
Is a wise face
Possessor of a face
Possessor of a heart
He is able and understanding. (*Códice Matritense del Real Palacio*, VI, fol. 215)

And finally, in this ancient writing, a father who participates in the raising of children by placing before them a large mirror (his example) is described as compassionate:

The father, root and origin of the lineage of men.
His heart is good, he is careful of things; he is compassionate, he is concerned, he is the foresight, he is support, he protects with his hands.
He raises children, he educates, he instructs, he admonishes,
He teaches them to live.
He places before them a large mirror,
A mirror pierced on both sides; he is a large torch that does not smoke.
(*Códice Matritense de la Real Academia*, VIII, 118, v.)

The above reference to a "large torch that does not smoke" speaks again to *palabra*, or word, that is honest and consistent.

These last two accounts clearly articulate the basis of what the traditional elders described as a *"macho"* in the true sense of *palabra*, or word.

"Possessor of a face"—*cara*.
"Possessor of a heart"—*corazón*.

So complex are these instructions that 14 volumes are devoted to these teachings alone in the Florentine Codex, an ancient indigenous document. The development of one's character, identity, or root essence was paramount to the ancients because they understood that if the root of the tree was not well grounded, then the tree would be weak and vulnerable to the winds. This identity root, based on the dual concepts of *cara y corazón*, is reflected in the four main values.

The *cara* reveals the significance of a man knowing his *destino* (purpose in life)—his role within the family and community—and a commitment to the interdependent functioning of the family. The two values that form the basis of cara are *dignidad* (dignity) and *respeto* (respect).

In balancing this duality, the *corazón* reveals the need for compassion and trust, a spiritual harmony and a sense of understanding and consideration for others. The two values that form the basis of *corazón* are *confianza* (interconnected bonding) and *cariño* (love, acceptance).

It is with this knowledge that the "true" definition of *macho*, based on the indigenous elders' teachings, can be understood:

Dignified
A Protector
Nurturing
Spiritual
Faithful
Respectful
Friendly
Caring
Sensitive
Trustworthy. (*Códice Matritense de la Real Academia, VIII,* 118, v.)

So the teachings are still there, even though many do not know they exist. If you destroy the semblance of a people's authentic self, you destroy their spirit. Thus, we truly begin to understand the tremendous trauma that was perpetrated and the disequilibrium that was manifested—so profound in nature that we feel it still, even today. This tremendous historical, multigenerational distortion of our way of life impacted us to the degree that we, as a people, still are attempting to rebalance from the over 50 million deaths, rapes, and severe abuses that were perpetrated on our people. The total disequilibriating impact of destroying a harmonious, interdependent identity has now resulted in some of us hurting, killing, and violating our own as a way of life. This brings extreme sadness and pain to so many. And if that were not enough, these oppressive forces have been successful in having many believe that these negative, spirit-destroying acts of violence against women, the center of our people, are part of our cultural identity, a spirit-destroying lie that evokes deep hopelessness.

The end result of this belief is shame, resulting finally in a total psychospiritual amnesia of one's true spirit. This long-term spirit-breaking process continues to have a devastating effect on Chicano/Latinos as a whole, and with reference to domestic violence, we see the harmful effects daily. Fortunately, the spirit of the ancients is very strong and thus we, as a people, have been able to maintain a semblance of our *destino* whereby the *mujer* (woman) and mother is still held with much respect and honor by many as an ideal, and in practice as well. This is not to say that the multigenerational oppression has not had its effect. Furthermore, I believe that unless we re-root the true essence of the ancient teachings quickly, we may lose our total rooted spirit.

We find in approaching this issue of *El Hombre Noble Buscando Balance* (The Noble Man Searching for Balance) that we have men at different points on the journey.

As part of this journey, there is a symbol of a "bridge crossing" rite of passage phase in every young person's life that is seen as critical in defining that person's development. The following is the way "The Bridge Story" came to me in a dream:

It was said that one of the greatest gifts of the dual forces coming together was that of creation—and so it was from woman and man in connection and commitment to each other and the community that the young ones were gifted to the world. It was man (father) who had as his role the raising and guiding of the children, and woman (mother) had as her role the nurturing and caring for the children, as did all the community. But after a time, when the crying woman's (La Llorona) prophecy had come true and the people were struggling, there was a young girl whose time it was to approach the bridge. Since woman/mother gave life, she was given the privilege of guiding her children to the bridge. So it was that this mother took her daughter to the woman's bridge (as there are two bridges), and she found a group of women standing in a circle at the foot of the bridge, talking and sharing. This was expected, as young girls are raised to share and care for each other, and to gather in circles.

The mother approached the women and asked them to help guide her daughter across the woman's bridge. The women readily accepted and encircled the young girl for the journey. A few days later, it was time for another to take her son to the man's bridge. As she approached the man's bridge, she looked but could find no one at the foot of the bridge. Needing someone to accompany her son, she continued to look and saw a group of men halfway across the bridge. They were arguing, drinking, and fighting with each other. She called out to them and asked them to accompany her son across the bridge. The men looked at each other in confusion, wondering to whom she was talking. Again, the mother called out to the men for assistance, and once again, they were dismayed. As boys, they had been raised to take care only of themselves and not to care for and nurture others. The mother called out again, asking if they would come and accompany her son across the bridge.

In the midst of this shouting, one man spoke up and said, "How do you expect us to take a young boy across the bridge when some of us grown men haven't even been across ourselves?"

"Then what should I do with my son?" asked the mother.

"Just leave him here with us," replied the man. So the mother left her son in the midst of the men who, themselves, were struggling.

As she went back to the village, very concerned, the other women noticed her worry and asked her, "Why?" She replied, "All the men I saw were arguing, fighting, drinking, lying, and cheating." She then turned to her young daughter and said, "Be careful with the men; they can't be trusted."

As she gave this advice to her daughter, her younger son also heard and learned to distrust men and, more importantly, to distrust himself.

Another mother approached the bridge with her son and was able to look through the men halfway across the bridge and see her husband, who had barely reached the other side. As she called out to him to come get his son, he said, "But I barely made it here myself! I just recently stopped drinking and going out. I'm afraid if I go past those men, I may get caught again because the pain that drew me to the middle is still present. I'm sorry; I can't."

There are many good men, but they hide themselves in their work, or in sports, or inside themselves. They spend very little time with their children, wives, or families, because to do this would open their hearts not only to love but also to their pain-ridden past. They may distance themselves emotionally from those they love most, only to explode unexpectedly someday.

There are many Chicano/Latino men, however, who have made it across the bridge, while maintaining their identity, values, traditions, and spirituality, but the oppressive society does not acknowledge or recognize them. These are not the men whom we generally see in domestic violence, alcohol, or drug treatment programs, because they are busy being good grandfathers, fathers, husbands, sons, brothers, and friends to their family and community.

"The Bridge Story" begins to explain the complexity of the issues as we attempt to understand the impact of multigenerational oppression in reference to working with Chicano/Latino men and domestic violence. What we find is that this sociohistorical trauma has affected them to different degrees whereby they fall at different places on what I have termed the Psychocultural Digressionary Scale. There are five stages to this process.

## 1. Psychocultural Confusion

This is a state in which the multigenerational effects of oppression confuse the people to the degree that their internal sense of spiritual identity still gives them signals that their aggressive, forceful ways are inappropriate to their true cultural base. Although they "know" that their aggression is culturally inappropriate, they are confused by society's message of male dominance, compounded by the lack of "true" knowledge in reference to their own culturally balanced sense of being *un noble hombre* (a noble male).

## 2. Internalized Anger

This often occurs as the traditional ceremonies and traditions of healing, cleansing, and rebalancing have been invalidated by society as being not necessary. This results in confusion about the changing values, the changing roles for men and women, along with continued invalidation by an oppressive society, which causes men to feel insecure and to begin questioning their *destino* (purpose in life). With the traditional extended support and healing systems (*compadres, temezcallis, hombres* circles) no longer in place, their inadequate feelings are internalized and manifested in several ways:

Generalized apathy (unmotivated)

Generalized fear (rigid)

Hypersensitivity (reactive, moody)

## 3. Internalized Oppression (Hate)

At this point in the digressionary process, men begin to believe that the oppression and mistreatment by society is deserved and is due to an inadequacy in the Chicano/Latino culture. Many people at this stage falsely believe that male dominance, sexism, and domestic violence are a part of the Chicano/Latino identity, thus validating their abusive behavior. Unconsciously, they begin integrating many oppressive processes: violence, infidelity, and negative coping methods (drugs, alcohol, fleeing) as a maladaptive way of attempting to survive and maintain their "value." To justify their behavior, they blame the victims. People at this stage encircle themselves with others who reinforce their behavior.

> Distrust in self and others (controlling, jealous)
>
> Anger turned outward (hostility, acting out)
>
> Self harm (drugs, alcohol, violence)

## 4. Dissociative Patterns of Behavior (Self-Hate)

At this stage, the oppression has been internalized so deeply that the expectations of male behaviors and treatment of women are based on the false, imbalanced sense of continuing the cycle. The cultural shame is so pervasive that there is a general mistrust, dislike, and avoidance of Chicano/Latino men. Gang violence, men fighting each other, and women stating, "I'll never marry a Chicano/Latino man" are symptoms. Individual day-to-day survival becomes the focus, and a systematic process of separating oneself from one's actions, and the harm caused by them, is common. People at this stage have trouble differentiating between self-sabotaging behavior and life-enhancing, culturally appropriate behavior.

> Anger turned inward (self-hate)
>
> Established alternative rules (survival)
>
> Fatalism (lack of hope)

## 5. Psychospiritual Amnesia (Rage)

At this point, men have no recollection or memory of true Chicano/Latino cultural authenticity. They believe their negative adaptive behaviors are part of the cultural expectations. This occurs many times when children are born into a family that is functioning at stage 3, 4, or 5. No one has taught the children the true cultural expectations of being *un hombre noble*, of being a *persona con palabra* (a person with credibility). Therefore, the children grow up with a false sense of who they are and what they should be. Rage-based, destructive behavior is a symptom of full-blown psychospiritual amnesia.

What makes the healing and rebalancing process more difficult and complex are the present-day oppressive processes that continue to torment the Chicano/Latino people. With the intensified immigrant bashing and English-only movements in full force, it makes it difficult to focus on the problem behavior without addressing the ongoing societal trauma. Any attempts to re-root the imbalanced, pain-ridden men in their true manhood identity are often seen by mainstream practitioners as not directly dealing with their behavior. In addition, the so-called leaders in the field of domestic violence, those who work with batterers, control the definition of what is acceptable theory, practice, and intervention, thus directly and indirectly continuing the oppression that has been perpetrated on the Chicano/Latino-community for generations.

With this in mind, we see how it becomes necessary not only to address the imbalanced, violent behavior that is a symptom of a deeper, self-denigrating, spiritual identity violation but to address it in the context of the total past and present-day social-historical oppression. More importantly, we must recognize that the effects of the oppressive trauma have been not only on the so-called abuser but on the family and community as well. This, therefore, necessitates encircling the entire healing process with a philosophy that is consistent with and indigenous to the identity ceremonies, traditions, and principles of the Chicano/Latino people themselves.

## LA CULTURA CURA/THE HEALING TREE PHILOSOPHY

Families, communities, and societies since the beginning of time have had to confront issues that appeared to threaten the very essence of their purpose. Even in those times when there seemed to be no hope for revitalization, a way has shown itself.

Traditionally, in all communities, there was a sacred tree where individuals, families, and the community as a whole would gather. That tree, the symbolic focal point, rod of life, or spiritual altar, in more recent times is seen as a church, synagogue, community center, or the home of the community healer/leader. Where this "place of the tree" truly served its community purpose, it became the reference point from which one gained clarity of purpose, healing, and strength. It then was the role of each person and family to take the spirit of this "tree" into their homes and instill its meaning into the members of their family. It is for this reason that many families have a spiritual altar in a special place in their homes.

At the same time, it was evident to all that the "weak wind," the "coyote spirit," or negative influences of the world were a constant threat to the harmony and balance of the individual, the family, and the community. It was for this reason that families and communities began to understand that in order to survive and grow, they, like the tree, must be re-rooted in positive principles.

People—men, women, elders—gathered in circles as a manner of honoring and keeping in harmony with those principles. In these circles, and through positive ceremonies, traditions, and customs, the principles were taught, reinforced, and strengthened. Therefore, the principles provided the way for the individual, the family, and the community to carry out their larger purpose in life, and the ceremonies and traditions ensured that they were taught and maintained.

Various tribes, subgroups of Chicano/Latino people, have developed interpretations of the principles and ceremonies based on the particular "way" of their rooted ethnic spirit. Although ceremonial expression of these rituals and principles is different, depending on the particular region, it is found that ethnic-centered people of all roots have gathered, and continue to gather, in circles (men, women, family/community) to strengthen, rebalance, and maintain harmony.

The healing tree philosophy (Codice Matritense del Real Palacio, n.d.) is used to symbolically emphasize the need for a positive, centering base of principles that assist Chicano/Latino males to maintain their balance, and grow. It is also used to illustrate the various elements that affect an individual and family/community, positively or negatively, in this process.

## 1. Purpose/*Destino*: Based on Individual, Family/Community Dignity (*Dignidad*)

A basic premise of individual, family/community dignity acknowledges that within the ancestral wisdom of a people are the teachings and medicine necessary for growth and healing. The teachings or healing elements inevitably come from the people themselves. Therefore, in order for healing, or rebalance, to be successful, and although the initial incentive may come from an outside person, the ongoing motivation for individual, family/community growth and rebalancing must come from within the circle of those who desire or need growth and change.

## 2. Responsibility: Based on Respect (*Respeto*) for Family/Community Vision

Individuals must have a vision that reflects the potential of their true self in reference to their family/community. If a person has only a negative view of himself and his culture, then he has no avenue for growth or development.

A person's primary ethnicity is the root of the vision. It is necessary for the person to dream, reflect, and rediscover the life-enhancing values and gifts of his own indigenous culture. It is necessary to know and understand his history in order to understand the process that created his present situation. By this process, and with the proper guidance, a person will be able to separate pain and dysfunction from the strength of its culture. As part of their indigenous heritage, all peoples have ceremonies and rituals for clarifying and rediscovering their vision of growth. These ceremonies and rituals must be integrated and practiced in a balanced, consistent manner.

## 3. Interdependence: Based on Individual, Family/Community Trust (*Confianza*)

The strengthening of a community, and the families within it, directly enhances the development and healing of its individuals. As individuals heal and grow, they reintegrate with the positive vision of the community. Families/communities, and the individuals within them, must develop interdependently. If one is missing, then disharmonious growth occurs, which leads to false hope and development. It is essential to know the difference between codependence, individualism, and indigenous cultural interdependence.

## 4. Development: Circular Learning Based on Love (*Cariño*) for Life

A love for life is the basis of a circular learning process. As times change, people must learn "new" ways (based on ancient teachings) to live in the world as individuals, families, and communities. There must be pride in one's root ethnicity and respect for those of another root. The new ways must be both life-preserving and life-enhancing. In addition, organizations, institutions, and dominant societal communities must learn to live in new ways.

## 5. Enthusiasm: Living Life with a Sense of Spirit (*Espíritu*)

Living life with a sense of spirit (spirituality) allows an individual, family/ community to approach life with an element of enthusiasm (*ganas*). Instilling or reinstilling that sense of spirituality in an individual, family/community allows one to deal with the difficult, and sometimes overwhelming, day-to-day pressures with a sense of hope and "greater spirit."

With the healing tree as the philosophy for reframing and addressing this issue of manhood and violence, the previous principles are used as a basis for re-rooting and recentering the behavior and spirit of the men. The true indigenous expectation of Chicano/Latino men as *hombres nobles* (noble men) begins to redefine the values and behaviors that are appropriate and acceptable. A traditional process of an extended kinship network, or *circulo de hombres*, a healing, rebalancing, and accountability process is reintroduced and initiated in these men's lives in order that, collectively, they can complete their journey across the bridge. In addition, establishing this circle of support (*compadres*) gives them a place to heal from the wounds of oppression and effectively confront the day-to-day stressors as *hombres nobles*.

One of the main elements of approaching an issue, such as domestic violence, is how you define it. In Western psychotherapeutic approaches to this issue, it continues to be standard to use a box-oriented framework to categorize, intervene, and evaluate progress. On the other hand, the traditional indigenous way is to look at things not in terms of good or bad, victim or perpetrator, but in terms of balance, of harmony, of the circular nature of life. That circular nature stresses an important point: If you share balance and harmony, they come back to you; if not, you must deal with what you have given. With the circular nature in mind, and based on the previous emphasis on healing from oppression and colonization, we acknowledge and recognize that most Chicano/Latino men in treatment are carrying not only their own unresolved baggage but that of their fathers, grandfathers, and so on back. This acknowledgment brings to light the choice for us, as men: to be a noble man and attempt to heal and balance the pain, or irresponsibly give the baggage to the next generation, thus abdicating our manhood expectation. In addition, based on the healing tree philosophy, we acknowledge that we all come to the circle with *regalos* (gifts) and *cargas* (baggage) and lessons to teach each other. This aspect of *nosotros* (all of us) having gifts and baggage and lessons to teach puts men in the role of being accountable but without reoppressing them with categories and labels.

## The Four Directions

The intervention process itself utilizes the traditional four dimensions of life: physical, emotional, mental, and spiritual, incorporated within a four-phase framework.

- *Conocimiento:* In this phase, the focus is the acknowledgment of who the person is and what he brings to the circle. What is his *palabra*, meaning who and what does he represent? This is the core element in building *confianza* (trust).
- *Entendimiento:* The aspect of understanding, or reunderstanding, the journey of each person in the circle is the emphasis here. The aspects of history, oppression, and uncovering the authentic *hombre noble* are the focuses.
- *Integration:* The application of being able to live and maintain balance and harmony, in spite of the "coyote's" presence, is the focus.

The "coyote spirit" is used as the trickster elements in one's life that attempt to draw the person off-balance.

- *Movimiento:* This final phase focuses on the ongoing reestablishment of traditions and customs that help maintain the balance. The interconnected lifelong responsibility of being an example and a *compadre* to other men is emphasized.

As in a circle, there is no beginning, no end. This reinforces the idea that the lessons of life will always be present and that one has the choice of how he can approach these lessons and handle them in life.

What is occurring is the regrounding and the establishment of *destino* (positive purpose) in the lives of men, with the interconnected checks and balances of positive traditions and customs. The *circulo* becomes the extended kinship network that supports but also makes all members accountable. The degree of healing and cleansing depends on a multitude of factors, but with the spirit reintroduced in their lives, men are given a viable option to continue to live their lives based on more than just day-to-day survival.

As one heals and grows, we all heal and grow, thus shedding a wounded layer of oppression that will make the lives of future generations much happier and more harmonious.

*Un Hombre Noble*/A Noble Man . . .

- *Es un hombre que cumple con su palabra* (Is a man of his word). *Tiene un sentido de responsabilidad para su propio bienestar y para otros en su circulo* (Has a sense of responsibility for his own well-being and that of others in his circle).
- *Rechaza cualquier forma de abuso: fisico, emocional, mental, u espiritual a si mismo o a otras personas* (Rejects any form of abuse: physical, emotional, mental, or spiritual, to himself or others).
- *Toma tiempo para refleccionar, rezar y incluir la ceremonia en su vida* (Takes time to reflect, pray, and include ceremony in his life).
- *Es sensible y comprensivo* (Is sensitive and understanding).
- *Es como un espejo, reflejando apoyo y claridad de uno a otro* (Is like a mirror, reflecting support and clarity to one another).
- *Vive estos valores honradamente y con amor* (Lives these values honestly, and with love).

## REFERENCES

*Códice Florentino.*
*Códice Matritense de la Real Academia.*
*Códice Matritense del Real Palacio.*
Duran, E. F., & Duran, B. M. (1995). *Native American post colonial psychology.* New York: SUNY Press.
Garibay Kintana, Á. M. (Trans.). (1943). *Huehuetlatolli, documento A.* Sacramento, CA: La Casa Editorial de Tlaloc.
Leon-Portilla, M. (1961). *Los antiguos mexicanos.* Mexico: Fondo de Cultura Económica.
Leon-Portilla, M. (1992). *The broken spears: The Aztec account of the conquest of Mexico.* Boston: Beacon Press.
Maruse, E. S. (n.d.)
Olmos, A. de. (n.d.). Mss en Nahuatl, fol. 112, r.
Olmos, A. de. (n.d.). Mss en Nahuatl, fol. 188, r.

Torquemada, J. de. (1943). *Monarquia indiana* (Mexico City: Editorial Salvador Chávez Hayhoe).

Zurita, A. de. (1891). Breve y sumaria relación de los señores y las maneras y diferencias que habia de ellos en Nueva España. In J. García-Icazbalceta (Ed.), *Nueva colección de documentos para la historia de México:, Vol. III*. (pp. 71–227). México: Imprenta de Francisco Diaz de Leon.

# 3

# Fire and Firewater: A Co-Occurring Clinical Treatment Model for Domestic Violence, Substance Abuse, and Trauma

RICARDO CARRILLO AND MARIA J. ZARZA

Intimate partner violence (IPV) is considered a major public health concern in the United States and worldwide. Estimates of the incidence of IPV in the United States find that approximately 1 out of 5 couples experience IPV during a one-year period (Schafer, Caetano, & Clark, 1998).

Several studies reveal higher rates of domestic and family violence among Latinos than among non-Hispanic Whites (Ellsberg, 1999; Straus & Smith, 1990), even when the socioeconomic status (SES) is controlled for in the samples (Field & Caetano, 2003). Communities of color such as Latinos and African Americans, and particularly women of color, are especially vulnerable to higher rates of violence for a variety of reasons including socioeconomic disadvantage and a history of oppression, sexism and racism (Field & Caetano, 2003; Sorenson & Telles, 1991; Hampton, Carrillo, & Kim, 1998). As a matter of fact, women of color suffer more severe and lethal rates of violence than Caucasian women, young Black men suffer more homicides than any other group, and the communities of color have the highest rates of incarceration and criminal justice involvement than other groups (Sokoloff & Pratt, 2005; Sokoloff & Dupont, 2005; Richie, 1996, 2000).

An analysis of five states (Arizona, California, Oklahoma, Oregon, and Texas) performed by the Violence Policy Center (2000) show that Hispanic females are killed at rates slightly above those of non-Hispanic

White females, but below those of Black females (this includes all homicides, not just those caused from family violence). Data on intimate partner homicide (IPH) reflect higher rates of fatalities among Latinas and higher rates of IPH perpetrators of Latino ethnicity in New Jersey (New Jersey Department of Community Affairs, 2003). Duncan, Stayton, and Hall (1999) reviewed data on police records and noted that Hispanic women were more likely to be injured during intimate partner violence incidents than non-Hispanic women.

On the other hand, there are studies that reflect no significant differences between Latinos and non-Hispanic Whites (Tjaden & Thoennes, 2000; Renninson & Welchans, 2000), especially when SES and other variables are controlled for in the samples (Kantor, Jasinski, & Aldarondo, 1994; Neff, Holamon, & Schluter, 1995). Despite the existence of contradictory findings of comparative studies, scholars consider that IPV is a serious problem that needs immediate intervention among Latinos.

In spite of the significance and magnitude of the IPV problem among the rapidly increasing Latino population, a paucity of culturally and linguistically relevant intervention and prevention curricula exists. The lack of available literature and scientific studies on program development and evidence-based models for Latino batterers' intervention programs is a clear reflection of the gap in culturally appropriate services nationwide. The National Latino Alliance for the Elimination of Domestic Violence states the following:

- Domestic violence in Latino populations must be understood within the context in which it happens. A legacy of multiple oppressions (some of which began centuries ago) such as poverty, discrimination, racism, colonization, and classism makes it imperative that domestic violence not be viewed as a unidimensional phenomenon. This important social issue requires that research, policy, advocacy, and services be approached with an understanding of the intersecting social forces that are at work in the occurrence of domestic abuse in Latino families and communities.
- In addition, cultural factors such as a strong orientation toward family and community must be central to interventions and programs that attempt to address the problem in a culturally competent, effective, and respectful manner. The most recent approaches to domestic violence research and intervention strategies in Latino and other racial/ethnic communities are beginning to shift their

focus from individual abused woman (or even the batterer or the couple) to the community problem that affects, and is affected by, many elements in the environment in which it occurs.

■ Culturally specific batterer intervention programs for Latinos are being developed within the context of a comprehensive family intervention approach. These programs view domestic violence as a violation of human rights and a social malaise that is allowed to take place in many families. The interventions consider that, in a majority of cases, abuse by men against women is a behavior that many males have learned at home and in a society in which violence is an accepted way of resolving differences. For more information, see www.dvalianza.org/resor/factsheet_dv.htm.

## CURRENT MODELS WITH LATINO OFFENDERS

Models that currently address Latino offenders fall into three different categories. The first category includes models based on the criminal justice context for mainstream offender populations, with some adaptations for cultural concerns. Safety and accountability are the guiding principles establishing the parameters for their work. The Duluth Abuse Intervention Project in Spanish and the Evolve Program in Connecticut fall into this category. An excellent example of the Spanish Duluth model is the Court Services and Offender Supervision Agency in Washington, DC. This agency uses bilingual and bicultural therapists who have a high success rate of reducing the resistance and using clinical vignettes to increase the cessation of violence with a varied Latino population of male and female offenders. The emphasis of all Duluth-oriented models is the reeducation of patriarchal beliefs that contribute to the oppression of women. The model is based on Freire's (2000) empowerment process for dealing with colonialization. The Evolve model has been evaluated and found to be effective with Latino and African American men (Lyon, 2007), primarily because the program presents a frame for discussing manhood, fatherhood, and the impact of violence on the men's children. The program also addresses issues of coparenting by the partner (victim) and raises awareness of substance abuse and its contribution to domestic violence (Williams, 2007; personal communication).

The second category of models was created by authors who reacted to the cultural limitation of mainstream models. These authors sought inspiration for their curriculum and program modes from Latin American theorists and feminists, as well as from the voiced needs of Latina victims of domestic violence and Latino men seeking to change their violent and oppressive behavior at home. Although safety and accountability remain the primary goal of these models, gender analysis, deconstruction of masculinity, and re-education for equity in relationships are the guiding principles. The three programs that illustrate this approach are CECVIM (Centro de Capacitación para Erradicar la Violencia Intrafamiliar Masculina/Training Center to Eradicate Masculine Intrafamily Violence) in San Francisco, Caminar Latino in Atlanta, Georgia, and CORIAC (Colectivo de Hombres por Relaciones Igualitarias/The Project of Men for Equal Relationships), a re-educative experience with men in Mexico.

Finally, the third category was created in response to the need for Latino men to heal from colonization, acculturation, witnessing family violence, self-wounding from violence and substance abuse, and suffering abandonment, abuse, and neglect. Safety and accountability remain paramount, but the framework expands to incorporate prevention, inclusion, and restorative justice as critical components for the Latino community's transformation to nonviolence. The National Compadres Network: Fire and Firewater, *El Hombre Noble Buscando Su Palabra* (The Noble Man Searching for His Word) (Alianza, 2003) is the program in this category.

This chapter will concentrate on the National Compadres Network model, which is a comorbidity treatment model for domestic violence and substance abuse with Latino men. The model is based on the assumption that intimate partner violence is a learned behavior that may be unlearned among Latino perpetrators with culturally sensitive interventions that address the most critical risk factors for this specific community.

## THE NATIONAL COMPADRES NETWORK MODEL

The model addresses the following risk factors for IPV among Latinos: (1) a culture of violence learned from the group history, society, and the family; (2) sexist values and sexist social rules: a culture of violence and oppression against women; (3) psychological factors and co-occurring conditions; (4) socioeconomic factors such as poverty, unemployment, and discrimination; (5) acculturation and acculturation stress;

(6) substance abuse; and finally (7) IPV as a private "family" issue, a view that is responsible in part for the perpetuation of violence in the family, Latino-style.

It is beyond the purpose of this chapter to discuss all risk factors related to IPV exhaustively. Therefore, this chapter focuses on only those variables linked to the National Compadres Network program rationale. In the same way, the model does not assume that perpetrators of IPV present all of the risk factors explained in the following sections. On the contrary, it is assumed that IPV may also occur in the absence of many of the factors herein presented. Therefore, a comprehensive evaluation of each participating individual throughout his treatment is necessary to address later his violent behavior and its causes and consequences.

## Historical, Environmental, and Intergenerational Violence

The program assumes that violence is a learned behavior and that it therefore can be changed through re-education of alternative, more functional conduct repertories; without that assumption, any psychoeducational intervention program would be worthless. Batterers' treatment programs have traditionally held that domestic violence can be changed through cognitive and re-educative approaches, which appear to be the most useful in the cessation of violent behaviors. Our belief is that the man has "learned well" (to be violent).

Domestic violence has its roots historically in child abuse (Miller, 1990), patriarchy (Martin, 1981), colonialization, racism, and oppression (Freire, 2000; Duran & Duran, 1971; Carrillo & Tello, 1998), and authoritarian political regimes (Martín-Baro, 1989). The unlearning of these exploitive and oppressive behaviors needs to be contextualized so that the attending population can understand where and how they learned these behaviors. The Atlanta Men Overcoming Violence program conducts similar classes on the co-learning of patriarchy and racist oppression and its relationship to domestic violence (Douglas & Nuriddin, 2002; Douglas, Nuriddin, & Perry, this volume).

The National Compadres Network program presupposes that violence and substance abuse are indeed learned from generations of violence and substance abuse in the family. It also assumes that historic variables such as centuries of colonization, political oppression, and trauma suffered in wars (such as the civil war in El Salvador and Nicaragua) constitute important variables that may influence the use of future violent behaviors (Freire,

2000; Duran & Duran, 1995; Duran, Duran, Yellow Horse, & Yellow Horse, 1998). Although it is imperative to have the participating individual understand his own personal family history and the intergenerational patterns of behaviors, the learning process is expanded ecologically to political and historical contexts to help people who use violence understand a broader picture of violence and how it is learned and reinforced. This framework is called "Domesticated Violence."

1. It takes a nation to raise children to become violent men; thus, it takes a nation to stop the violence by raising children not to become violent men.
2. Violence is a learned behavior that has been reinforced nationally, economically, politically, and socially. Nationally, we must remove the reinforcements and teach nonviolent conflict resolution by example.
3. There is a historical correlation between oppression and the domestication of violence, replicating among the oppressed-oppressor relations. There has been a historical resistance to oppressive ways, exposing the oppressor.
4. *La cultura cura* (the culture cures) vs. a culture of oppressive violence.
5. Oppression is a spirit-breaking process of objectifying others.
6. Oppression has an inherent pathology of addiction.
7. The end goal must be honoring all our sacred relationships as we heal generations of oppressive pain and harmful ways.

## Gender Power Imbalance

Numerous scholars have explained the critical role of traditional patriarchal values that place Latino women at a heightened risk of IPV (Perilla, Bareman, & Norris, 1994; Perilla, 1999; Torres, 1991; Zarza & Froján, 2004; Zarza, Adler, & Martínez, 2004). The culture of violence and socioeconomic oppression against women reduces women's role to marital obligations, household chores, and childbearing.

This suffocation of women's rights prevents them from having opportunities, choosing their future, and enjoying independence from fathers and husbands. For instance, Latina immigrants in abusive relationships who are dependent on men for their socioeconomic power and residential status face clear impediments to leave, which creates a vicious cycle of abuse and oppression (Zarza et al., 2004; Zarza & Adler, 2007). This oppressive environment preserves an imbalance of power in gender relationships and therefore plays a critical role in the maintenance of violence in intimate relationships and within the family. Once violence is reinforced and employed to obtain desired outcomes, it becomes a destructive behavioral pattern (Zarza & Froján, 2004).

The culture of violence against women in Latin America is reflected in the traditional Spanish *dichos* or *refranes* (proverbs) such as *"La mujer como la escopeta siempre cargada y en la esquina"* [women and guns always loaded (pregnant) and at home] and *"La mujer en la casa y el hombre en la Plaza"* [the man out in the street and the woman at home]. Many Mexican songs attribute blame and pain to women. Examples of misogynous songs include "Usted" (music by Gabriel Ruíz, words by Jose Antonio Zorillo) and "El Rey" (words and music by José Alfredo Jiménez).

A society that tolerates and even rewards violence against women constitutes a high-risk environment where intimate partner violence is part of the natural social and family life. The right of men to punish their wives emotionally or physically in many Latin American countries is socially acceptable, making it less likely that abused women even self-identify as abused (Heise, Raikes, Watts, & Zwi, 1994; Torres, 1991). Social tolerance to violence and oppression against women influence men toward using abusive behaviors against their wives.

## Co-Occurring Conditions

Although IPV can occur in the absence of emotional distress and mental health problems, multiple studies explain the role of psychological dys-functions and mental health problems on IPV occurrence likelihood, as well as its frequency and severity. Impulsivity, stress, and frustration are only a few of the many psychological and emotional problems identi-fied by different scholars as directly influencing violent behavior among perpetrators (Dutton, 2002; Gelles & Straus, 1979; Hamberger, Lohr, Bonge, & Tolin, 1997). Zarza and Froján (2004) identified also that jeal-ousy and the need to control the victim were common factors of ini-tiation of fights and violent incidents against immigrant Latino women. However, violence against women can start for no apparent reason or previous discussions or disagreements.

Childhood trauma and a history of violence in childhood were also identified by the literature as common to many perpetrators (Sonkin, Martin, & Walker, 1985). Child abuse and the experience of violence in the family (e.g., a child who witnessed a father abusing his mother) may be related both to trauma and to the learning of violent behaviors as an acceptable way to solve conflicts in the family. In addition, many immigrant men come from war-torn situations in Latin America, especially in Central America and Mexico. Posttraumatic stress disorder is an undiagnosed problem for this population (Carrillo & Goubaud-Reyna, 1998). This model assumes that a "co-occurring condition exists" and continual assessment of the trauma and of mood and thought disorders are part of the ongoing observations of the client's progress through treatment.

## Attachment Theory

Recent developments in neurobiology and attachment theory have significant relevance for domestic violence offenders. Research in domestic violence suggests that male batterers represent all three insecure attachment classes: avoidant, preoccupied, and disorganized or fearful (Sonkin & Dutton, 2003).

Each form of insecure attachment has particular defense mechanisms as a method of coping with attachment anxiety. Batterers with an avoidant style present as disconnected emotionally, lacking empathy, cold and uninterested in intimate relationships. They can vacillate between being distant and cut off emotionally and being critical and controlling. These clients need to incorporate an "emotional soundtrack," as one client put it, into their life.

Batterers with a preoccupied style try to please others in order to receive approval. They can present as extremely self-controlled, except when experiencing loss anxiety, when they can become extremely clingy and angry.

Disorganized clients are also known as "borderline" (Dutton, 2002). Many batterers exhibit significant impairment in their early attachments, which places them in the borderline or disorganized group (Van der Kolk, McFarlane, & Weisaeth, 1996). This is a group of individuals who have experienced terror in their interpersonal relations, and they may have sustained neurochemical damage in various aspects of their cortical functioning.

Sonkin and Dutton (2003) advocate for a "safe and secure base" to work with batterers. They also advocate for an attuned approach to deal with the possibility of lethal behavior in batterers. A safe and secure approach allows for the maintaining of the clinical relationship with potentially lethal offenders by helping clients manage their anxiety. An attachment approach is essential to the client who suffers from co-occurring conditions. The impact of trauma, direct abuse, or the witnessing of abuse sets the stage for the use of substances. The attempt to block out or self-medicate contributes to the impairment of attachments. Therefore, a precursor to learning about the sacredness of attachments requires that the men learn about *palabra* (word). The facilitator of a *palabra* program models how to use it. The counselor, facilitator, therapist, or other professional working with the man must be the "one"—the one who will be securely attached to the wounded man until he can rely on himself and others for support. This is not just clinical alliance. The "one" has given his or her *palabra*—a commitment to being present for the man and his *familia*.

## Poverty, Unemployment, and Related Stressors

Recent findings identify the importance of poverty as a strong predictor of violence among different groups, including Latinos (Cunradi, Caetano, & Schafer, 2002). Latinos are disproportionately affected by poverty, unemployment, low-paid jobs, and low education levels (Ramirez & De la Cruz, 2003). Stressful living conditions such as these may influence IPV. According to the social structural theory of Gelles and Straus (1979), those with lower SES might be more affected emotionally by negative life events and may have greater exposure to childhood violence, substance abuse, and depression, as well as poorer coping mechanisms, than upper SES-individuals (Straus, 1990). Current studies also support the idea that poverty is a strong predictor of IPV along all ethnicities in the U.S. (Cunradi et al., 2002).

In addition, Latinos are disproportionately affected by other factors such as crime, violence, and institutionalization (Amaro, Messinger, & Cervantes, 1996; Rice & Dolgin, 2002), lack of health insurance (Newacheck & McManus, 1989; Brindis, Driscoll, Biggs, & Valderrama, 2002), increasing health problems (Freid, Prager, MacKay, & Xia, 2003), STDs (Buzi, Weinman, & Smith, 1998), and HIV/STD infections (Brindis et al., 2002; Centers for Disease Control and Prevention, 2002; Berger & Rivera, 1993). These conditions are at the base of increasing mental health problems among Latinos in the United States related to acculturation stress, trauma, racism, and marginalization. All these factors combined might be playing an important role to the increasing rates of male-to-female intimate partner violence (MFIPV) among long-term Latino immigrants and new generations of U.S.-born Latinos.

## The Role of Acculturation

Different studies emphasize the increasing rates of IPV among Latinas who immigrate to the United States (Dutton, Orloff, & Aguilar Hass, 2000) and U.S.-born Latinas (Lown & Vega, 2001a; Sorenson & Telles, 1991). Some studies focus on the influence of acculturation. Violence seems to rise when women are more acculturated such that men perceive a loss of control over their spouses (Kantor et al., 1994; Perilla et al., 1994; Sorenson & Telles, 1991). According to Walker (1999), the adaptation to a new culture, which results in exposure to new social roles between men and women, can lead to acts of violence on the part of men toward women, in order to gain control over them.

In addition, findings on epidemiology among Latinos show that Latinas born in the United States report suffering more IPV than Latino immigrant women (Kantor et al., 1994; Sorenson & Telles, 1991). Sorenson and Telles (1991) found that Mexican-Americans born in the United States reported a rate of violence 2.4 times higher than immigrants born in Mexico. They explain these results in part by conflicts between two cultures. A more recent study with 1,155 women of Mexican origin (Lown & Vega, 2001a) also reflected higher rates of IPV among U.S.-born Mexicans than among immigrants from Mexico. Aguilar-Gaxiola et al. (2002) found mental illness, alcoholism, and domestic violence to be prevalent in Mexican immigrants after 13 years of living in the United States. In essence, the longer the migrant stays in the United States, the more impaired he or she becomes. It appears that the significance in prevalence rates becomes similar to the general population on these variables.

Carrillo and Tello (1998) suggest that there exists a degree of resistance toward cultural change and a propensity to maintain certain aspects of the Latino culture, so that as people assimilate into U.S. society and culture, rigid gender roles and patriarchal leadership of the family pass down from generation to generation. Flores-Ortiz, Esteban, and Carrillo (1994) have described the rigid patterns of sex role identification, use of violence, substance abuse, and indirect, dysfunctional communication as *"la cultura congelada"* (frozen culture).

## Acculturation Stress

The migration experience may be extremely stressful (acculturation stress) and even contribute to the onset of posttraumatic stress disorder

(PTSD) (Cordova & Kury, 2001). Posttraumatic stress has been found in many Central American immigrants and now gang-involved Latinos (Rodriquez, 2001; Carrillo, 2005). Furthermore, extended exposure to chaotic, violent environments causes a number of psychoneurological impairments, including impaired attachments, uncontrolled impulsive behavior, increase in substance abuse, and an overactive cingulate gyrus, which results in obsessive/angry negative thoughts, jealousy, anxiety, and depression. As previously discussed, stress, including acculturation stress and PTSD, may also contribute to the onset of IPV and other violent behaviors.

## THE ROLE OF SUBSTANCE ABUSE

Substance abuse, and specifically the use of alcohol, has been identified as one of the most powerful predictors of domestic violence (Cunradi et al., 2002; Schafer, Caetano, & Cunradi, 2004). In addition, alcohol problems have been found among victims of IPV in various studies (Lown & Vega, 2001b). Gondolf (1998) has identified a high correlation of reoffense with alcohol and substance abuse in his evaluative study of batterer treatment programs.

Latinos have high rates of substance abuse (e.g., alcohol, cocaine, and metamphetamine) in the United States (de la Rosa, 2002; Kandel, 1995). The impact of being raised in a chaotic, chemically dependent, and violent environment significantly impairs the ability for safe, secure adult attachments. Modeling of substance abuse and family violence contributes to chronic chaos. The correlation of love and pain paired together is the most difficult experience to unlearn in recovery (Carrillo, 2005). Substance abuse appears to contribute to increases in lethality, emotional abuse, physical abuse, impulsivity, and criminal behavior (Sonkin & Dutton, 2003). The combination of substance abuse and domestic violence requires a dual-disorder approach or comorbid treatment, such as the integrated model used by the National Compadres Network.

## VIOLENCE AS A PRIVATE FAMILY ISSUE

According to the findings of the literature about prevalence of MFIPV, data based on self-reporting greatly underestimate the prevalence of violence against Latina women in the United States (Carrillo & Tello, 1998;

Perilla et al., 1994; Tjaden & Thoennes, 1998; Walker, 1999). One of the main reasons for this underreporting is that violence is traditionally perceived as a private family matter within the Latino family (Perilla et al., 1994). Therefore, the perpetrator never receives social and legal punishment for his actions. On the contrary, when violence results in positive consequences such as power and control over the others, the likelihood of its occurrence increases. In this way, the perpetrator will repeat his behavior to control the victim and obtain a desired outcome.

Latina women are reticent to report the abuse because of this perception of IPV as a "private matter," but also out of feelings of shame, guilt, loyalty to their partners, and fear. Latina immigrant women, principally because of social or economic pressures, lack of legal residence status, language and cultural barriers, isolation, and mothering responsibilities, find it extremely difficult and unsafe to report the abuse and seek help. There also exist a multitude of impediments such as language barriers; social isolation; fear of deportation, discrimination, or change; and cultural stigma against divorced/separated women that prevents Latina immigrant women from talking about their abuse, much less reporting it to authorities (Bauer, Rodriguez, Skupinski-Quiroga, & Flores-Ortiz, 2000). Furthermore, reporting the abuse can lead to negative socioeconomic, legal, and familial consequences that make their lives worse, including the risk of more severe violence as retaliation. In fact, the majority of homicides occur when victims separate or intend to separate from their abusers (Zahn & Cazenave, 1986).

## EL HOMBRE NOBLE BUSCANDO SU PALABRA

The main goal of this intervention model is to prevent or reduce the rate of domestic and community violence and its consequences in Latino communities in the United States and in Latin America. The intent is to train offenders to become safe and secure men (*Hombres Nobles,* or Noble Men), standing up against domestic violence and becoming "peace keepers" or "keepers of the culture" in their respective communities, providing the mentorship and role modeling to other men and youth in their respective communities.

The Compadres Network has over 20 men's *circulos* (circles) throughout the nation, providing a variety of mentorship, fatherhood, and community building efforts from California to Washington, D.C. Our emphasis has been in the states of California and Texas to develop domestic violence programs, rites of passage programs, and fatherhood centers to assist in the development of safe and secure communities. Our goals are to make the men safe, help them make amends, and model how to become a "man who knows" (*mazitle*), not a man who batters or offends. The National Compadres Network shares the vision of other international groups such as CORIAC in Mexico and *Hombres Contra la Violencia* in Nicaragua, to make the men responsible and accountable for their behavior and to make communities safe from domestic and community violence.

The theoretical framework of this model is the view that violence is a learned behavior that is transferred from generations and societies where violence is reinforced and taught as an acceptable way to control others. This behavior is described as "Domesticated Violence" because it is based on the societal history of violence and oppression used to control people and ultimately used in the family to control its members. Since violence is a learned behavior, people can relearn alternative ways to solve conflicts with their intimate partners and other family members. The model is sensitive to the history of sociopolitical situations: the history of colonization, religion, language, and culture of Latino men.

## Comprehensive Assessment

Prior to implementing the intervention stage of this model, it is critical to complete a thorough assessment of the offender that includes information on his violent behavior toward an intimate partner and other family members, the history of child abuse and witnessed violence, substance abuse, stressors related to work, economic problems, family issues, involvement of children in violent incidents (child abuse and children witnessing violence in the family), and other dysfunctional behaviors. In addition, it is critical to conduct a mental health assessment of the offender in order to rule out conditions that may contribute to lethal, dangerous situations, as well as to assess his amenability to treatment.

The differential diagnostic assessment also includes a lethality assessment checklist of 12 items (Campbell, 1995), designed to be completed by the therapist, including increase in severity and frequency of violence, obsession with the victim, use and accessibility of weapons, threats to commit suicide, a history of substance abuse, death rituals, PTSD, and other indicators of risk of lethality.

A new addition to the assessment section is the evaluation of the acculturation level and acculturation stress experienced by the client.

As discussed earlier in the chapter, a higher acculturation level has been identified by the literature as a risk factor for the employment of violence in U.S.-born Latinos and Latino immigrants with longer residence time in the United States. The assessment of acculturation level and acculturation stress should be conducted regardless of the offender status as immigrant of first, second, or more generations (Aguilar-Gaxiola et al., 2002).

It is critical in the initial phase to assess the degree of the *cargas y regalos* (wounds and strengths) the participant carries. Since the focus of this work is on developing and maintaining "sacred relationships," thus maintaining the safety and security of those persons interconnected with the participant, it is imperative that we assess where he is in terms of his relationships, thus determining his ability and willingness to continue with the healing and learning process. Some participants come with generations of internalized trauma complicated by active substance abuse, which does not allow them to be open or ready to receive an intervention of this type. For this reason the overall assessment, the lethality assessment, and clinical rule-outs are all essential at the beginning of the treatment program.

## Curriculum

Once a thorough assessment is conducted, the offender starts the program, which consists of 52 sessions, held once per week. This ethnocultural model design attends to four phases of the process of cognitive and behavioral change:

1. Knowledge (*conocimiento*) of the person: Who is he? What is the best approach to new learning? What is his motivation for change? What is his level of attachment?
2. Comprehension (*comprensión*) of the causes and risk factors related to the employment of violence.
3. Integration (*integración*) of tools, knowledge, and resources to stop the violent behavior and start alternative, well-adapted conduct.
4. Movement (*movimiento*), or display of alternative behaviors and resolution of conflicts.

Lessons address risk factors identified as directly or indirectly responsible for the use of violence by Latino males. The goal is to reduce negative attitudes and irrational cognitions (i.e., sexism, control, jealousy) and the use of any negligent, emotional, physical and sexual abuse against family members and their intimate partner. The approach to substance abuse is abstinence oriented (with simultaneous referral to a detoxification program if necessary), includng 12-step referral, mandatory drug screen administered randomly, and a motivational interviewing orientation that fits nicely with the humanistic cultural perspective.

## Phase I: Knowledge (Conocimiento)

New participants go through the *Conocimiento* sessions, which introduce them to a definition of violence and oppression and further determine if they are ready for the *círculo* (support group) treatment process and ready to work on their own relationship development. This initial phase is critical in maintaining the men's attendance to the program, reducing the dropout level by promoting an environment of mutual respect and understanding between therapists and participants. Self-respect and respecting each other in the group is always encouraged, positively reinforced, and modeled through the entire program.

This phase focuses also on encouraging the men to look into their own personal *cargas y regalos* (wounds and strengths) and violent behavior rather than blaming, accusing, or punishing them for their conduct. Participants are instructed to understand that violence is a learned behavior and therefore it can be changed. They are instructed that they will be presented with tools and techniques to change irrational cognitions, such as sexism, and the need to establish power and control, and solve conflicts in a peaceful and fair way in intimate and family relationships.

This phase is composed of 10 lessons with the main goal of making the men aware of their attitudes and fears; the violent techniques they employ to control and maintain power in their relationships; the consequences of abuse for their victims and themselves; the mechanisms of denial, minimization, and blaming others for their behaviors; and their rage as well as mechanisms or tools to control these and guide the anger toward alternative behaviors and conflict resolution techniques.

During this phase, offenders will establish a plan to change violent behavior that will be constantly reviewed during the entire program. This personal plan engages the offender, who gives his *palabra* (word) to accomplish the agreement. The plan includes the offender's list of behaviors and commitments that he can change. It also includes things that he cannot change and therefore will accept with serenity. It also includes problems that he will have to solve instead of accepting and the barriers that he will encounter in order to complete these tasks.

**Manuel:** Mira, the bitch, does not understand me. She was born here and does not know how to serve and take care of her man. She is always at her mother's house, and complains that we don't own our own home. *No me respeta.* [She does not respect me.]

**Group:** Hombre, primero, she is not a "'bitch," she is your companera, your partner, your lover, the mother of your children. That's the way your father talked to your mother, que no? You have shared that it was painful to you to hear that from your Papi to your mom. She is not in group, brother, but you are, and we are listening to your *carga*, about not providing for your *familia*. You appear conflicted about not owning your own home, but not conflicted about spending money on booze or other women? What's up with that?

## Phase II: Comprehension (Comprensión)

The second phase of the intervention process brings an understanding or critical analysis of how it is "we" have come to integrate violence as a part of our relationships. To some extent, this is the beginning of a re-*conocimiento* (reframing) of how the participants see themselves, their family, their culture, and their situation. Differentiating "true" culture and manhood, true *machismo* from false culture and false *machismo* is the basis of this group of teachings. This is the phase where participants are pushed to see their actions interconnected with that of the group, meaning that their actions affect more than just themselves. This begins to assist the participants to redevelop a positive group consciousness, *El circulo* (as reflected in the Spanish saying *"Dime con quien andas y te diré quien eres"*—"tell me who you run with and I will tell you who you are"). It is important for the facilitator, in this phase, to guide the group to share as much cross-reflection with each other as possible and to "teach" participants how to do this in a good way. It is suggested that the facilitator be as creative as possible in integrating storytelling, music, video clips, real-life situations, and so forth as part of the teaching process to make this phase very experiential, and push the participants to look within for a deeper understanding of who they are.

**Group Facilitator:** (*plays Tony Touclf's "Sofrito Mama": "Mira quien entro, Conio, El Dominicano mas Malo; Yo, . . . mano de pierda, te saco la . . .")*
  . . . . . . If your wife, *compañera*, girlfriend wants to work, *do you let her,* or does it not matter to you?
  *(The group discusses this and the majority agreement is that the group allows her to work, or not, but the emphasis is that they give her permission. "* Yo la dejo trabajar. No la dejo trabajar. *[I let her work, I don't let her work.])"*
**Group Facilitator:** *Que interesante.* [How interesting]. Is that not what the *hacendando*/plantation owner does to the *peon*/slave? *He lets him work?*
**Group's Response:** *Hay Doctor*, you know, that's from *El Machismo.*
**Facilitator:** What is *Machismo*?

The group then engages in a discussion of *machismo,* and it is highlighted that the men's understanding of being womanizers, drunks, addicts, loyal to their friends is a distorted view of manhood. *El hombre macho* is actually a man of his word, faithful and loyal to his wife and children and respectful of his elders. The work, then, is to elicit from the group where on a continuum of distorted *macho* vs. *hombre noble* they want to be. Most group participants want to learn how to be *hombres de palabra* (men of their word). We have successfully engaged them in the clinical process at that point, and we can develop an individual treatment plan.

This phase is composed of 13 sessions with the main goals of giving Latino offenders a framework on the genesis of violence in society, the history of violence and dominance in Latin America, the oppression suffered through centuries, and the power and control of conquerors and society. The history of the oppression in the Latino offenders' countries is provided as a reflection of the violence in the family with the purpose of reframing violence. This phase of comprehension (*entendimiento*) discusses the historical genesis of sexist attitudes (e.g., *machismo, marianismo, hembrismo*), provides a new definition of manhood (*ser hombre* [being a man] implies being dignified, protective, responsible, nurturing, spiritual, faithful, respectful, friendly, caring, sensitive, trustful, and a provider), and encourages offenders to demolish the myth of *machismo* as entitlement and superiority over women. Several lessons also discuss offender's personal conducts and attitudes related to patriarchy, male dominance and male privilege, roots of power, control, and violence. The goal is to make offenders aware of their dominance toward their partners in order to change attitudes and dysfunctional cognitions and behaviors. This phase also stresses that blaming their culture for their violent behavior is only part of the denial and minimization of their violent behavior. This phase also discusses the erosion of cultural values as a consequence of the use of violence. The assumption of this model, that *la cultura cura* (culture cures), is based on the recuperative values of the Latino culture such as *familismo* (family loyalty), *respeto* (respect), *confianza* (trust), *dignidad* (dignity), *cariño* (love), and *coraje* (courage) and helps toward the elimination of domestic violence (i.e., a man who hits his wife is considered a coward in the Latino culture). Other cultural values and sayings such as *el rey de la casa* (the king of the house) or *ser muy macho* (being very macho) are discussed and reframed again as a song of patriarchy and male dominance/privilege, not as an indication of respect for a father/husband figure. This is the foundation for helping the men develop the understanding of the *Sacredness of Relationships.* Since many of the men in treatment have not observed or lived this value, it is a difficult concept to grasp. They always ask, "Do you have a movie or something where I can see a healthy relationship?"

Pre-Columbian cultures emphasized the teaching of *cara* (face) and *corazón* (heart) for well-educated and cultured individuals (Tello, 1998). Both concepts are employed in this phase of the program. "Face" reflects the values of respect and dignity. "Heart" indicates that the individual has affection and warmth and is trustworthy. Many offenders of domestic violence who also are chemically dependent have not had the life experience of being raised in an environment of safety, security, or attunement with *cara y corazón.* Therefore, an approach that teaches this developmental process is beneficial to learning new behaviors and teaching them about parenting and marital relationships (Carrillo, Goubaud-Reyna, Martinez, & Tello, 2000). In turn, this teaches a foundation for effective parenting. The men father the other men in the group, while they learn how to parent their own children with *cara y corazón.*

A new curriculum has been added to for this phase specifically. It is called *Padres Nobles,* in which the men listen to their children describe how the violence has affected them. The men learn to take responsibility and become accountable for the intergenerational impact of passing violence onto the next generation. They can "arrest" it. In addition they learn specific parenting skills that are nonviolent and worthy of an "elder, with *cara y corazón.*"

**Padres Nobles Lesson:** I love my Papi. But sometimes he turns into a monster, his eyes are red, and he has smoke coming out of his ears.

I'm scared that he will hit my mommy again or leave and never come back (*feedback from one of the children of the men in group*).
(*The group responds to the fear of the child and they share the shame and familiarity of being raised in the violent home.*)

**Manuel:** *Madre,* that's how I felt when I was little too. My father drank, beat my mother almost to death, then beat my uncle up, and we always thought we would be next. When he was murdered and never came back, I had a hole inside of me. I want to be a better father, *ayúdame* [help me, please].

## Phase III: Integration (Integración)

This is the process of assimilation of a new philosophy of life as *hombre noble* (noble man). Integration involves the incorporation of learned skills and resources such as adjusting behavioral repertoire, techniques to control emotional distress and anger, and knowledge of risk situations learned through the program into practice. The 11 sessions in this phase of the process challenge participants to refocus their lives and commit themselves to nonviolent intimate relationships.

If the program has an ongoing *círculo de hombres* (support group), it is important that the participants begin attending on a regular basis to assist them in developing a positive support system. This is the phase where participants are also encouraged to become involved in community service activities and/or positive volunteer activities allowing them to "give back" to their community and become a positive example to others. At the same time, the teachings in this phase of the program will continue to challenge participants' *cargas* while developing their *regalos*.

## Phase IV: Action (Movimiento)

This final phase of the intervention process attempts to ensure that functional behavior, cognitions, attitudes, and skills learned during the entire program become habits. During this phase of the program, participants should become aware of the consequences of their violent behavior, denial, and minimization. Once participants have integrated this knowledge and become aware and understanding of IPV, then they should be ready to ask for forgiveness from all those they hurt. At this stage, it is imperative that participants are well integrated in a *círculo de hombres* to establish an ongoing support and reinforcement of these teachings. Finally, if at all possible, programs should attempt to reintegrate successful participants as cofacilitators or presenters in the community as examples of *hombres* who have healed and are examples of *hombres nobles.*

## SUMMARY AND CONCLUSIONS

In sum, the intervention model of *El Hombre Noble Buscando Su Palabra* addresses risk factors linked to the use of violence against an intimate partner by Latino men recently revealed by the scientific community. The risk factors addressed include a culture of violence and sexism, psychological and emotional factors, socioeconomic problems, immigration and acculturation issues, substance abuse, and the perception of IPV as a private matter. This culturally sensitive model assumes that violence is a learned behavior that can be modified with alternative conducts to solve conflicts and cope with negative emotions.

The main components of the intervention include a comprehensive assessment, cognitive and behavioral strategies and coping skills, which are delivered both in individual and support groups. The desired outcomes are changing the offender's sexist and positive attitudes towards violence, making the offender aware of the consequences of his violent behavior, and causing the offender to understand the roots of violence and develop the necessary coping skills and social support to deal with the everyday frustrations and stress. Ultimately, the goal is to prevent further incidents of emotional, physical, or sexual abuse and help offenders to solve conflicts peacefully with their intimate partner and other family members.

### REFERENCES

Aguilar-Gaxiola, S., Zelezny, L., Garcia, B., Edmonson, C., Alejo-Garcia, C., & Vega, W. A. (2002). Translating research into action: Reducing disparities in mental health care for Mexican Americans. *Psychiatric Services, 53,* 1563–1568.

Alianza. (2003). *Forum on Latinos who batter: Hope for those who hurt others.* New York: National Latino Alliance for the Elimination of Domestic Violence.

Amaro, H., Messinger, M., & Cervantes, R. (1996). The health of Latino youth: Challenges for disease prevention. In M. Kagawa-Singer, P. Katz, & D. Taylor (Eds.), *Health Issues for Minority Adolescents* (pp.80–115). Lincoln: University of Nebraska Press.

Bauer, H., Rodríguez, M., Skupinski-Quiroga, S., & Flores-Ortiz, Y. (2000). Barriers to health care for abused Latina and Asian immigrant women. *Journal of Health Care for the Poor and the Underserved, 11*(1), 33–44.

Berger, D. K., & Rivera, M. (1993). Risk assessment for human immunodeficiency virus among pregnant Hispanic adolescents. *Adolescence, 28*(111), 597–608.

Brindis, C. D., Driscoll, A. K., Biggs, M. A., & Valderrama, L. T. (2002). *Fact sheet on Latino youth: Health care access.* San Francisco: University of California, San Francisco, Center for Reproductive Health Research and Policy, Department of Obstetrics, Gynecology and Reproductive Health Sciences and the Institute for Health Policy Studies. Retrieved from http://reprohealth.ucsf.edu/publications/internal.htm#FactSheets.

Buzi, R. S, Weinman, M. L, & Smith, P. B. (1998). Ethnic differences in STD rates among female adolescents. *Adolescence, 33,* 130, 313–319.

Campbell, J. (Ed.). (1995). *Assessing dangerousness: Violence by sexual offenders, batterers, and child abusers.* Thousand Oaks, CA: Sage.

Carrillo, R. A. (2005). *Attachment theory and gang violence.* San Francisco: Department of Social Services.

Carrillo, R., & Goubaud-Reyna, R. (1998) Clinical treatment of the Latino domestic violence offender. In R. Carrillo & J. Tello (Eds.), *Family violence and men of color: Healing the wounded male spirit* (1st ed.). New York: Springer Publishing Co.

Carrillo, R., & Tello, J. T. (Eds.) (1998). *Family violence and men of color: Healing the wounded male spirit* (1st ed.). New York: Springer Publishing Company.

Carrillo, R., Goubaud-Reyna, R., Martinez, S., & Tello, J. (1998). *El hombre noble buscando balance. The noble man searching for balance; Healing family violence.* Los Angeles, CA: National Compadres Network.

Centers for Disease Control and Prevention (2002). *HIV/AIDS Among Hispanics in the United States.* Centers for Disease Control and Prevention, National Center for HIV, STD, and TB Prevention. Retrieved 2002 from http://www.cdc.gov/hiv/pubs/facts/hispanic/htm

Cordova, C. B., & Kury, F. (2001). Salvadorans. In A.G. Lopez & E. Carrillo (Eds.), *The Latino psychiatric patient: Assessment and treatment.* Washington, DC: American Psychiatric Press.

Cunradi, C. B., Caetano, R., & Shaffer, J. (2002). Socioeconomic predictors of intimate partner violence among White, Black, and Hispanic couples in the United States. *Journal of Family Violence, 17*(4), 377–389.

De la Rosa, M. (2002). Acculturation and Latino adolescents' substance abuse: A research agenda for the future. *Substance Use and Misuse, 37*(4), 429–485.

Douglas, U., & Nuriddin, S. (2002). Black men and domestic violence: What do we know, where do we go? *Conference Proceedings of the Institute on Domestic Violence in the African American Community's Spring 2002 Forum, May 30–31, 2002* (pp. 27–28). St. Paul: University of Minnesota Institute on Domestic Violence in the African American Community.

Duncan, M. M., Stayton, C. D., & Hall, C. B. (1999). Police reports on domestic incidents involving intimate partners: Injuries and medical help-seeking. *Women Health, 30*(1), 1–13.

Duran, E., & Duran, B. (1995). *Native American postcolonial psychology.* New York: SUNY Press.

Duran, E., Duran, B., Yellow Horse, M., & Yellow Horse, S. (1998). Healing the American Indian soul wound. In Y. Danieli (Ed.), *International handbook of multigenerational legacies of trauma* (pp. 291–311). Madison: University of Wisconsin Press.

Dutton, D. (2002). *The abusive personality: Violence and control in intimate relationships* (2nd ed.). New York: Guilford Press.

Dutton, M. A., Orloff, L. E., & Aguilar Hass, G. (2000). Characteristics of help-seeking behaviors, resources and service needs of battered immigrant Latinas. *Georgetown Journal on Poverty Law & Policy, 2*(2), 245–305.

Ellsberg, M. (1999). Domestic violence and emotional distress among Nicaraguan women; results from a population-based study. *American Psychologist, 54*(1), 30–36.

Field, C. A., & Caetano, R. (2003). Longitudinal model predicting partner violence among White, Black and Hispanic couples in the United States. *Alcoholism, Clinical and Experimental Research, 27*(9), 1451–1459.

Flores-Ortiz, Y. G., Esteban, M., & Carillo, R. A. (1994). La violencia en la familia. Un modelo contextual de terapia intergeneracional. *Revista Interamericana de Psicología, 28*(2), 235–250.

Freid, V. M., Prager, K., MacKay, A. P., & Xia, H. (2003). *Chartbook on trends in the health of Americans. Health United States, 2003.* Hyattsville, MD: National Center for Health Statistics. DHHS Publication No. (9/03) 2003–1232.

Freire, P. (2000). *Pedagogy of the oppressed.* New York. Continuum Press.

Gelles, R. J., & Straus, M. A. (1979). Determinants of violence in the family: Toward a theoretical integration. In W. R. Burr, R. Hill, F. I. Nye, and I. L. Reiss (Eds.), *Violence in the home: Interdisciplinary perspectives* (pp. 549–581). New York: Brunner/Mazel.

Gondolf, E. W. (1998). *Assessing women battering in mental health services.* Thousand Oaks, CA: Sage Publications.

Hamberger, L. K., Lohr, J. M., Bonge, D., & Tolin, D. F. (1997). An empirical classification of motivations for domestic violence. *Violence Against Women, 3*(4), 401–423.

Hampton, R.; Carrillo, R., & Kim, J. (1998). Violence in communities of color. In R. Carrillo & J. Tello (Eds.), *Family violence and men of color: Healing the wounded male spirit* (1st ed., pp. 1–30) New York: Springer Publishing Co.

Heise, L. L., Raikes, A., Watts, C. H., & Zwi, A. B. (1994). Violence against women: A neglected public health issue in less developed countries. *Social science and medicine, 39,* 1165–1179.

Kandel, D. B. (1995). Ethnic differences in drug use patterns and paradoxes. In G. J. Botvin, S. Schinke, & M. A. Orlandi (Eds.), *Drug abuse prevention with multiethnic youth* (pp. 81–104). Thousand Oaks, CA: Sage.

Kantor, G. K., Jasinski, J. L., & Aldarondo, E. (1994). Sociocultural status and incidence of marital violence in Hispanic families. *Violence and Victims 9*(2), 207–222.

Lown, E. A., & Vega, W. A. (2001a). Prevalence and predictors of physical partner abuse among Mexican American women. *American Journal of Public Health, 91*(3), 441–445.

Lown, E. A., & Vega, W. A. (2001b). Alcohol abuse or dependence among Mexican American women who report violence. *Alcoholism: Clinical & Experimental Research, 25*(10), 1479–1486.

Lyon, E. (2007). *Impact evaluation of Special Session Domestic Violence: Enhanced advocacy and interventions.* Washington, DC: National Institute of Justice.

Martín-Baro, I. (1989). Political violence and war as causes of psychocial trauma in El Salvador. *Journal of La Raza Studies 2*(2), 5–15.

Martin, D. (1981). *Battered wives.* San Francisco: Volcano Press.

Miller, A. (1990). *For your own good: Hidden cruelty in child rearing and the roots of violence* (3rd ed.). New York: Farrar, Straus, and Giroux.

Neff, J. A., Holamon, B., & Schluter, T. D. (1995). Spousal violence among Anglos, Blacks and Mexican Americans: the role of demographic variables, psychosocial predictors, and alcohol consumption. *Journal of Family Violence, 19,* 1–21.

New Jersey Department of Community Affairs (2003). *NJ Domestic Violence Fatality Review Board Report (February).* Retrieved 2005 from www.nj.gov/dca/dow/dowprograms.shtm#dvfrb

Newacheck, P. W., & McManus, M. A. (1989). Health insurance status of adolescents in the United States. *Pediatrics, 84*(4), 699–708.

Perilla, J. (1999). Domestic violence as a human rights issue: The case of immigrant Latinos. *Hispanic Journal of Behavioral Sciences, 21*(2), 107–133.

Perilla, J. L., Bareman, R., & Norris, L. (1994). Culture and domestic violence: The ecology of abused Latinas. *Violence and Victim 9*(4), 325–339.

Ramirez, R., & de la Cruz, G. P. (2003). *The Hispanic population in the United States: March 2002* (pp. 20–520). Washington DC: U.S. Government Printing Office.

Renninson, C. M., & Welchans, S. (2000). *Intimate partner violence. Bureau of Justice Statistics; Special Report.* Retrieved April 19, 2005, from http://ojp.usdoj.gov/bjs/

Rice, P. F., & Dolgin, K. G. (2002). *The adolescent. Development, relationships, and culture.* Boston: C. O. Merril-Allyn and Bacon.

Richie, B. (1996). *Compelled to crime: The gender entrapment of battered Black women.* NewYork: Routledge.

Richie, B. (2000). A Black feminist reflection on the antiviolence movement. *Signs, 25,* 1133–1137.

Rodriquez, L. (2001) *Hearts and hands: Creating community in violent times.* New York: Seven Stories Press.

Schafer, J., Caetano, R., & Clark, C. L. (1998). Rates of intimate partner violence in the United States. *American Journal of Public Health, 88,* 1702–1704.

Schafer, Caetano, & Cunradi. (2004). A path model of risk factors for intimate partner violence among couples in the United States. *Journal of Interpersonal Violence, 19,* 127–142.

Sonkin, D. J., Martin, D., & Walker, L. (1985). *The male batterer: A treatment approach.* New York, Springer Publications.

Sokoloff, N. J., & Dupont, I. (2005). Domestic violence at the intersections of race, class, and gender. *Violence Against Women, 11,* 38–64.

Sokoloff, N. J., & Pratt, C. (Eds.) (2005). *Domestic violence at the margins. Readings on race, class, gender, and culture.* New Brunswick, NJ: Rutgers University Press.

Sokoloff, N. J., & Dupont, I. (2005). Domestic violence at the intersections of race, class, and gender. *Violence Against Women, 11,* 38–64.

Sonkin, D., & Dutton, D. (Eds.) (2003). *Intimate violence: Contemporary treatment innovations.* (2003). New York: Haworth Maltreatment & Trauma Press.

Sonkin, D. J., Martin, D., & Walker, L. (1985). *The male batterer: A treatment approach.* New York: Springer Publications.

Sorenson, S. B., & Telles, C. A. (1991). Self-reports of spousal violence in a Mexican-American and non-Hispanic white population. *Violence and Victims, 6*(1), 3–15.

Straus, M. A. (1990). Social stress and marital violence in a national sample of American families. In M. A. Straus and R. J. Gelles (Eds.), *Physical violence in American families.* New Brunswick, NJ: Transaction Publishers.

Straus, M. A., & Smith, C. (1990). Violence in Hispanic families in the United States: Incidence rates and structural interpretations. In M. A. Straus & R. J. Gelles (Eds.), *Physical violence in American families: Risk factors and adaptations to violence in 8,145 families* (pp. 341–367). New Brunswick, NJ: Transaction.

Tello, J. (1998). *El hombre noble buscando balance:* The noble man searching for balance. In R. Carrillo & J. Tello (Eds.), *Family violence and men of color: Healing the wounded male spirit* (1st ed., pp. 31–52). New York: Springer Publishing Company, Inc.

Tjaden, P., & Toennes, N. (2000). *Extent, nature and consequences of violence against women: Findings from the National Violence Against Women Survey.* The National Institute of Justice and the Centers for Disease Control and Prevention. Retrieved April 19, 2005, from http://www.ncjrs.org/txtfiles1/nij/183781.txthttp://www.ncjrs.org/txtfiles1/nij/183781.txt

Torres, S. (1991). A comparison of wife abuse between two cultures: Perceptions, attitudes, nature, and extent. *Issues in Mental Health Nursing, 12,* 113–131.

Van der Kolk, B. A., McFarlane, A. C., & Weisaeth, L. (Eds.). (1996). *Traumatic stress: The effects of overwhelming experience on mind, body, and society.* New York: Guilford Press.

Violence Policy Center (2000). *When men murder women: An analysis of 1999 homicide data.* Washington, DC: Violence Policy Center.

Walker, L. E. (1999). Psychology and domestic violence around the world. *American Psychologist, 54,* 1, 21–29.

Zahn, M., & Cazenave, N. A. (1986). *Women, murder and male domination: Police reports of domestic homicide in Chicago and Philadelphia.* American Society of Criminology Meeting. October 29–November 1, Atlanta, Georgia.

Zarza, M. J., & Adler, R. (2007). Latina immigrant victims of interpersonal violence in New Jersey: A needs assessment study. *Journal of Aggression, Maltreatment and Trauma, 16,* 1.

Zarza, M. J., & Froján, M. X. (2004). Estudio de la violencia doméstica en una muestra de mujeres latinas residentes en Estados Unidos. *Anales de Psicología, 21*(1), 18–26.

Zarza, M. J., Adler, R., & Martínez, I. (2004). *Violence in the Latino family: Risk factors and consequences.* Paper presented at the Latin American Studies Association (LASA) International Conference. Las Vegas, NV.

Zarza, M. J., & Adler, R. (2007). Latina immigrant victims of interpersonal violence in New Jersey: A needs assessment study. *Journal of Aggression Maltreatment and Trauma, 16,* 1.

# Healing and Confronting the African American Male Who Batters

4

OLIVER J. WILLIAMS

## FISH IN A BARREL

Once there was a scientist who studied the health and behavior of fish. To track the health status of the fish on a consistent basis, the scientist went to the ocean, caught 12 fish, and put them in a barrel. Over time he noticed that one of the fish developed a spot on its back fin. He recorded its occurrences and noted this was unusual for this type of fish. A few days passed, and more fish developed spots and became ill. Eventually, all but one fish developed a spot in the same location and got sick. After numerous efforts to treat the fish, the illness would not go away. The scientist concluded that the fish without symptoms was immune to the disease; the other fish were unhealthy and the disease emanated from them. Because few scientists studied this type of fish, he considered himself to be an expert, and deemed the illness-free fish as the standard for fish of its kind. All descriptions defining the normal state of being for this type of fish were modeled from the scientist's report.

The "normal" fish was eventually set aside in its own container. To cross-check his results, the scientist returned to the ocean, caught 12 more fish, and put them in a barrel; the same thing happened. This time, two fish were without symptoms. The scientist concluded that these fish had become contaminated and issued a report to the public that "until further notice, these fish are unsafe." The cause of the illness and the key to immunity were unknown.

Another scientist, concerned with the health of the fish, sought to determine the reason for the illness. He posited that the community of fish and natural environments may have been protective factors. Fish tend to flourish in environments that match their natural capacities. The barrel represented a change that the fish could not negotiate. One potential healing approach was to return the fish to their natural environment, but this could result in more contaminated fish. A second approach was to create another healthy environment and community of fish that simulated the ocean conditions. The second option was selected, and the fish were restored to health.

## INTRODUCTION

Violence in intimate partner relationships is a crime that results in the injury or death of thousands of women each year. Although pro-arrest policies, jail time, and group treatment have emerged as approaches to confront men who batter, strategies must be developed to encourage more of these men to take responsibility for their destructive behavior. Also, pro-arrest policies and group treatment approaches cannot be seen as the only models to address such violence. We must develop a full range of primary, secondary, and tertiary prevention and intervention models to reduce violence among African American men who batter.

It is incumbent for those who work in this field to expand the way in which they view the causes and solutions to partner abuse. Current interventions in partner abuse treatment are often defined by theories of violence arising out of a singular point of view. These theories tend to promote a one-size-fits-all perspective related to men who batter and do not account for the entire important intersection of race, culture, and violence (Williams & Becker, 1995; Williams, 1999a). Nor have community models and collaborations that reach and engage this community and population been tried enough. This is especially true regarding African American men who batter. Men of color, as a group, drop out of treatment sooner and complete treatment at lower rates than their white counterparts do (Saunders & Parker, 1989; Tolman & Bennett, 1990). The present theories that explain male violence in partner relationships ignore key explanations for maladaptive behavior among African American men. Yet both conventional partner abuse and culturally focused perspectives

provide important information about abusive behavior in intimate partner relationships involving African American men. Although this chapter
was originally written over ten years ago, it still offers important contribution in thinking about how to respond to African American male violence, with some additional considerations. In the previous iteration of
this chapter, it spoke to men who are much older now and the issues and
challenges in their generation. A whole new group of African American
men have come of age. Many of the issues and challenges are the same,
but some of the ways in which a younger group articulates or views their
reality and issues have evolved. In this chapter, I will restate the issues
that remain relevant but also discuss new ideas, challenges, and thinking
for an older and a younger generation. Age, race, class, culture, and social
context are important considerations in theory building too. Accordingly,
this chapter will examine the theories that explain violence in the field
of partner abuse and those that address maladaptive behavior among
African American men. From these premises, this chapter will highlight
a theoretical framework for designing appropriate and culturally congru-
ent treatment models for African American men who batter.

## EXPLANATION FOR VIOLENCE IN THE PARTNER ABUSE LITERATURE

The battered women's movement has helped scholars, researchers, and
practitioners understand that theory and practice must be focused on
the lives of battered women when developing models for ending male
violence against women. This grassroots movement has raised our society's consciousness to the problem of domestic violence on many levels.
It has produced battered women's shelters, has informed society about
the impact of family violence on children, and was instrumental in the
creation of treatment for men who batter (Edleson & Eisikovits, 1996;
Peled, 1996; Edleson & Graham-Berman, 2001; McAlister, 2007).

The battered women's movement and a feminist critique of theories of violence have shaped the explanations for male battering behavior
(National Research Council, 1996) as well. Two theories seem to stand out
from this literature: structural theory as it relates to sexism, and the theory of learned behavior. From a feminist perspective of structural theory,
violence toward women is explained in terms of gender inequality (Yllo
& Bogard, 1988). It has been viewed as a symptom of another problem,
sexism, which is the devaluation and subordination of women by men

(Rothenberg, 1988). Historically, sexism has been embodied in laws and cultural norms that have given men license to be abusive toward women physically, emotionally, economically, and legally (Oppenlandar, 1981). In a review of mainstream history concerning partner abuse, laws have typically been a hindrance to women's capacity to address this problem and have implicitly and explicitly supported male violence. Historically, there had been few sanctions for partner abuse. Violence has been a choice men who batter make because the benefit is control, the results are immediate, and the legal consequences have been minimal. Ellen Pence (1989) explains how men use power and control in intimate relationships. She has influenced many in the field of domestic violence through her explanation of violence toward women. Gondolf (1985) also supports that a shared characteristic among men who batter is their need to control their female partner. Although some researchers suggest that violence for certain men also can be influenced by physical illness, brain injury, or personality disorders, most in the field acknowledge that the abuse of women is perpetrated by men who appear, in other ways as typical of men in society (Sonkin, Martin, & Walker, 1985; Saunders, 1992; Gondolf, 1988; Holtzworth-Munroe & Stuart, 1994; Roy, 1982). From this perspective, abuse is not considered merely a random act but a behavior focused specifically on a female partner. The protection of women and development of laws that will hold men who batter accountable for their abusive behavior have been major objectives of the battered women's movement.

According to the theory of learned behavior, violence is taught in relationships among members of a subgroup or community. When a person witnesses violence in a community or subgroup setting, he may imitate the behavior in anger, believing it a normal strategy to employ in conflict situations. Once the behavior is learned, it is passed on from generation to generation (Bandura, Ross, & Ross, 1963; Berkowitz, 1983; Rich & Stone, 1996; Rosenberg & Mercy, 1991; and Hammond & Yung, 1993). In the field of domestic violence, scholars specifically describe what behaviors men have learned and how their abusive behavior is directed toward women (Straus, 1980; Gelles, 1979; Martin, 1976; Flynn, 1977; Steinmetz, 1980). Violence is considered a male prerogative (Straus, 1980; Williams, 1989). Male socialization tends to make men, as a group, more accepting of violence (David & Brannon, 1976; Cicone & Ruble, 1978). Still much of the research suggests that partner abuse is learned within the family of origin. In many cases, young boys who observe their mother being abused by an adult male role model are at higher risk to abuse their female partners as adults (Rosenbaum & O'Leary, 1981). In batterers' treatment groups, some of the themes of treatment include the following: developing male alternatives to violence, increasing perpetrators' awareness of their need to control, and reducing their sexist attitudes and behavior. One clear message from the field has been that men who batter must be accountable for their behavior. Another is that men who behave poorly toward their partner are at higher risk for abusing or alienating others, such as children, other family members, neighbors, and colleagues. Often, group treatment encourages personal awareness, responsibility and accountability. Although this perspective is important and, in my opinion, must be a primary focus of treatment, scholars and practitioners must integrate such explanations with other realities including social context, cultural experiences, and problem solving. This requirement is as true today as it was years ago.

## AFRICAN AMERICAN MALE PERSPECTIVES ON MALADAPTIVE BEHAVIOR

The intersection of race, social status, social context and violence creates a set of issues that have typically not been discussed in the literature on domestic violence (Williams, 1994a; Tubbs & Williams, 1998; Oliver & Williams, 2005; Griffin & Williams, 1992). Few theories are specific regarding partner abuse among African American men. In fact, scholars who explore theories of African American men and maladaptive behaviors select this group because of their high rates of suicide, homicide, and acquaintance violence rather than their involvement with partner violence.

Still among the explanations for maladaptive behaviors in African American men, two theories stand out: structural theory and interactional theory. In these theories, scholars explore the experiences of young African American men in oppressive or violent social environments. They report that an oppressive social environment encourages violence (Blake & Darling, 1994; Hammond & Yung, 1993; Hawkins, 1987; Lemelle 1995b; Oliver, 1994; Rich & Stone, 1996; Roberts, 1994; Gibbs, 1988; Williams & Griffin, 1991; and Wilson, 1992).

Many African American men are uniquely affected by violent social environments. Homicide is the leading cause of death among African American men aged 15 to 34; they also have high rates of acquaintance violence and suicide (Oliver, 2000; Jenkins & Williams, in press). African

Americans are more at risk for physical harm by other African Americans than by Whites (Blake & Darling, 1994; Hammond & Yung, 1993; Hawkins, 1987; Rich & Stone, 1996; Roberts, 1994). Trey Ellis, in a work entitled, "What Does It Feel Like to Be a Problem?" comments on the plight of African American men in society. In order to intervene with these men he makes the following observation:

> Ironically, African American men have more right than anyone else to run and hide when other black men head our way on the sidewalk. Yet, we don't (most of us anyway), because we bother to separate the few bad from the legion of good. . . . I'm not making excuses for the black criminal—I despise him for poisoning and shooting more of my people than the cowardly Klan ever did. But we need to understand him as a human being if we're ever going to save him, or at least, save his younger brother or his son (Ellis, 1995).

Writers who are concerned about maladaptive behaviors in African American men attempt to discern the social realities and antecedents that produce this behavior among these men without excusing their negative behavior. There is a convergence of opinions among many scholars that African American men are not the sole cause of their destructive behaviors. In fact, many scholars imply that to understand African American male deviance, it is imperative to understand societal oppression. An oppressive structural social context creates hostile living environments that produce a range of maladaptive reactions among some African American men. The violence that results is predictable. Although most of the writers in this area chronicle other forms of interpersonal violence and problem behaviors, Staples (1982) and Gibbs (1988) note that violence toward women may be one maladaptive behavior that results. Still today, these conditions exist for a disproportional number of African American men (Oliver, Williams, & Hairston, 2005; Oliver, Williams, Hairston, & Crowder, 2004).

## STRUCTURAL THEORY AND AFRICAN AMERICANS' MALADAPTIVE RESPONSES

Staples (1982) and Wilson (1992) suggest that before one can truly understand violence perpetrated by African American males, there must be a critique of the African American man's experience in the United States. Violence in the lives of African Americans is allowed and even promoted because historically their lives have been devalued in American society (Hawkins, 1987). It is, therefore, imperative to recognize the types of societal violence the African American man experiences to understand the violence some African American men perpetrate (Wilson, 1992). Violence and oppression unleashed on African Americans every day goes unnamed (Gary, 1995; Lemelle, 1995a; Staples, 1982; Gibbs, 1988; Wilson, 1992). Wilson (1992) observes the following:

> The history of physical and psychological violence of White America against Black America which began with Afrikan slavery in America has continued to this moment in a myriad of forms: wage slavery and peonage; economic discrimination and warfare; political-economic disenfranchisement; Jim Crowism; general White hostility and Klan terrorism; lynching; injustice and "legal lynching," the raping of Black women and the killing of Black men by whites which have not been addressed by the justice system; the near-condoning and virtual approval of Black-on-Black violence, differential arrest, criminal indictments and incarceration . . . segregation; job, business, professional and labor discrimination; negative stereotyping and character assassination; housing discrimination; police brutality; addictive drug importation; poor and inadequate education; inadequate and often absent health care; inadequate family support, etc. (p. 7)

Lemelle (1995b) states that the study of African American male deviant behavior highlights the individual's relationship to production. He argues that the study of "Black male deviance" should focus on the organization of labor under capitalism. This requires an examination of U.S. social and cultural history viewed from the perspective of class struggle. A societal structure built on a dominator/subordinate model seeks to maintain the status quo where African Americans are the subordinate group and part of the underclass. In this context, the values of the dominator are to be internalized and reinforced, while the values of the subordinates are devalued and rejected (Lemelle, 1995b; Roberts, 1994). African Americans become frustrated attempting to follow all the rules while still facing the barriers to access (Chestang, 1972).

Oppressive experiences faced by African Americans occur within a sustaining environment. In sustaining environments, African Americans earn a living, are educated, obtain goods and services, and are involved in other activities that support their capacity to exist in society. They also endure institutional and other challenges in such environments. In contrast, a nurturing environment could be counted on to assist most African Americans in negotiating societal oppression in all its forms (Chestang,

1976; Norton, 1978). This nurturing environment consisted of African American families, media, neighborhoods, business, churches, and community. During the1940s through the 1970s, the African American community could rely on the presence of a nurturing environment. Since that time, the level of violence has increased significantly.

Many of the social supports that had constituted the nurturing environment have eroded (Gibbs, 1988). Many mobile African Americans (working-class, middle-class, and educated) left the former segregated neighborhoods and moved to integrated environments. Although opportunity and mobility can be considered good, the consequence is that it created a greater gap in economic diversity, advocacy programs, role models, social supports, social networks, and community leadership and a greater gap and physical distance between middle-class and poor African Americans. The results created increasingly stressful community and living environments, with fewer supports and resources for those who were left behind. Furthermore, these environments were at increased risk for poverty, stress, frustration, crime, and violence.

It should also be noted, however, that the gap in social support could be experienced by those who left, as well as those who were left behind. Although more mobile African Americans had greater financial resources, they were not necessarily connected to enriched family or community support, and advocacy. All African American males experience social oppression regardless of social status, but low-income men may feel it more intensely (Gary, 1995). Any African American male who is not connected to a healthy, nurturing support system is at risk for displaying maladaptive responses.

## AFRICAN AMERICAN MEN AND INTERACTIONAL THEORY

One consequence of an oppressive societal context is stressful and violent community environments that foster violent interactions among men. Nicholson (1995) and McCall (1994) describe their experiences in violent African American community environments and explain that violence was a behavioral imperative among their peers. They further explain that to move away from violence was a personal struggle and evolution to self-awareness. Rich and Stone (1996) describe the meaning of "being a sucker" for young African American male victims and perpetrators of violence. They interviewed African American men in hospital emergency rooms who were victims of violence. Respondents

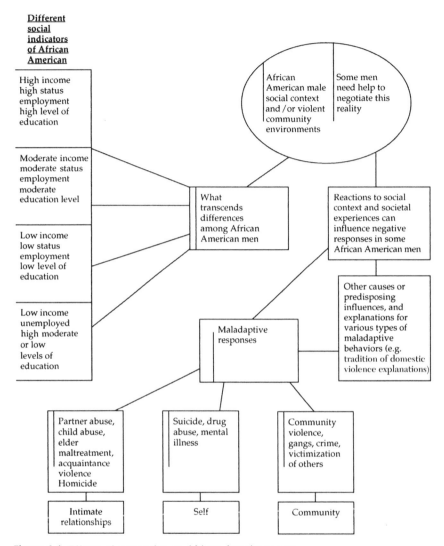

**Figure 4.1** Effects of oppression on African American men.

reported that either an unwillingness to use violence or the perception of "weakness" and vulnerability could result in more danger and increase the potential for abuse, more so than the actual use of violence. Oliver (1994) describes the tough-guy personality that develops from exposure to a violent environmental context. Violence may ensue based on one's perceptions of others, within this context. Such perceptions can be triggered by verbal and nonverbal interactions with others. What is important to recognize is that most people in that environment are operating on the same set of cognitive and behavioral imperatives. Violence for some is viewed as a rule for living and/or survival. The attributions for violence are then generalized to other contexts, such as family or intimate relationships (Williams, 1994a). Violent behavior, therefore, may result either from a reaction to oppression or through learned behavior from a hostile and violent community environment. Williams and Griffin (1991) suggest that the violence that results can be directed at the self, at intimate relationships, or at the community (see Figure 4.1).

## BLENDING CONVENTIONAL WISDOM IN THE FIELD WITH AN AFRICAN AMERICAN MALE–SPECIFIC APPROACH

Separately, theories concerning partner abuse or maladaptive behaviors and African American males offer only partial explanations concerning the behavior of African American men who batter. Regarding domestic violence, sexism, male socialization, and social learning are the underlying conditions for violence; controlling and abusive behavior are the results. Legal accountability is used to sanction and control maladaptive behaviors. Group treatment is a method used to reform and educate men who batter. Societal and internalized oppression and a social learning from a violent family, peer, and community environment can produce a range of maladaptive behaviors in any man, including African American men. These maladaptive behaviors can include problems such as crime, poor interpersonal relationships, poor conflict resolution skills, substance abuse, and violence. Several writers in this field suggest that such behaviors require holistic treatment. Instead of focusing on isolated behavior change with individual behavior problems, more could be accomplished through healing and teaching African American men to live a balanced life within a community of self and others (Akbar, 1985; Blake & Darling, 1994). Men who are emotionally out of balance tend to substitute one maladaptive behavior for another (Blake & Darling, 1994). Other researchers recommend that attention to the African American male's social realities is imperative. Violent African American men must develop skills to negotiate violent and oppressive experiences and environments in adaptive ways (Williams, Boggess, & Carter, 2001). Nicholson (1995), McCall (1994), and Brown and Edwards (2005) describe a time in which they did not see violence as a choice, but they eventually learned that there were alternatives to violence. Gibbs (1988) and Wilson (1992) recommend sanctions for the negative behavior, but they also suggest providing resources and development information for men who live in highly stressed urban communities. Treatment approaches with violent African American men must make the link between the oppression and social context they experience and the oppression they perpetuate, because violence toward women through abusive and violent behavior may be a result of displaced anger from their social context (Williams, 1993; Wilson, 1992); it is also determined by rules of manhood from the streets (Oliver, 1994; Oliver et al, 2004, Brown & Edwards, 2005). Taken together, the two theoretical perspectives provide greater insight on multiple levels in understanding and responding to African American men and violence and those men who batter. A broader, integrated perspective on violence encourages the development of more effective models and intervention. Still, there is no language to discuss the blending of these perspectives. Those who write about domestic violence usually do not refer to the work of scholars of African American maladaptive behaviors, and vice versa. In order to confront male battering effectively in this population, practitioners and researchers must become familiar with the literature of both fields. Models of practice with African American men who batter must emerge from these combined theories (refer to Figure 4.2).

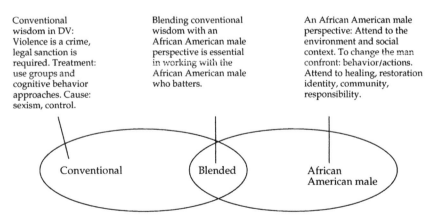

**Figure 4.2** Demonstrating how conventional methods must be blended with an African American male perspective.

## WHAT SHOULD A BLENDED PERSPECTIVE EMPHASIZE?

Because there is not a common reality between the two fields of violence, it is truly a challenge to address the question of what a blended perspective should emphasize. The question itself sparks a debate, because the perspective on what is most important differs so drastically based on the perception of needs. Clearly the safety of women is paramount. Those who work with female victims of domestic violence understand, all too well, the nature and behavior of men who batter and demand that the destruction done to women every day be addressed. To listen to women's stories about their experiences of abuse and humiliation helps one recognize that sanctions, accountability, and consequences for men who batter are essential to stop maladaptive behaviors from continuing and to send a message that such behavior is not allowed. In contrast, those who work with African American men see boys and men either hurt or dying at the hands of other African American men. They also see the destruction and the breeding ground for anger and hostility. They, too, ask the question of primary interest in partner abuse: How do you stop people from abusing and re-abusing, and how do you prevent men from ever starting violent and abusive behavior? Although sanctions and jail time constitute one response, they cannot be the only response. The model of addressing domestic violence has stayed, basically, the same for more than 25 years. Without updating and contextualizing current models, by itself the present model cannot be expected to respond to abusive behavior of all men in America who are African American, Latino, White, Native American, Asian, Arab, African, South Asian, South East Asian, or of other groups with both similar and differing worldviews, orientations, and sets of realities and differing brands of sexism. It is necessary to develop models of practice that take into consideration the influences and context of the population of diverse groups of men one serves. A common unifying theme is that there is no justification for abuse, but we must understand how men view their world and react in it and at the same time shape models of practice. Another unifying theme from the Duluth model is that men must be taught alternatives to violence, develop insight to their behaviors, develop skills in addressing those abusive behaviors, develop a set of alternative, nonabusive sets of behaviors, and to know when to employ them through a responsibility plan.

Sanctions must be a consequence for maladaptive behaviors, but they cannot be the only strategy. Scholars who write about violence among African American men as well as those who change their abusive behavior refer to a type of healing that is essential in order for change to occur. Still today, the notions of sanctions and of healing appear to be unlikely partners. The debate over punishment versus rehabilitation in criminal justice reflects a similar conflict. Given the nature of the problem, helpers must find a way to make it work. The realities of battered women and African American men are important. For change to occur, it is imperative that we do not get caught in a zero-sum perspective; that is, either one approach or the other. The debate must center on a framework of inclusion. The message must be sent to African American men, as well as all men who batter, that destructive behavior is not acceptable, and changing such behaviors is imperative in supporting healthy communities.

A common philosophy must emerge between scholars and practitioners in the partner abuse field and African American male violence field. A blended perspective captures the essential elements for responding to partner abuse among African American men. In addition, programs must assess their capacity to work with African American male clients (Williams & Becker, 1994). A common philosophy should include the following points. A blended approach must take everything we have learned over the last 30 years about addressing domestic violence among all men who batter (sexism, male socialization to violence, power and control, creating responsibility plans, developing a monitoring system that reviews the man's behavior, teaching alternatives to violence, creating consequences for continued abuse, and the like) but also address other themes and issues of this group (such as examining and challenging the men's worldview, their particular brand of sexism, and other issues).

## CHALLENGES IN IMPLEMENTING TREATMENT MODELS WITH AFRICAN AMERICAN MEN WHO BATTER

### Limited Endorsement from the Field

The field of domestic violence has gone through various developmental stages. In the early days of the domestic violence movement, the safety of women and raising consciousness were among the first issues to be addressed. Although issues of race, culture, and diversity were important, they were not attended to because not enough attention, information, or support existed about the primary issue—domestic violence.

In the late 1960s and early 1970s, the developing field of domestic violence emerged as an effort to keep women safe from abuse. Generally speaking, female family members, friends, and neighbors took abused women into their homes to protect them from attack. This grassroots movement organized because traditional helping professions and systems, including law enforcement, courts, marital therapy, psychology, and social work, frequently ignored the plight of the battered woman, identified her as the problem, or provided little support for her. In the early 1980s, I recall that court systems would order divorcing couples, including those that experienced domestic violence, to meet with individual and family therapists at the family agency where I worked as a clinician before a divorce would be granted. The judges wanted to know whether counseling could be an alternative for any couple seeking a divorce. The battered woman was usually frightened of her partner and had endured the abuse for years and wanted out of the relationship. The husband tended to be confused by her concerns over abuse and would recount how he had apologized for his behavior and did not understand why she was being so difficult. Prior to the mid 1970s, psychology labeled battered woman as masochistic without labeling the man or viewing him as the source of the problem. Many marital therapy or couples counseling practitioners saw the resolution of the violence as negotiating the conflict between couples and improving poor skills in communication and interactions between them. In the 1970s and 1980s, helpers in a range of professions did not recognize that the woman would be a target no matter what she did, and they failed to see the man as the carrier of abuse from relationship to relationship. The battered women's movement encouraged batterer intervention programs (BIPs) to challenge abusive men to take ownership for the abuse/violence and end it prior to addressing the conflict. In the BIP groups I conducted, a number of men who battered would report how couples counselors would have their female partners agree to change their behavior in a particular manner and then the men would promise not to hit them. The men learned through batterer groups that the responsibility for the abusive behavior was theirs and reported that this philosophy helped them to alter their thinking and abusive behavior.

In the mid to late 1980s, as information developed about the disparities associated with domestic violence rates, the service needs of African American battered women, and the severity of domestic violence they experienced, researchers and practitioners began to explore the impact of this problem on African American battered women (Asbury, 1987;

Coley & Beckett, 1988; Sullivan & Rumptz, 1994; Donnelly, Smith, & Williams, 2002; Campbell, Campbell, King, Parker, & Ryan, 1994; Straus & Gelles, 1986; Hampton, Gelles, & Harrop, 1989; Lockhart, 1985; Uzzell & Peebles-Wilkins; 1989; Williams, 1989).

The emerging view about diversity was not widely embraced by the entire field, which tended to feel more comfortable with a one-size-fits-all approach to serve all women. Pathology was the implicit method of explaining the disparities in the rates of violence. Still, little effort was made on how to reconcile the violence or reach out to those African American communities most affected or with the greatest disparities.

One contributor to this problem has been a tendency to operate from a singular reality about how we see the problem and their solutions. For example, Oppenlandar (1981) described the development of the domestic violence field and how laws have been among the greatest contributors to disenfranchisement and abuse of women. The information was accurate, but the history tended to be shaped around either a European perspective or White American woman's reality. It tended to ignore how the problem emerged among various cultural groups and how women of color may experience multiple issues and oppressions regarding the type of sexism they experience, the lack of protection under the law, or the influence of issues such as slavery, racism, and other forms of disenfranchisement during the same period of time. As it relates to domestic violence, little information was available regarding the important intersection of race, class, gender, ethnicity, culture, violence, and oppression.

Attention to diversity today is still not widespread, but there is evidence this trend is changing. National culturally specific organizations have emerged, such as the Institute on Domestic Violence in the African American Community (IDVAAC); Alianza (a national Latino organization for the elimination of domestic and sexual violence); and the Asian Pacific Islander Institute on Domestic Violence (API), which encourage better understandings of the issues facing African American, Latino, and Asian/South Asian/Pacific Islander groups, respectively. Further, scholarship associating diversity and battered women's needs, and acceptance of that scholarship in the field, are gradually increasing. Still, the extent that we embrace and integrate these concepts into our practice is variable (refer to Figures 4.3–4.5).

Information and practice models associated with African American men who batter in these populations also follow a similar trajectory and void over the years. Few studies have been funded to understand and identify methodologies, and models that work from researchers who are

**Developmental stages of the field of Intimate Partner Violence**

**Grassroots movement: All in the same boat**

| **Pre-1974:** | $\longrightarrow$ | **1974 to Present:** | $\longrightarrow$ | **1994: VAWA** |
|---|---|---|---|---|
| Women helping women (safe houses) | | Battered women's shelters | | Expanding the ways we do our work |

| ↑ | ↑ |
|---|---|
| **BIPs** | More scholarship and organizations began around diversity issues; disparities in IPV became more visible |
| In the mid-80s questions about inclusiveness, diversity and disparities begin to surface | |

**Today, the extent that we understand, trust, articulate and integrate this knowledge into the field is variable**

**Figure 4.3** Status of diversity related to intimate partner violence.

steeped in the realities of those groups or that represent those communities. Disparities in the rates of violence, success in batterer intervention, among African American men and other cultural groups, compared to white still must be explored. And people from around the country want to know what to do and how to work effectively with these groups.

Research indicates that batterers intervention programs has some success for men who batter, as it relates to African American men, research concerning models have been mixed. Not enough studies have been conducted to give us a clear picture concerning what to do. Gondolf (2007) reports that culturally specific models have mixed results, but in this study there where concerns over the implementation of the model. In contrast, Lyon (2007) found that a culturally responsive model had some success with African American and Latino men.

# Status of Diversity Related to Intimate Partner Violence

## • Developmental stages of the field of Intimate partner violence

### Expanding the ways we do our work

**Today the extent that we understand, trust, articulate and integrate this knowledge into the field is variable, although more scholarship is available on diversity issues.**

**There is a difference between consciousness raising and acceptance or believing and doing. The field must be more action oriented. Work with diversity must be more effectively and consistently communicated with in the field of IPV**

Dr. Oliver J. Williams © 2005

**Figure 4.4** Challenges related to diversity in today's practice in domestic violence.

Frank and Ben (2007) state that domestic violence have limited effectiveness; they recommend a law enforcement incarceration strategy as the approach of choice. But given how law enforcement interacts with communities of color, we might expect greater disparities in incarceration rates as well (Maver, 1999). Over the last few years, some efforts also encourage the use of a social justice model for engaging men who are already predisposed to be nonviolent and encourage their participation in a campaign to end violence against women. In my opinion, we cannot afford to use only one model. We must use them all, including batterer intervention. Investment in culturally responsive approaches on this continuum must emerge and be tested to determine how to achieve more successful outcomes among African American men and other cultural groups.

A public health model of primary, secondary, and tertiary prevention for African American male populations should be considered. Primary prevention consists of public education and information directed at all African American men at various ages and developmental stages,

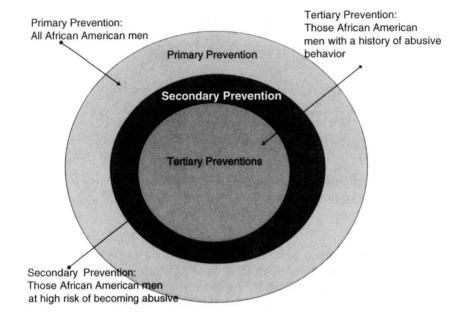

Primary Prevention:
All African American men

Tertiary Prevention:
Those African American
men with a history of abusive
behavior

Primary Prevention

Secondary Prevention

Tertiary Preventions

Secondary Prevention:
Those African American men
at high risk of becoming abusive

**Additional themes to address in each category of men include:**

1. **Definitions of respect**
2. **Identity of self**
3. **Acknowledging and addressing their brand of sexism, beliefs about the purpose of women and behaviors and attitudes toward women**
4. **Fatherhood and DV**
5. **Street codes about resolving conflict**
6. **Co-parenting and DV**
7. **Alternatives to violence—given social context and situation—man to man, family, community**
8. **Problem solving skills**
9. **Connections with parts of the community that support nonviolence and adaptive behaviors**

**Figure 4.5** The Public Health model and approaches to reach African American males related to domestic violence.

education levels, and socioeconomic statuses. Secondary prevention also considers the same grouping as in primary prevention, but approaches are constructed to target African American men who are high risk for becoming abusive and violent. We know the age groups that are most at risk; we know the influences on men and the locations of communities most at risk for varying forms of violence. The challenges to this form of prevention are that we do not often describe the potential barriers to success, use models that accurately reflect their realities, or agree on issues to include in interventions. We have been short on approaches that will engage and reduce the potential for violence, given the realities and influences on this community. Finally, tertiary prevention focuses on developing models and approaches for African American men with a history of violence and abuse. With this population of abusers, there is no magic or definitive model that guarantees success. Still, it is essential to find models that increase the possibilities for success among these abusive men. Without engaging these men too, we can be assured of the continued abuse of women from one relationship to another.

## Not Solution Oriented Enough?

We often study failure more frequently than success. Often, researchers give us a snapshot of what occurs in the population or interventions. In the name of objectivity, there are those who have no particular commitment to a particular troubled community to identify what works. They do not consider how to report or reconcile important challenges the African American communities face. They see the problem of domestic violence in a vacuum. In contrast, there are models created by researchers who have continued to search for answers that include communities of color in all their complexities. Funders must consider how to support researchers who are themselves steeped in the realities of the communities they study as well as researchers who also represent those diverse communities and are committed to finding models that work for these populations.

Further, cultural competence must be utilized and integrated with lessons learned about what ends male violence. While asking some BIP providers about men who have been successful or changed from being abusive, some have been able to identify men who have changed, while other providers reported that they do not look for it. Lessons learned from those who have changed (given their social and cultural context) should help shape BIPs too. In 2007, in *Assembling the Pieces* (the

IDVAAC newsletter), men with histories of violence against a female partner reported on their change. The abusive man and other key informants (present partners and community members who could validate their change) were interviewed about his violent and abusive sobriety. In another project titled the Safe Return Initiative (a project of IDVAAC and the Office on Violence Against Women), one of the early activities was to identify and interview African American men who had histories of incarceration and violence toward other men and women and had transformed. In the newsletter and project, men described their path to change. Understanding the guidepost for change has been important in many other recovery and change efforts, addictions programs, and self-help efforts such as Alcoholics Anonymous or Narcotics Anonymous. We have been reluctant to consider a range of models and approaches with men who batter, because of the philosophy about what constitutes safety, content, and success and the consequences for battered women of relapse of violent men. We fear women may be encouraged to stay in abusive relationships. Although staying should not be encouraged, we know that many women leave violent relationships, but many also stay. We must support the woman regardless of her choices. We should also defend against women believing that a batterer's participation in any change effort will guarantee change; we know better. We must not proclaim any one model as the answer. At the same time, finding a range of approaches to end men's violence is the goal; we should thoroughly consider several strategies to reduce this violence, including culturally competent approaches.

## LACK OF UNDERSTANDING ABOUT WHAT IT MEANS TO BE CULTURALLY COMPETENT

Over the years I have heard some BIP practitioners and researchers dismiss cultural competence in batterer intervention as endorsing men, from a particular cultural group, sitting in a room and complaining about racism and White folks. The practitioners believed that it took the focus off of the primary concern—the men's own violence against women. In contrast, the practitioner who understands cultural competence recognizes that it is an effort to discuss and problem-solve around various social context and life challenges and their direct relationship to displaced anger and violence against women. Traditional approaches are not sacrificed; in fact, a blended approach of our traditional models of BIP with enhanced themes is recommended. Williams (1994b) notes that men who completed culturally competent treatment groups rather than groups conducted according to a mainstream model felt as though the group facilitator understood their reality better and confronted them on issues that were relevant to their culture and social context. Williams (2007) broadly defines cultural competence as a set of behaviors on the part of practitioners and/or organizations that maximize a client's capacity to benefit from social services through an understanding of racially or culturally diverse clients' values, social context, definition of help-seeking behaviors, barriers to service delivery, and understanding of service needs. Practitioners and organizations that are culturally competent are knowledgeable, responsive, and intentional about addressing issues from diverse client groups. Cultural competence on issues discussed in treatment groups emerges from understanding these men's perspective on issues that result in conflict or violence and how the men justify their behavior, including intimate partner violence. Providers are better able to engage these men and discuss issues that result in abusive behaviors, in a way that more closely and authentically approximates the men's reality (Hairston & Oliver, 2005; Oliver et al., 2004; Brown & Edwards, 2005), particularly, among African American men who are at high-risk of being abusive and who come from high-stress, low-income communities.

In talking to these African American men with histories of violence toward other men and women, several common themes have emerged. One theme is a particular brand of sexism in attitude and behaviors manifest toward women (Oliver et al., 2004; West & Rose, 2000; Bell & Mathis, 2000). The role and latitude prescribed to women is limited and specific. Bell and Mathis (2000) describe the iconography that influence how the beliefs and behaviors emerge. This is different from conventional social and societal contribution to sexism; rather, it comes from a specific social context. Brown and Edwards (2005) describe growing up in a violent African American community and how gang culture discouraged being "soft" or taken advantage of by other men. They noted that this was even more specific regarding the role of women. Hairston and Oliver (2005) describe how men they interviewed had multiple co-occurring romantic relationships with women who had a particular role and purpose for them. The following are some of the other themes:

- The meaning of being a sucker
- Identity of self and manhood in the culture

- Definition of respect within society, in the community, man to man, and in the family
- Fatherhood
- Co-parenting
- Reconciling street codes of negotiating conflict and survival and replacing them with alternative responses to address conflict
- Connecting men to a healthier community environment and support systems that support better choices.

## Lack of Supportive Treatment or Agency Environments

Cultural competence is an effort to enhance a client's capacity to benefit from programs offered through social services, yet some organizations are resistant to it. I have encountered programs and practitioners that regard cultural competence as racist or unfair to White clients because they perceive it as giving a particular racial or cultural group an advantage or undue attention, despite disparities in completion and dropout rates, victims' sense of safety, or recidivism of this client group.

As mentioned above, some organizations and providers define cultural responsiveness as encouraging a cultural group of people merely to get together and complain about racism rather than educate themselves, develop skills, and solve problems of particular relevance related to their rationalizations about conflict or violence against women. Practitioners who do not represent the groups they are working with have been resistant to cultural competence because they feel it marginalizes them and discounts their contribution to engage and reach a specific client cultural group. Rather than valuing the potential benefit of this approach, administrators and practitioners may be so resistant to it that they sabotage the potential for success. In one case, an administrator who, along with a probation officer, supervised and assigned men to treatment groups told African American men assigned to a culturally specific treatment group that they were being assigned to the "racist" group. The men reported that upon hearing this, they were distrustful and reluctant to participate because they thought they were being singled out for poorer treatment because of their race. The reality was that there were other groups that used a mainstream approach with all or mostly African American men without concern over configuration. Being around other African Americans by itself was not a concern—it fact it was commonplace; the men referred to all these groups lived in a predominantly African American community. The men noted that they did not mind being in a culturally specific group, but that they did not want to be placed in what the administrator and probation officer cited as a "racist" group. The administrator of that BIP believed that cultural competence was by definition racist and explicitly attempted to interfere with efforts to reach the men.

Williams (1994b) reported that African American men in heterogeneous BIPs with group facilitators who were unaware of their community or cultural experiences were less able to engage them. They reported that they would feel more favorably about the facilitator if the facilitator was a good listener, but they did not feel this person understood them or could confront them on issues that mattered. This does not mean that culturally specific groups are the only model; Williams (1999b) describes healthy heterogeneous groups. He reports that people in differing cultural groups can be culturally competent as long as they are steeped in the realities, issues, and challenges of the populations they work with. Lyon (2007) reports on the Evolve BIP in Connecticut, in which African American and Latino men were reported to have a successful outcome with multicultural facilitators who addressed themes and issues associated communities. This project and model were also based in a supportive agency environment with intense facilitator supervision.

## Teaching Alternatives to Violence in Multiple Life Contexts

In conventional approaches to domestic violence treatment, men learn alternatives to violence. Group treatment facilitators explore the predisposing influences for conflict situations that can result in violence toward women. The content of treatment for African American men who batter must expand to include the ways that social oppression and social learning from hostile community environments result in violence toward women. African American men who batter must examine their reactions to social oppression and social context. They should examine their code of conduct and rules for living, then make the link between frustration and their displacement of that anger onto women. They also must gain skills for negotiating a stressful oppressive social context. In particular, African American men who batter must learn the connection between violence among peers and the generalization of that violence to intimate partner relationships.

## No Narrative in Treatment about Displaced Anger and Scapegoated African American Women

Battered African American women report that their partners attribute their violence to experiences with racism and oppression in society. African American men who batter must consider that if social oppression influences their life, African American women are affected by that same oppression. In fact, African American women experience a double oppression: societal oppression and the oppression of sexism and partner abuse. Violence toward African American women may be a form of displaced frustration; however, she is being the scapegoat because of his frustrations. If an African American man who batters is mindful of the oppression he experiences, he must also be mindful of the oppression he commits against a female partner. (Williams, 1994b).

Richie (1995) in her gender entrapment theory encourages us to examine what families, particularly African American families, do to deny sexism and abusive behavior to women in order to protect male perpetrators. African American women know that the men's oppression is real. Moreover, Asbury (1987) describes the double bind many African American women and families face—being concerned about how their man will be treated in a legal system that historically has been unjust. At the same time, they hate being victimized by his violence. So, often, a woman endures a hostile, violent relationship to support her partner (or family member) in order to keep the family together, or because she believes she can heal him or that he will change. For safety's sake, African American battered women must not accept this rationale as a reason to stay with someone who is out of control. She must be informed that she is at risk for violence if she stays. She cannot heal his pain through loyalty because he must heal himself. Men who batter are 100% responsible for their behavior. African American men must be reminded that African American women face social oppression, too.

## Challenges to the Notion of Healing and Restoration

Roberts (1994) asserts that African American men's positive ways of relating to women can contribute to an understanding of men's realities and possibilities. Furthermore, rarely is the public (including certain African American males) exposed to African American men as playing more positive roles in healthy and constructive relationships: as models, nonviolent parents, providers, workers, partners, and husbands (Blake & Darling, 1994; Hare, 1964; Staples, 1986). Yet these positive behaviors and images are realities among African American men, as well.

The idea of healing and restoration is based on the reality that there are powerful positive models of African American manhood that all African American men must strive toward. Havenaar (1990) states that psychotherapy models can provide healing if they are based on the morals, cultural values, and realities of a client group. He notes that every culture has its own *Menschanschauung* (view of the human being) that its uses to resocialize and heal its people. Unless African American men have healthy definitions of manhood, based on what can be described as an African American set of values, problems will occur (Akbar, 1989; Asante, 1981; Madhubuti, 1984; Roberts, 1994). hooks (1995) and Roberts (1994) state that African American men must define themselves based on a healthy definition of masculinity, rather than on a destructive, sexist, or borrowed definition. hooks (1994) reminds African American men not to recreate the power and control paradigm that scapegoats and oppresses women. She reminds us that oppression is destruction to everyone. Roberts (1994) reports that when African American men adopt or recreate negative definitions of masculinity, they are embracing Euro-American symbols of masculinity that define male and female as mutually exclusive components. African American men, in contrast, historically have valued African American women as assertive, independent, and competent, and have embraced a duality of role identity for women and men. Asanti (1981), Akbar (1985), and Roberts (1994) describe a set of enduring values that characterize African Americans. These include the importance of group and community above competition and individual aspirations. Furthermore, sharing, respect, and reciprocity are valued in interpersonal relationships. Madhubuti (1984) suggests, in a poem titled "Black Manhood: Toward a Definition," that an African American man must live a life of balance. Akbar (1989) expands on this theme and encourages African Americans to live in balance within a community of self and others. Waldram (1993) suggests that for one to attain balance and healing he or she must actively focus on behaviors and action steps. To transform African American men who batter, these men must have accurate information about their history as healthy (nondysfunctional, nonpathological) people. They must meet and interact with healthy models. Men who batter must be taught the rules for African American male health, which include living in balance, learning how to negotiate life's challenges adaptively and without violence, and being respectful and inclusive of African American women and children. Finally, as they follow the action steps, they must strive to become models themselves.

## SUMMARY

An enriched perspective retains the beliefs presently held in the field of partner abuse, but it differs because African American male perspectives are included as ingredients that shape the treatment content and design. For example, there is no justification for partner abuse; men who batter must take responsibility and be held accountable for their behavior; violent men must learn alternatives to violence and controlling, sexist attitudes and behaviors. Accordingly, culturally competent programs will also include traditional and alternative explanations for violence among African American men who batter in approaches to treatment. Treatment interventions must incorporate these explanations and make the link between these explanations and the man's behavior. Violent African American men must learn how to negotiate life challenges arising from social context and environment. In domestic violence treatment groups and in the African American community, it is essential to address healing, identity, and community responsibility.

Engaging and confronting African American men who batter requires the capacity to respond to the dual realities of battered women and of African American men who batter. First and foremost, we must protect women from abuse. We must also develop a language to talk about alternative perspectives to confronting domestic violence. We must expand the present perception for the causes and solutions of violence. We must enrich present methods of treatment to be more inclusive: A one-size-fits-all approach is not always appropriate. Scholars and practitioners who study African Americans and those in the domestic violence community must talk to each other, work with each other, and learn from each other. Finally, African Americans are caught in a peculiar predicament. Oppression and social context shape their experiences, perceptions, and interactions in profound ways that continue to endure. Some survive these challenges better than others. Those who do not withstand them may turn against themselves through destructive responses to self, to those they profess to love, and to the community. Such destructive behavior can be seen as another tool of internalized oppression. For some African American men, violence may be due to sexism, internalized oppression, and displaced anger; for others, it is male socialization and control. There must be legal sanctions to protect women from abuse in addition to community-based interventions and sanctions appropriated by African Americans, which protect women and confront men who batter. Violence erodes a community's capacity to care for itself. At a speech in 1998 at the University of Minnesota, Dr. Robert Allen, the author of *Black Awakenings* and co-author of *Brother Man*, made the following comments regarding domestic violence and African American men:

> African American men know intimately the violent capabilities of other men. It is a tragedy that some of us have internalized the violence of this racist/sexist society and brought it into our communities and our homes. The injuries done by racism to black men's bodies and spirits are sometimes devastating, but this can never justify transforming that hurt into rage and violence against black women's bodies and spirits. We may not yet be able to stop the violence of the racist state, but self-inflicted violence in our communities and homes we can stop. Black men, who well know the lash of white male violence, have a special responsibility to stand with black women and children against all forms of violence. Black men must hold each other responsible for challenging sexism in our community as we all challenge the racism of white America . . . at the Million Man March, disavowing wife abuse, abuse of children, and the use of misogynist language was an affirming and healing gesture.

The domestic violence field and the community of African Americans must collaborate in affirming and healing gestures to reduce this problem in this community. To end this problem in African American, White, Latino, Asian, and Native American communities, we must value our similar and unique realities with this problem and support our communities' recovery efforts.

## REFERENCES

Akbar, N. (1985). Our destiny: Authors of scientific revolution. In H. P. McAdoo & J. L. McAdoo (Eds.), *Black children: Social educational, and parental environments*. Beverly Hills, CA: Sage.

Asbury, J. (1987). African American women in violent relationships: An exploration of cultural differences. In R. Hampton (Ed.), *Violence in the black family: Correlates and consequences* (pp. 89–106). Lexington, MA: Lexington Books.

Asante, M. (1981). Black male and female relationships: An Afrocentric context. In L. Gary (Eds.), *Black men*. Beverly Hills, CA: Sage.

Bandura, A., Ross, D., & Ross, S. A. (1963). A comparative test of status envy, social power, and secondary reinforcement theories of identificatory learning. *Journal of Abnormal and Social Psychology, 67*, 527–534.

Bell, C., & Mathis, J. (2000). Importance of cultural competence in ministering to African American victims of domestic violence. *Violence Against Women's Journal, 6*(5), (May), 515–532.

Bell, Y. R., Bouie, C. L., & Baldwin, J. A. (1990). Afrocentric cultural consciousness and African-American male-female relationships. *Journal of Black Studies, 21*(2), 162–189.

Berkowitz, L. (1983). The goals of aggression. In D. Finkelhor (Ed.), *The dark side of families.* Beverly Hills, CA: Sage.

Blake, W. M., & Darling, C. A. (1994). The dilemmas of the African American male. *Journal of Black Studies, 24*(4), 402–415.

Brown, P., & Edwards, W. (2005). *Safe Return Initiative: From the prison to the community. Interviews.* St. Paul: Institute on Domestic Violence in the African American Community, University of Minnesota.

Campbell, D. W., Campbell, J. C., King, C., Parker, B., & Ryan, J. (1994). The reliability and factor structure of the index of spouse abuse with African-American battered women. *Violence and Victims, 9*(3), 259–274.

Chestang, L. (1972). *Character development in a hostile environment.* Chicago: University of Chicago Press.

Chestang, L. W. (1976). Environmental influences on social functioning: The Black experience. In P. Cafferty & L. Chestang (Eds.), *The diverse society: Implications for social policy.* New York: Association Press.

Cicone, M., & Ruble, D. (1978). Belief about males. *Journal.of Social Issues, 34*(1), 5–15.

Coley, S. M., & Beckett, J. O. (1988). Black battered women: Practice issues. *Social Case Work, 69,* 483–490.

David, D., & Brannon, R. (1976). *The forty-nine percent majority: The male sex role.* Reading, MA: Addison-Wesley.

Donnelly, D., Smith, L., & Williams, O. J. (2002). Batterer's education curriculum for African American men. In E. Aldorando & F. Mederos (Eds.), *Programs for men who batter.* Kingston, NJ: Civic Research Institute.

Edleson, J. L. (1984). Working with men who batter. *Social Work* (May/June), 237–241.

Edleson, J. L., & Eisikovits, Z. (Eds.) (1996). *Future interventions with battered women and their families.* Beverly Hills, CA: Sage Publications.

Edleson, J., & Graham-Berman, S. (Eds.) (2001). *Future directions for children exposed to domestic violence.* Washington, DC.: American Psychological Association.

Ellis, T. (1995). What does it feel like to be a problem? In D. Belton (Ed.), *Speak my name: Black men on masculinity and the American Dream.* Boston, MA: Beacon Press.

Flynn, J. (1977). Recent findings related to wife abuse. *Social Case Work, 58,* 13–20.

Gary, L. E. (1995). African American men's perceptions of racial discrimination: A sociocultural analysis. *Social Work Research 19*(4), 207–217.

Gelles, R. J. (1997). *Intimate violence in families.* Thousand Oaks, California: Sage.

Gibbs, J. T. (1988). *Young, Black, and male in America: An endangered species.* Westport, CT: Auburn House Publishing.

Gondolf, E. W. (1985). *Men who batter: An integrated approach for stopping wife abuse.* Learning Publications Inc.

Gondolf, E. W. (1988). Who are those guys? Toward a behavioral typology of batterers. *Violence and Victims, 3*, 187–203.

Griffin, L. W., & Williams, O. J. (1992). Abuse among African American elderly. *Journal of Family Violence, 7(1)*, 19–35.

Hairston, C., & Oliver, W. (2005). *Safe Return, domestic violence and prisoner reentry: Experiences of African American men and women. Discussion group Reports.* St. Paul: Institute on Domestic Violence in the African American Community, University of Minnesota.

Hammond, R. W., & Yung, B. (1993). Psychology's role in the public health response to assaultive violence among young African American men. *American Psychologist, 48(2)*, 142–154.

Hampton, R. L, Gelles, R. J., & Harrop, J. W. (1989). Is violence in the Black family increasing? A comparison of 1975–1985 national survey rates. *Journal of Marriage and the Family, 51*, 969–979.

Hare, N. (1964). The frustrated masculinity of the Negro male. *Negro Digest, 13*, 5–9.

Havenaar, J. M. (1990). Psychotherapy: Healing by culture. *Psychotherapy & Psychosomatics, 53(1–4)*, 8–13.

Hawkins, D. F. (1987). Devalued lives and racial stereotypes: Ideological barriers to the prevention of family violence among Blacks. In R. L. Hampton (Ed.), *Violence in the Black family: Correlates and consequences.* Lexington, MA: Lexington Books.

Holtzworth-Munroe, A., & Stuart, G. (1994). Typologies of male batterers: Three subtypes and the differences among them. *Psychological Bulletin, 116(3)*, 476–497.

hooks, b. (1994). *Outlaw culture: Resisting representations.* New York: Routledge.

hooks, b. (1995). *Killing rage: Ending racism.* New York: Owl Books.

Jenkins, E., & Williams, O. J. (in press). Culture, domestic violence and mental health: Issues facing African-American women in addressing mental health consequences of domestic violence. *Violence Against Women.*

Labriola, M., Rempel, M., & Davis, R. (2005). Testing the effectiveness of batterer programs on judicial monitoring. *Center for Court Innovation.* (November) New York, New York.

Lemelle, A. J. (1995a). *Black male deviance.* Westport, CT: Prager.

Lemelle, A. J. (1995b). The political sociology of Black masculinity and tropes of domination. *Journal of African American Men, 1(2)*, 87–101.

Lockhart, L. L. (1985). Methodological issues in comparative racial analysis: The case of wife abuse. *Social Work Research and Abstract, 21(2)*, 35–41.

Lyon, E. (2007). *Impact evaluation of Special Session Domestic Violence: Enhanced advocacy and interventions.* Washington, DC: National Institute of Justice.

Madhubuti, H. R. (1984). *Earthquakes and sunrise missions: Poetry and essays of Black renewal 1973–1983.* Chicago: Third World Press.

Madhubuti, H. R. (1990). *Black men obsolete, single, dangerous? The Afrikan family in transition.* Chicago: Third World Press.

Martin, D. (1976). *Battered wives.* San Francisco: Glide Publishing.

Mauer, M. (1999). *Race to incarcerate: The Sentencing Project.* New York: New York Press.

McAlister, B. G. (2007). Deciding on fathers' involvement in their children's treatment after domestic violence. In J. Edleson & O. J. Williams (Eds.), *Addressing fatherhood in batterers after violence: Opportunity for improving the lives of women and children.* New York: Oxford University Press.

McCall, N. (1994). *Makes me wanna holler: A young Black man in America.* New York: Random House.

National Research Council. (1996). *Understanding violence against women.* Washington, DC: National Academy Press.

Nicholson, D. (1995). On violence. In D. Belton (Ed.), *Speak my name: Black men on masculinity and the American dream.* Boston: Beacon Press.

Norton, D. (1978). The dual perspective. In *The dual perspective: Inclusion of ethnic minority content in social work curriculum.* New York: Council on Social Work Education.

Oliver, W. (1994). *The violent social world of African American men.* New York: Lexington Books.

Oliver, W. (2000). Preventing domestic violence in the African American community: The rationale for popular culture interventions. *Violence Against Women, 6,* 533–549.

Oliver, W., Williams, O. J., & Hairston, C. F. (2005). Prisoner reentry and intimate partner violence in the African American community: The case for culturally competent interventions. *Journal of the Institute of Justice & International Studies, 4,* 147–158.

Oliver, W., Williams, O. J., Hairston, C. F., & Crowder, L. (2004). Prisoner reentry and intimate partner violence in the African American community: The case for culturally competent interventions. *Journal of the Institute of Justice & International Studies, 4,* 147–158.

Oppenlandar, N. (1981). The evolution of law and wife abuse. *Law and Policy Quarterly, 3*(4), 382–405.

Peled, E. (1996). Secondary victims no more: Refocusing interventions with children. In J. L. Edleson & Eisikovits, Z. (Eds.), *Future interventions with battered women and their families.* Berkeley, CA: Sage Publications.

Pence, E. (1989). Batterer programs: Shifting from community collusion to community confrontation. In P. L. Casear & L. K. Hamberger (Eds.), *Treating men who batter: Theory, practice, and programs:* New York: Springer.

Pleck, J., & Pleck, E. (1980). *The American nail.* Englewood Cliffs, NJ: Prentice-Hall.

Rich, J. A., & Stone, D. A. (1996). The experience of violent injury for young African American men: The meaning of being a sucker. *Journal of General Internal Medicine, 11,* 77–82.

Richie, B. E. (1996). *Compelled to crime: The gender entrapment of Black women.* New York: Routledge.

Roberts, G. W. (1994). Brother to brother: African American modes of relating among men. *Journal of Black Studies, 24*(4), 379–390.

Rosenbaum, A., & O'Leary, K. D. (1981). Children: the unintended victims of marital violence. *American Journal of Othopsychiatry, 51*(4), 692–699.

Rosenberg, M. (1990). Change to participants: From analysis to action. *Public Health Reports, 106,* 233–235.

Rosenberg, M., & Mercy, J. (1991). Assaultive violence. In M. Roesenberg & J. Mercy (Eds.), *Violence in America: A public health approach.* New York: Oxford University Press.

Rothenberg, P. S. (1988). *Racism and sexism: An integrated study.* New York: St. Martin's.

Roy, M. (Ed.), (1982). *The abusive partner: An analysis of domestic battering.* New York: Van Nostrand Reinhold.

Saunders, D. G. (1992). A typology of men who batter women: Three types derived from cluster analysis. *American Orthopsychiatry, 62,* 264–275.

Saunders, D. G., & Parker, J. C. (1989). Legal sanctions and treatment follow through among men who batter: A multivariate analysis. *Social Work Research and Abstracts, 25*(3), 21–29.

Sonkin, D. J., Martin, D., & Walker, L. E. (1985). *The male batterer: A treatment approach.* New York: Springer Publishing.

Staples, R. (1982). *Black masculinity: The Black male's role in American society.* San Francisco: Black Scholar.

Steinmetz, S. K. (1980). Women and violence: Victims and perpetrators. *American Journal of Psychotherapy, 33*(3); 334–339.

Straus, M. (1980). Victims and aggressor in marital violence. *American Behavioral Scientist, 23*(5), 681–704.

Straus, M., & Gelles, R. (1986). Societal changes and changes in family violence from 1975 to 1985 as revealed in two national surveys. *Journal of Marriage and the Family, 48,* 465–479.

Sullivan, C. M., & Rumptz, M. H. (1994). Adjustment and needs of African American women who utilized a domestic violence shelter. *Violence and Victims, 9*(3), 275–286.

Tolman, R. T, & Bennett, L. (1990). A review of quantitative research on men who batter. *Journal of Interpersonal Violence, 5*(1), 87–118.

Tubbs, C., & Williams, O. J. (1998). *Community Insight Report: San Francisco.* St. Paul: Institute on Domestic Violence in the African American Community, University of Minnesota.

Uzzell, O., & Peebles-Wilkins, W. (1989). Black spouse abuse: A focus on relational factors and intervention strategies. *Western Journal of Black Studies, 13*(1), 10–15.

Waldram, J. B. (1993). Aboriginal spirituality: Symbolic healing in Canadian prisons. *Culture, Medicine & Psychiatry, Sept. 17*(3), 345–362.

West, C., & Rose, R. (2000). Dating aggression among low income African American youth: An examination of gender differences and antagonistic beliefs. *Violence Against Women, 6*(5), 470–494.

Westra, B., & Martin, H. (1980). Children of battered women. *Maternal and Child Nursing,* 41–53.

Williams, O. J. (1989). Spouse abuse: Social learning, attribution and interventions. *Journal of Health and Social Policy, 1*(2), 91–109.

Williams, O. J. (1992). Ethnically sensitive practice in enhancing the participation of the African American man who batters. *Families in Society: The Journal of Contemporary Human Services, 73*(10), 588–595.

Williams, O. J. (1993). Developing an African American perspective to reduce spouse abuse: Considerations for community action. *Black Caucus: Journal of the National Association of Black Social Workers, 1*(2), 1–8.

Williams, O. J. (1994a). Group work with African American men who batter: Toward more ethnically-sensitive practice. *Journal of Comparative Family Studies, 25*(1), 91–103.

Williams, O. J. (1994b). Treatment for African American men who batter. *Cura Reporter, 25*(3), 6–10.

Williams, O. J. (1999a). The African American man who batters: Treatment considerations and community response. In R. Staples (Ed.), *The Black family* (pp. 265–279). Belmont, CO: Wadsworth Publications.

Williams, O. J. (1999b). Working with groups of men who batter. In L. Davis (Ed.), *African American men: A practice guide* (pp. 229–242). Thousand Oaks, CA: Sage Publications.

Williams, O. J. (2007). *Concepts in creating culturally responsive services for supervised visitation centers.* St. Paul: Institute on Domestic Violence in the African American Community, University of Minnesota.

Williams, O. J., & Becker, L. R. (1994). Domestic partner abuse treatment programs and cultural competence: The results of a national study. *Violence and Victims, 8*(3), 287–296.

Williams, O. J., Boggess, J., & Carter, J. (2001). Fatherhood and domestic violence: Exploring the role of men who batter in the lives of their children. In J. Edleson & S. Graham-Berman (Eds.), *Future directions for children exposed to domestic violence* (pp. 157–188). Washington, DC: American Psychological Association.

Williams, O. J., & Griffin, L. W. (1991). Elder abuse in the Black family. In R. L. Hampton (Ed.), *Black family violence: Current research and theory* (pp. 117–127). Lexington, MA: Lexington Books.

Wilson, A. N. (1992). *Understanding Black adolescent male violence: Its remediation and prevention.* New York: Afrikan World InfoSystems.

Yllo, K., & Bogard, M. (Eds.) (1988). *Feminist perspectives on wife abuse.* Newbury Park, CA: Sage.

# 5

# African American Men Who Batter: A Community-Centered Approach to Prevention and Intervention

ULESTER DOUGLAS, SULAIMAN NURIDDIN, PHYLLIS ALESIA PERRY

## INTRODUCTION

Race matters.

This is one of the core organizing principles that informs the practices of Men Stopping Violence (MSV), a 26-year-old, Atlanta-based organization that works to end male violence against women.

As part of that overarching mission, we challenge systems that oppress both men and women because of class, gender, sexual orientation, age, and/or race/ethnicity. MSV asserts that violence against women is not an individual pathology, but a systemic control tactic that cannot be uncoupled from other oppressive systems of control, such as racial discrimination or heterosexism. The work of MSV is based on the premise that these systems are integrated and, therefore, should be addressed as parts of a whole.

In working with African American men, facilitators for MSV's Men's Education Program (MEP) acknowledge the reality of the racial and class oppression that the men experience while simultaneously challenging them to engage in rigorous self-examination and be accountable for their abusive and violent behavior toward women. Our experience with African American men indicates that they are more willing to be engaged in this process and more open to the intervention experience when they are part of a homogeneous group.

The limited research in this area supports these observations. A small study conducted in 1995 found that African American men who participated in a racially homogeneous group, in which the facilitator was also African American, were more likely to feel comfortable participating, trust the feedback they received, accept challenges from other men, and connect with the facilitator (Williams, 1995).

More research is needed on outcomes for African American men who participate in racially homogeneous batterer intervention classes/groups. However, studies that have examined outcomes for other types of work involving African Americans also point to the need for what Williams and Gondolf (2001) have termed culturally focused counseling. They write:

> According to clinical observations and research findings in other fields, cultural issues may explain the poor outcomes associated with African American men in conventional batterer counseling. Practitioner-researchers recommend culturally focused batterer counseling as an appropriate response to these issues. (Williams and Gondolf, 2001, p. 283)

One of the classes that MSV conducts for men as part of our 24-week program (part of the MEP) is made up entirely of African Americans, including facilitators. The aim of the class is not to isolate or segregate but to provide a setting that facilitates deeper engagement and encourages increased participation from Black men. (This does not mean that issues related to racial oppression are not addressed in the two other, mixed-race, classes that we conduct as part of the 24-week program. All men can benefit from a deeper understanding of the ways in which racism and sexism are related.)

MSV also conducts a class, Tactics and Choices, for men who have been arrested on domestic violence charges in DeKalb County, Georgia. Men are required by the courts to attend this class as a condition of being released on bond. Routinely, African Americans make up more than 98% of this one-time, three-hour class, although the total African American population of the county is about 56%, according to 2005 U.S. Census figures. The men in this class represent mainly the working poor and working class. The makeup of these classes is clearly a reflection of racism and classism within the criminal-legal system. Whether they are in the 24-week program or in the one-time Tactics and Choices class, for these men racism is the presenting issue.

MSV also has a number of programs that engage men who have not been identified as batterers. They include the Internship Program, in which MSV mentors young men who are interested in organizing to end violence against women; the Because We Have Daughters® (BWHD) Program, which strengthens relationships between fathers and daughters while educating fathers about challenges faced by women and girls; the Mentor Training Program, for men who want to mentor boys; and education and training for practitioners, researchers, policymakers, and other community stakeholders interested in ending violence against women. The dearth of African American male facilitators, advocates, and researchers working in the area of violence against women has spurred MSV to seek assertively to engage African American men in these programs, especially young men recruited into the Internship and Mentor Training programs.

All of these efforts reflect MSV's view that strategic, community-based engagement is necessary for changing the social and cultural climate in which violence against women occurs. This view is also reflected in the analytical tools we use—specifically the Men Stopping Violence Community-Accountability Model—to assess the problem and create effective solutions.

This chapter will explain MSV's philosophical framework as it relates to African-American men, including the Community-Accountability Model; present the Core Principles of MSV's work with African-American men; and discuss programs and practices based on those principles.

## PHILOSOPHICAL FRAMEWORK

Many practitioners who work with batterers are still reluctant to explore the question, "Why do some men batter?" And, given the focus of this chapter, "Why do some African American men batter?"

MSV shares this concern and asserts that it is more instructive to focus on the function of a batterer's abuse. One of the risks in asking "why" is that the batterer—and his justifications and story—become the focus, and his female victim becomes invisible. The batterer becomes recast as a victim—of the system and perhaps of what he sees as her use of the system to victimize him. It might appear that facilitators who focus on "why" are supporting the batterer at the expense of the female victim, with the effect being that his abuse is justified.

This is one reason why facilitators and educators might resist examining the psycho-social context in which African American men's violence against women occurs. MSV examines that context, considering how historical, cultural, and social factors have influenced individual behavior and perception, not because it justifies African American men's abuse, but because it informs that behavior. This awareness allows facilitators to design intervention and prevention strategies that deepen African American men's engagement—in the classroom and in the community.

## Historical Context

MSV identifies the direct cause of men's violence against women as the cultural assumption that manhood is defined by the ability to dominate and control people, situations, and environments. Our culture has as its foundation a patriarchal system that demands that females be viewed as inferior to males and subject to male control. African American author and activist bell hooks (2004) defines patriarchy as

> A political-social system that insists that males are inherently dominating, superior to everything and everyone deemed weak, especially females, and endowed with the right to dominate and rule over the weak and to maintain that dominance through various forms of psychological terrorism and violence. (hooks, 2004, p. 18)

Given that cultural mandate, is the man who perpetrates violence against a woman engaging in aberrant behavior, which is the common view? Or, rather, is he being loyal to the patriarchal system that educated him? MSV ascribes to the latter view. The batterer is—consciously or unconsciously—using coercion and violence to secure his place in a patriarchal system.

hooks's definition implies that patriarchy is ideological. Anyone, regardless of sexual orientation, gender, class, and race can internalize patriarchal values, though men are more encouraged and nurtured to internalize these ideals, and patriarchy requires all men to develop the will to use violence to sustain the system.

African American males, like all males, are told from birth to death, directly and subliminally, that to be female is to be inferior. Very early in life the African American male gets the message that to be vulnerable is to be weak, and to act compassionately and lovingly is inviting others to take advantage of you and possibly destroy you. These "soft" traits are traditionally assigned to females, and the overriding message is that the worst thing you can do as a male is to act "like a girl."

MSV intervenes with approximately 100 African American men in any given month. Some of these are part of our one-time Tactics and Choices class and others are part of the 24-week class. Facilitators who work with these men week after week observe how consistently these messages are presented. African American men have so deeply internalized these patriarchal messages that alternatives to this way of being seem unimaginable. This is especially evident in men who reside in communities where the life philosophy is "survival of the fittest." Any invitation to consider nonaggressive, nonviolent ways of living is experienced as a threat to their very survival.

As we will see later, the MSV Community-Accountability Model illustrates the ways in which African American males are socialized through primary, micro, macro, and global systems to, essentially, go to war. The psychological indoctrination that soldiers undergo to enable them to fight wars mirrors the ways in which the African American male's socialization is carried out. Unfortunately, girls and women are often the enemy targets.

In its work with African American men, MSV acknowledges that some of these men are in partnerships with women of all ethnicities. However, since most of the African American men MSV encounters are partnered with African American women, and most interpersonal violence occurs intraracially, this analysis focuses on intraracial relationships between African American men and women.

## Roots of Male-Female Tension in African American Communities

While African American males are socialized in similar ways to other racial and ethnic groups, their historic and cultural experiences have shaped their gender relations in a unique way. African-American males' particular brand of sexism has been shaped by racism, with its deep roots in slavery. Many social scientists continue to document the impact of slavery on African American family life. Some assert that the tensions between African American men and women today can be traced to the slave experience.

Sociologist Donna L. Franklin (2000) argues that healing the rifts between African American men and women requires an understanding of slavery and its aftermath and a strategy for attending to the effects that are deeply present in the minds, bodies, and souls of Black folk. Slavery had a devastating impact on the Black family. Franklin writes:

> The roots of black gender conflict can be traced to this experience of powerlessness during slavery. Stripped of the most fundamental control over their family lives, slaves could not ordinarily choose how to fulfill the human roles of husbands and wives, fathers and mothers, sons and daughters. (Franklin, 2000, p. 28)

Africans' experiences in America took away the roles that defined men and women in West African culture. African men could no longer expect to fulfill their roles as warriors, husbands and, most importantly, fathers. African women had no protection from any quarter: no protection under marriage, none from forced liaisons with White men, no protection under the law, no right to marry or raise children.

These injustices continued after emancipation, with Whites in power exploiting the tensions between Black men and women. Former slaves were challenged with reinventing and constructing new family life in the new conditions of freedom. White men—former slave masters and other men in power—exploited the relationships between Black men and Black women, engendering distrust between them and encouraging Black men to use any means necessary, including violence, to control Black women.

Franklin describes how gender relations between Black men and women were complicated by the Freedman's Bureau:

> The bureau was established by the Republican Congress in 1865, ostensibly to protect the rights of former slaves by providing them with education and medical care. It was the bureau's responsibility to monitor labor contracts and oversee "problems" encountered by this new labor force. It soon became clear, however, that the primary aim of the bureau was to protect the interests of the planters, not the interests of black families, and still less the interests of black women. Southern whites saw the aspirations of black women to attend to their own households and care for their own children as jeopardizing agricultural productivity. Dismayed by the dramatic reduction in the black labor force, with black women withdrawn, planters appealed in writing to the Freedman's Bureau for measures that would ensure their return to the fields. (Franklin, 2000, p. 49–50)

Franklin further asserts that once the Freedman's Bureau made the commitment to protect White planters' interests by mandating Black women's return to the fields, it reinforced that directive by strengthening its relationship with Black men. The bureau gave Black men authority over their wives, designating the husband as head of the household and establishing his right to sign contracts for the labor of his entire family. Families without a male head of household were allotted less land. Black husbands were also held accountable by bureau agents for their wives' work performance. Black women were paid a lower wage than Black men for the same labor.

> This Faustian bargain struck by white and black men, was the first signal after emancipation of the erosion of gender relations in the African-American community. The bureau reported receiving hundreds of complaints from black women of battery, adultery and nonpayment of child support. (Franklin, 2000, p. 51–52)

An examination of social-political and economic policies and practices over recent decades shows that they mirror those of the nineteenth-century Freedman's Bureau. There are institutional policies and practices that facilitate tensions between Black men and Black women and encourage patriarchal structural arrangements in African American communities. MSV theorizes that African American men's use of violence or the threat of violence is, in part, both an unconscious and a conscious attempt to regain their perceived lost or diminished rightful place in the home.

A century after Reconstruction, U.S. government policies were still influencing the structure of the Black family. One of the most well-known analyses of Black poverty was authored by Daniel Patrick Moynihan, who at that time was Assistant Secretary of Labor in the Johnson Administration. What came to be known as "The Moynihan Report" identified Black female-headed households as a major factor in creating and perpetuating Black poverty and in essence described such familial arrangements as anti-American if not pathological. In a section of the report headed "The Tangle of Pathology" it was stated:

> In essence, the Negro community has been forced into a matriarchal structure which, because it is too out of line with the rest of the American society, seriously retards the progress of the group as a whole, and imposes a crushing burden on the Negro male and, in consequence, on a great many Negro women as well.
>
> . . . Ours is a society which presumes male leadership in private and public affairs. The arrangements of society facilitate such leadership and

reward it. A subculture, such as that of the Negro American, in which this is not the pattern, is placed at a distinct disadvantage. (U.S. Department of Labor, Office of Policy Planning and Research, 1965)

The Moynihan Report seemed to place the blame for Black poverty squarely on the shoulders of Black women, who, the report implied, would be in much better circumstances if they were in families led by men. This attitude continues to carry weight as government policies and private initiatives alike seek to promote traditional patriarchal, hierarchical families as the norm, in essence sustaining the Faustian bargain.

## The "Code of Silence" Within African American Communities

The historical facts of slavery, segregation, and the continuing discrimination that occurs at every level of American life demand a thoughtful and thorough examination of race and how it influences the work to end male violence against women. In acknowledging that we all live and operate within cultural and political systems based on inequality, domination, and patriarchal values, we begin to get to the root causes of male violence against women and have a clearer picture of how that violence affects everyone.

Many African Americans have developed a code of silence about dysfunction within their communities to counter the negative ideas and images that traditionally have been part of the American cultural conversation about Black people.

African Americans' experiences with the criminal-legal system have also prompted them to shield problems within African American communities from the larger society. Given the use of law enforcement, the court system, and other authorities to control, manipulate, and unlawfully abuse and imprison African Americans, Black women have reason to mistrust the state and its proposed solutions. Therefore, many of them have not been comfortable relying on the criminal-legal system to resolve domestic violence cases in their communities. Many African Americans have advocated for and developed alternative approaches and models.

Given race relations in this country, there are few occasions where African Americans and Whites discuss these issues in any meaningful way. Most Whites continue to deny and reject African Americans' experience of America as racist. Poll after poll document diametrically opposing views over whether certain events had anything to do with race. A recent event that provided an illustration of this point was the government's ineffective response to Hurricane Katrina in 2005. In an ABC News poll conducted in September 2005, 76% of African Americans said that race affected the government response to the hurricane, whereas 73% of Whites said race did not affect the response (Langer, 2005).

The persistent denial and minimization of racism and slavery's aftermath must be rigorously challenged if we are to effectively address violence against women in African American communities.

## MSV'S COMMUNITY-ACCOUNTABILITY MODEL

Patriarchal and racist ideologies have demanded that we address the problem of male violence against women by focusing on the few men who get caught (mostly the poor and men of color) rather than on the structural inequalities, policies, and practices that encourage and nurture male violence. As discussed in the previous section, MSV views African American males' violence against women as a problem deeply rooted in historical and societal values.

MSV's Community-Accountability Model of Male Violence Against Women offers a view of the cultural and historical mechanisms that support male violence against women and includes information on the ways in which multiple oppressive systems intersect. The model, and the strategies and programs related to it, demonstrate the potential for disrupting traditions of abuse and dominance at the individual, familial, local, national, and global community levels.

The model invites African-American men to consider the many unique social and cultural messages that they receive about women and about their male roles. The model also shows the relationships between social systems and individuals, and how the systemic oppression of people—whether they are women, lesbians, gay or transgendered people, people of color, or some other marginalized group—informs the culture of violence against women.

By showing how familial and community systems rooted in patriarchy are connected, men gain insight into the way their life patterns are formed and informed by those systems, which helps them begin to disrupt destructive patterns.

## Ecological Models

The Community-Accountability Model is an ecological model. Ecological models have been influential in sociological and psychological research and the formation of social policy since psychologist Urie Bronfenbrenner began his work on human ecology, using a model that showed the ways in which family, culture, and environment shaped how children developed into adulthood. His theories (Bronfenbrenner, 1979) have had widespread influence on the study of how people interact with their environments.

Variations of Bronfenbrenner's model began to be applied to a number of research subjects, including male violence against women. A review of these and several other published models of violence and violence against women shows that they have in common an emphasis on identifying risk factors in order to excavate the causes of violence and, consequently, predict individual behavior so that interventions can be developed.

Rather than attempting to predict individual violent behavior by identifying risk factors, the MSV model identifies the socializing messages and behaviors that help create a climate of violence by pressuring individuals to be loyal to a patriarchal, hierarchal value system. This approach helps MSV craft responses that advocate individual responsibility at the same time that it looks beyond the individual to encourage necessary cultural change (see Figure 5.1).

## Interconnected Community Systems

The MSV model identifies patriarchy and colonialism as root causes of male violence against women. It also illustrates the ways in which gender, racial, and class hierarchies support the use of violence to maintain oppressive systems, and how sociopolitical systems instruct individuals at different levels of community to enforce and reinforce the messages used to maintain those systems.

The model is organized around the different levels of influence at which hierarchies based on patriarchy, gender, race, and class assert themselves, and identifies those levels at which cultural norms can be disrupted. MSV names the function of each level of socialization and focuses on the messages conveyed by each community represented. How these communities interconnect and how their messages are interpreted, acted upon, and redeployed back throughout the system

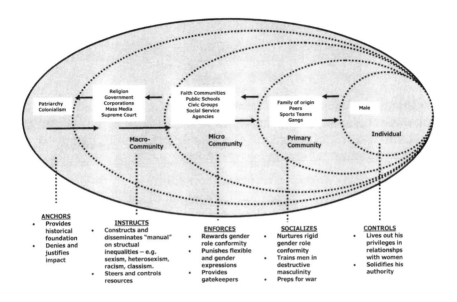

©Men Stopping Violence, Inc.

**Figure 5.1**  The Men Stopping Violence Community-Accountability Model of Male Violence Against Women.

of communities is vital to understanding how individual men are influenced and how, in turn, they influence the communities of which they are a part.

This analysis views this political-social system as a global one that is sustained and strengthened by smaller, related systems that control smaller spheres of influence. The analysis focuses on the roles of interconnected community systems in both socializing men and reinforcing patriarchal male behavior.

This model allows MSV to view African American men—batterers or not—not only as individuals who are abusive, but as people in relationship with their environment and with other individuals and groups that perform socializing functions. MSV's work seeks not only to intervene at different community levels to encourage individuals to change, but to train African American men to become catalysts that shift social norms toward nonviolent, nonsexist, and nonpatriarchal manifestations. MSV views community accountability in this sense as more than sanctions imposed by the criminal-legal system, social service agencies, and other government entities. MSV strategies seek to encourage nongovernmental actions initiated by individuals making up a number of different kinds of communities—family, the workplace, faith communities, schools, and others.

## Levels of Community Influence

MSV's Community-Accountability Model depicts five levels of community influence: the individual and the primary, micro, macro, and global communities. The individual male, his actions, and the forces that act upon him are represented by the smallest ellipse in the model. The primary community is that group just outside of the individual, consisting of his family of origin, school friends, clubs, gangs, or any group that fulfills a familial role. Beyond this is the micro community (workplace, legal system, faith communities, social service agencies); the macro community (governments, mass media, high level courts such as the U.S. Supreme Court, corporations); and the global community (patriarchy and colonialism).

The arrows indicate the flow of energy and influence among these communities, how they act upon each other, and how actions at each level influence the other levels. Energy and influence flows not only from the global community through smaller levels down to the individual but in the opposite direction; the individual's actions may either help maintain the system or have the potential to effect social change.

The colonial and patriarchal cultural systems upheld by interactions between communities ensure that African American boys and men encounter powerful messages establishing male supremacy as the historical and cultural norm. They internalize the notion of male privilege and use it in their everyday lives. Major and minor norm-setting institutions send explicit and implicit messages to boys and girls, men and women, about the superiority of men. Girls and women also internalize the message that male dominance is an established norm that must be either accepted or resisted, and neither choice ensures a woman's safety from male violence.

Such a reality points to a need for strategies that acknowledge the limitations of practices to address African American men's violence against women that do not account for racism and colonialism. MSV developed Core Principles to guide practitioners, organizers, and other community stakeholders interested in working to end male violence against women in African-American and other communities.

# PRINCIPLES AND PRACTICES

The principles and practices of MSV center around community-based strategies for addressing male violence against women. The classes/groups act as laboratories in which we stay connected to the core issue of male violence against women. The lessons learned are integrated into theory and practices in all parts of our community organizing.

In the next section, we describe five Core Principles that have been developed, reviewed and refined over two decades.

## Principle 1: We Are the Work

Commitment to the cause of ending violence against women means committing to conducting ongoing personal work. This awareness is necessary in order to advocate for women and confront men about their sexist beliefs and behaviors. While facilitators/organizers are unlikely to engage in blatantly abusive behaviors, they can collude with the system of patriarchal masculinity in a number of subtle ways.

African American male facilitators, for example, may instinctively identify with men in their classroom and subtly validate their beliefs and behaviors in order to strengthen that identification and also to maintain their own male privilege. Personal work (a lifelong process) allows practitioners to take responsibility for their own behavior, examine the ways in which they collude, and to hold themselves and others accountable. It also helps facilitators explore their motivations for working with African American men.

In the classroom or in the community organizing with men, whatever our gender or ethnicity/race, we are more likely to enhance victim safety and increase accountability for men when we engage in honest and critical introspection.

### Application of Principle

There are a number of ways in which MSV practitioners engage in the work of self-examination.

The foundation for this practice is laid when male potential staff members for MSV enter the Men's Education Program's 24-week class. Any male interested in working at MSV is required to complete this program, which has male accountability and self-examination as core practices.

Men who work for MSV continue this process in regular Men's Accountability Meetings. In these gatherings, men recount circumstances in which they may have used sexist, racist, or heterosexist behavior in their day-to-day lives. The meeting is an opportunity for men to be accountable for this behavior and to hold other men accountable in a respectful and assertive way. Staff members also provide each other with feedback outside of these meetings.

MSV also encourages men to practice self-care. Creating safety and justice for women includes challenging men to take care of their own physical and emotional needs. As part of their patriarchal training, men have been socialized to view women as their caretakers, and because women cannot adhere to this unreasonable expectation, many men resort to violence or the threat of violence to punish them.

Self-examination is important and useful for practitioners who work with or plan to work with African American men since the culture promotes racist ideas about black men and racist and sexist ideas about black women. African American facilitators and practitioners are not immune; they often carry these racial biases about African Americans as well. So for them self-examination is also necessary.

In our trainings, MSV uses exercises to challenge practitioners around their beliefs. One tool we often use in trainings is a "sentence stem exercise," which requires participants to complete statements about Black men. For example, a sentence might start out with "I wish Black men would _____" and participants are asked to fill in the rest of the statement with the first thing that comes to mind, which assists in bypassing the conscious mind. Many White participants who may have viewed themselves as progressive or nonracist often express surprise at the beliefs they hold about Black men. Some Black women participating in the exercise also find this exercise illuminating as well and express surprise at the level of the anger they hold toward Black men.

It makes sense that practitioners, no matter how conscious they are, might still hold damaging beliefs about race and gender; it is extremely difficult not to internalize what the culture says about African American men and women. The work of practitioners is to be aware that such internalized beliefs could affect their work with African American men and to, therefore, engage in ongoing self-examination.

## Principle 2: African American Women's Voices Must be Central to the Work

The primary goal of MSV in working with African American men is to enhance the safety of African American women. As previously noted, most interpersonal violence is intraracial. Therefore, we seek out the voices of African American women in order to hear how they are affected by male violence. When African American men are the focus of this work, it is easy for the voices of African American women to become lost.

African American women develop a clear understanding of patriarchy and how it works. They must in order to keep themselves safe in a culture where the threat of male violence is so pervasive. At the same time, they are very familiar with the ways in which African American men use their experiences with racism to avoid accountability for their violence against women. Being able to hear the truth of African American women's experiences and being given opportunities to empathize with their physical and emotional pain is important for both practitioners and African American class participants, who so often hide their abusive actions behind the pain of their own experiences with oppression.

### Application of Principle

African American women have been part of the conversation at MSV since early in the organization's life. In the late 1980s and early 1990s, MSV began the African American Initiative to ensure that African American women's voices were heard and that MSV's work was informed by Black women's experiences and reality. A group of African American women from the board and community and African American men from staff and the board met monthly.

In addition to being a laboratory for learning about and addressing gender relations in African American communities, these meetings provided the foundation for a number of practices at MSV.

The African American Initiative recommended that MSV begin an all–African American men's class, and this class continues to be a critical part of our mission. As stated earlier, the aim of the class is not to isolate African American men, but to create a climate that enhances the participants' willingness to attend to gender oppression.

Another recommendation was for MSV to be proactive in seeking and encouraging African American leadership in the organization. By

1998, one of the co-executive directors of MSV was an African American man, and African Americans continue to fill leadership positions at the organization.

MSV was also advised to fill more Board of Directors positions with African American women. Since then, Black women have continued to be active on the MSV board, and three immediate past board presidents have been African American women.

Another way that MSV invites input from African American women is to maintain strong relationships with the Women's Resource Center to End Domestic Violence (WRC), a Georgia-based organization that serves domestic violence victims. One of the recommendations of the WRC and other advocates was that MSV should cease "accountability checks" with the female partners of men in the 24-week program. Instead, the WRC, which has a predominantly African American staff and client base, provides liaisons between female partners of batterers and MSV. This allows the voices of African American women victims to be heard without jeopardizing their safety.

Another way that African American women's experiences are heard is through the use of materials—readings, music, and video—in the classroom. Often, a piece is used to open the class session. This material includes work by such women as bell hooks, Beverly Guy-Sheftall, Johnetta Betsch Cole, Evelyn White, Gladys Knight, and Aretha Franklin.

Beginning class with women's voices sets the tone, keeping women's reality present. Once the material is shared, men have an opportunity to respond. Often the reading serves as a discussion topic. The men are encouraged to respond to what they are feeling, thinking or remembering.

## Principle 3: Race Matters

In the work to end violence against women, race matters because, although it is a social construct, race has meaning for how people are treated. The concept of race affects MSV's work with African American men in a number of ways.

When working with African American men, race is always in the room. As stated earlier in the chapter, MSV conducts a class, Tactics and Choices, for DeKalb County, Georgia, and men are required to attend as condition of their bond posted for a family violence offense. We conduct this course every two weeks, and out of approximately 45 men per session,

98% of them are Black. That is not representative of the demographics of DeKalb County nor an accurate breakdown of men who are committing domestic violence-related crimes.

For the 24-week class, some men come, theoretically, by choice and some men are court-ordered. Most White men state that they are coming by choice, and most men of color—and poor men in general—state that they are court-ordered. This shows that White men and men with more economic power have the privilege to avoid incarceration and can be perceived as more willing to attend because they did not need a court order. However, MSV facilitators observe no difference in the degree of willingness to take responsibility for abusive and controlling behaviors and make positive changes.

Ignoring race gives men another justification for denying, minimizing, or otherwise detaching themselves from their violence against women. Without a frank discussion of the realities of race, African American men can fall back on their own victimization by a racist culture. While it is important to validate these men's struggles because of oppression, MSV's work calls for facilitators to use skills to hold these men accountable for their abuse of women.

Without attending to race, including examining their own racist beliefs and attitudes, practitioners run the risk of participating in the marginalization of African American women's voices.

Even within movements to end abuse against women, there have been differences between the experiences of White women victimized by male abuse and those of African American women victims. Also, women of color in the Violence Against Women's Movement have always insisted that race be addressed. However, the White, middle-class narrative tended to dominate, and issues of race were marginalized.

Also, the historical use of law enforcement to oppress African Americans means that African American women are unlikely to view law enforcement in the same ways as White women do. The Battered Women's Movement worked very hard for the recognition of battering as a serious crime that required serious attention from the criminal-legal system. However, African American women may be reluctant to rely on a system that they perceive as racist and in which African Americans are disproportionately represented. Instead of placing their trust in the state, they may first seek other systems of support that they recognize as being valid, such as churches, sororities, families, and extended families.

All of these factors make it imperative that practitioners who work with African American men not adopt a "colorblind" strategy but develop practices that attend to race without undermining the work to end violence against African American women.

## Application of Principle

The all–African American class that MSV conducts is a way of enhancing the safety of African American women by creating an environment that helps men take responsibility for their actions. MSV has two mixed-race classes also, and the observation has been that African American men have a higher level of willingness to take responsibility for their actions when they are among other Black men, including Black facilitators.

For African American men even to begin to take on sexism, their struggles as victims of racism have to be acknowledged and validated. The oppressive nature of the criminal-legal system must be named. However, the MSV facilitators of this class, both African American, do not allow men to stay grounded in their own victimization.

The use of African American male facilitators for this class and other educational settings is one way that MSV signals that attending to race is critical to the work of ending violence against women. Another way is the use of educational materials that reflect African American interests, for example, readings by African American writers such as bell hooks and videos that depict African American subjects.

Outside of the classroom, MSV is intentional about seeking out, organizing, and engaging African American men for all our programs. The Training and Community Education Program works with African American men in congregations, civic organizations, and other groups; African American fathers are actively recruited for the BWHD Program; and we recruit men of color for the Internship Program so that the next generation of practitioners will be more diverse.

MSV also maintains a diverse staff and has African Americans at the leadership level who have roles in policy making, decision making, and organizational structure. MSV facilitators are encouraged to undergo antiracism training on an ongoing basis, and they regularly engage in antiracism work in the community.

In addition, we provide training and support for African American men who are doing the work, through our programs and through our relationships with other African American organizations doing domestic violence work. These include such groups as A Call to Men and the Institute on Domestic Violence in the African American Community.

Absent the presence of African American facilitators, organizations that work with African American men should ensure that their staff has a high level of knowledge and consciousness about race issues. That means engaging in accountability work around race and attending the appropriate workshops and trainings. MSV has provided training that specifically addresses working with African American men in both classroom and community. The Office on Violence Against Women (OVW) of the U.S. Department of Justice has supported that work.

## Principle 4: Intersectionality (Race, Gender, Class, Sexual Orientation) Matters

All forms of oppression are interconnected. Intersectionality is the relationship between oppressions, including those based on race, gender, class, and sexual orientation. Racism cannot be ignored when working with men from different cultural backgrounds. Homophobia cannot be ignored when grappling with the ways in which we define manhood. Class hierarchies affect the ways in which men enter a program like MSV's and how men are viewed once there. Organizing to end violence against women requires that advocates be aware and educated about these "isms."

Our commitment to change begins with an awareness of how we ourselves move in the world, because we cannot organize in a meaningful way without exposing our own roles in maintaining inequities. By educating ourselves about the interrelatedness of oppressions, advocates have a more complete set of tools when addressing violence in all of its forms.

The point of being attentive to intersectionality, therefore, is to better understand the factors that are at work in African Americans' lives at any given moment. Although various issues of oppression are framed in the media and in some organizations as separate, an individual's experience cannot easily be broken apart and categorized.

Activist Ami Mattison wrote:

> Within current political parlance, we are bombarded by nonsensical distinctions among questions of freedom and justice: It's a gay issue, a black issue, an Asian/Pacific Islander issue, a women's issue, an immigrants issue, a homeless issue, an AIDS issue, a welfare issue, etc. While we must assert the specificity of our causes and concerns, we know that justice cannot be compartmentalized in this way. (Mattison, 1997, p. 1)

## *Application of Principle*

In our trainings and classes, race and gender, particularly as they relate to African-Americans, are placed in the broader context of oppression, those restrictions and assaults on humanity suffered because of not only race and gender, but because of class, sexual orientation, age, education level, country of origin, language barriers, and many, many other identifiers.

At national trainings, MSV has used the Anita Hill/Clarence Thomas story to illuminate the issue of intersectionality. We show excerpts from a PBS documentary about the 1991 confirmation hearings for Thomas's Supreme Court nomination. Hill, who had worked for Thomas when he headed the Equal Employment Opportunity Commission, testified before a Senate committee about Thomas' alleged sexual harassment.

Some of the African Americans interviewed for the PBS film made it clear that they thought that any possible sexism suffered by Anita Hill should be subordinated to concerns about possible racism suffered by Clarence Thomas. Classism played a role as well in some African Americans' view of the hearings. Many African Americans thought that it was inappropriate for any Black person to go public with such accusations. But they were especially uncomfortable hearing highly educated, upper middle-class African Americans like Hill and Thomas "airing dirty laundry."

Another exercise MSV uses, "The Myth of the Level Playing Field," demonstrates how all kinds of oppressive, hierarchical ideas come into play as people navigate their lives. This activity, by illustrating areas of privilege and marginalization, has been an eye opener for many training participants. For example, at the end of the exercise, many African American men in attendance are surprised to recognize their own privilege. In considering oppressive hierarchies, other factors besides gender and race need to be part of the conversation.

To help men in the classroom consider the relationship between sexism and other oppressions, we use an exercise in which we begin by asking men to cite negative messages they have heard about women. Once we have a substantial list of negative messages, we label this list "Gender Prejudice." We then invite men to name some of the powerful institutions in this country that set the norms for the socialization of men and women (government, media, religion, etc.). When we think of who is responsible for how these powerful institutions are created and operated, we see that most are run or governed by White males. We present the men in class with the equation: Gender Prejudice + Power = Sexism.

Once men are clear about this definition, we change part of the equation. We change the word "gender" to "race" and then ask men how this change affects the list of negative messages that was developed about women. Men begin to realize that the list of messages can also be applied to their experiences with race prejudice; there is little difference between most of the negative messages about women that men hear and internalize and the negative messages about Black people that White people hear and internalize.

When we now look at the list of powerful institutions, again we see that White men are responsible for establishing and operating these institutions. Thus we have created a new equation: Race Prejudice + Power = Racism.

For many African American men, it is the first time they have considered that their treatment of women is an act of oppression comparable to that of racists.

Another way that MSV is attentive to issues of intersectionality is by engaging in activities that, at first glance, are seemingly outside the work of ending male violence against women. That includes participating in activities celebrating the Martin Luther King Jr. Holiday, in particular the annual King Day March, and the annual Gay Pride celebration in Atlanta.

## Principle 5: Community Accountability Is Key

MSV advocates a shift from a sole focus on intervention to prevention strategies that seek to educate a critical mass of African American men to work in their communities. In this way, the analysis of the problem and the strategies that grow out of that analysis benefit not only men who attend batterer intervention programs (BIPs), but all men.

BIPs as we know them generally have not taken on the work of community and social change as a way of working to end violence against women. The majority of them have no connection to the community except through the criminal-legal system. MSV's experience has led us to believe that community-based strategies aimed at identifying and educating more male allies and strengthening collaborative ties between men and women are key to creating safety for women.

There are a number of reasons for this community-based focus. First, there are a significant number of women who are affected by male violence who are not being helped by BIPs, and nationally the number of men attending BIPs represents only a fraction of those who commit violence against women. Most BIP participants are court-referred. The National Institute of Justice (NIJ) has reported that approximately 80% of the men participating in BIPs surveyed nationwide were court-referred (Healy, Smith, & Sullivan, 1998). However, a significant number of incidents of violence against women never make it to the courts. Information gathered by the Bureau of Justice Statistics (BJS) shows that between 1993 and 1998 an average of 47% of the incidents of intimate partner violence that occurred in the United States (about 400,000 incidents) were never reported to the police (Rennison & Welchans, 2000).

These statistics illustrate a need for solutions that engage a greater number of men in order to increase the safety of those women and girls who do not turn to the criminal-legal system for safety and justice.

## Application of Principle

MSV has expanded or begun programs that take the work even deeper into communities, actively challenging men of conscience to accept responsibility for the problem and the solutions. In educating *all* men about male violence against women, MSV brings communities to the classroom and the classroom to communities.

Community accountability is a strong brick in the foundation of the 24-week program. We view the classroom not as a cocoon of confidentiality, but as part of the community in which we live and work. The classroom is open to those interested in doing the work and witnessing the work of violence intervention and prevention.

The course work of the 24-week program requires men enrolled to hold each other accountable and also requires them to bring men from their congregations, workplaces, families, and other communities into class as witnesses and accountability partners. Currently, men in the program are required to bring men two times during the 24 weeks.

The aim of inviting these community witnesses is, in part, to help men who complete the program to sustain change. But, just as importantly, the inclusion of men from outside the program provides those men with opportunities to question and challenge themselves and exposes them to the work of ending violence against women.

The classroom is, therefore, open to advocates, facilitators, and others interested in witnessing the educational process. MSV was identified by the Judicial Oversight Demonstration Initiative (JODI), a project of OVW, as a program that was using innovative practices to work with African American men. Representatives from the Dorchester County, Massachusetts, and Washtenaw County, Michigan, JODI sites visited to observe the work. Several of the attendees, who included judges, defense attorneys, advocates, and facilitators, commented later that the visit was a powerful experience that changed the way they looked at themselves and changed their work with African American men. That visit and others like it also has the effect of providing us with feedback about our practices, so that we may be held accountable for how we work.

MSV also routinely arranges opportunities for men in the 24-week program to interact with communities outside the classroom. The all–African American class, for example, has held a session on the campus of Morehouse College, a male, predominantly Black college in Atlanta. Students observed the class and afterward participated in a facilitated discussion of what they witnessed. The African American class has also been required to attend forums and community events related to the work of ending violence against women, including a candlelight vigil for victims of domestic violence murders, a book event for author/activist bell hooks, film screenings, and more. Some fathers in the class have participated in MSV's BWHD Program.

Upon completion of the 24-week program, men are invited to join the Community Restoration Program (CRP). CRP allows men—most of whom have been through the 24-week program or are former MSV interns—to continue to support each other and the work of MSV. For the past few years, this group has also been seriously involved in community education on the issue of male violence against women. They have lobbied lawmakers in Georgia and nationally about legislation that affects the safety of women and children.

MSV also conducts ongoing work within African American communities—with churches, civic organizations, educators, and others interested in the issue—to assist in helping these groups define the problem and formulate their own strategies for tackling it. MSV continually challenges communities to be educated and to get creative about ways to take on this problem without total dependence on the criminal-legal system.

Media appearances are also vital to linking the work we do to community. MSV staffers are regularly called upon to discuss male violence against women in both electronic and print media, both locally and nationally.

## CONCLUSION: A CASE STUDY

The following example illustrates how work done in MEP classrooms can galvanize community groups, which, in turn, helps create safety for women who might not ever depend on the criminal-legal system.

Several years ago, an African American MSV facilitator invited one of the ministers from his church to visit the Tactics and Choices class that our organization conducts for men arrested on domestic violence charges in DeKalb County, Georgia. The minister was Black, and the church was predominantly Black.

The minister attended the class and participated in discussion. One of the exercises conducted during the class helps men to identify tactics they have used to control and dominate women. The minister shared with the class one of the tactics he has used in his relationship and how he believed his partner was affected because of his actions.

The minister was so affected by his experience and by the high level of interaction that the men engaged in that he decided to attend a session of the all-African American class that is part of the 24-week program. Here he witnessed men taking responsibility for their actions and challenging each other around their choices to use aggression, control, and violence in relationships.

Inspired by the depth of the work the men were doing, he announced to the class that night that he was going to share his experience with his congregation and talk to his pastor about the church finding a way to address male violence against women.

As a result of this man's witnessing of the work being done in the classes, his church created a ministry to address the concerns and needs of women in the congregation who were involved in abusive and controlling relationships. The ministry grew into a support network for women, who come together to meet and share their experiences and to be in a safe space where their experiences are acknowledged and taken seriously.

MSV conducted an informational meeting with men in the congregation to educate them and raise awareness about issues of intimate partner violence. Conversations about how men conduct themselves in relationship to women are now an ongoing part of the monthly meeting of the church's men's group.

Recently, the women of the women's support group initiated a meeting with men from the men's group to develop a protocol for addressing domestic violence within the congregation. One of the issues discussed in that meeting was the importance of our pastor speaking to the issue of intimate partner violence on Sundays during services, and since that meeting the pastor has intentionally named male violence in relationships as unacceptable behavior during the Sunday service.

Subsequently, the female and male church members developed a protocol to provide safety for women and to hold men accountable for any abusive or violent behavior.

This is one of a number of examples of how the work of MSV has moved beyond the conventional work of just working with men who batter. Our commitment to community accountability, community involvement, and community creativity is an acknowledgment that true safety for African American women means thinking differently. The ongoing challenge is to promote a view of prevention and intervention that gives more than lip service to the idea that violence against women is a community problem that demands a community-based response.

It is no small task. African American communities and communities of all sorts have in the past been willing to deny ownership of the epidemic of violence against women. Part of that denial takes the form of diverting men into BIPs without attempting to examine and challenge the social context in which their violence takes place.

MSV is advocating for no less than a paradigm shift away from a methodology that focuses primarily on BIPs and toward one that provides all men with opportunities to become change agents within their communities.

## REFERENCES

Bikel, O. (Producer). (1992)., Clarence Thomas and Anita Hill: Public hearing, private pain [Television series episode], In *Frontline*. Public Broadcasting Service.

Bronfenbrenner, U. (1979). *The ecology of human development*. Cambridge, MA: Harvard University Press.

Franklin, D. L. (2000). *What's love got to do with it?* New York: Simon & Schuster.

Healy, K., Smith, C., and O'Sullivan, C. (1998). Batterer intervention: program approaches and criminal-legal strategies. *Issues and Practices in Criminal Justice*. Washington, DC: Department of Justice, Office of Justice Programs, National Institute of Justice. [Electronic version.]

hooks, bell. (2004.) *The Will to Change: Men, Masculinity and Love*. New York, NY: Atria Books.

Langer, G. (2005). *Poll: Bush approval drops*. Retrieved July 2, 2007, from http:// abcnews.go.com/Politics/PollVault/story?id=1117357

Mattison, Ami (1997). Pieces of Us. *Etcetera, 13*(5). Retrieved July 5, 2007, from: http://www.menstoppingviolence.org/LearnMore/articles/PiecesOfUs.pdf

Rennison, C. M., and Welchans, S. (2000). *Bureau of Justice Statistics Special Report: Intimate partner violence.* Washington, DC: Department of Justice, Office of Justice Programs, Bureau of Justice Statistics. [Electronic version.]

U.S. Census Bureau (2005). *State and county QuickFacts.* Retrieved July 5, 2007 from: http://quickfacts.census.gov/qfd/states/13/13089.html

U.S. Department of Labor, Office of Policy Planning and Research. (1965). *The Negro family: The case for national action.* Retrieved July 2, 2007, from http://www.dol.gov/oasam/programs/history/webid-meynihan.htm [*sic*]

Williams, O. J. (1995). Treatment for African American men who batter. *CURA Reporter, 25* (3), 6–10.

Williams, O. J, and E. W. Gondolf (Eds.). (2001). Culturally focused batterer counseling for African American men. *Trauma, Violence and Abuse, 2*(4), 283–295.

# 6 A Postcolonial Perspective on Domestic Violence in Indian Country

EDUARDO DURAN, BONNIE DURAN,
WILBUR WOODIS, AND PAMELA WOODIS

## DREAM*

I was sitting on a hill overlooking a river, and gazing into the distance I could tell I was sitting on the north side of the river. Looking to my left, I could see that it was the east, south was straight ahead of me, to my right was the west, and behind me was the north.

I was sitting there watching things—the clouds, the wind blowing, the river down below—and all of a sudden the earth started shaking and everything just started moving. Clouds rolled in, and there was thunder and lightning. It was really interesting because everything was shaking and things were noisy. It was getting darker and darker. Then I realized I kind of saw something making a movement to my left. I looked and the place I was sitting turned into a bunch of kivas (Anasazi ceremonial structures, partly underground). I looked and there were people popping out of the ground, jumping from the kivas. They were actually running toward me, and past me, up to the highest point of the hill. So I got up and joined everybody else on this plateau area. It was still dark and stormy, and all kinds of people were there. All of a sudden, out of the sky came a yucca plant. It was really long, and the tip of it was on fire. As soon as it hit the ground, everything stopped. There was just complete silence.

I looked down and saw the tip of the yucca burning and went to pick it up. As I bent down to touch it, a voice said, "Don't touch that." So I backed away, and in just a few seconds there was a couple of Pygmy-like people coming from the south over the hill. They were painted in shades of greens and reds. There were two of them, and they both had an evergreen plant or a tip of a young piñon in their hands. They came running and then just stopped. They seemed like they were having fun, really. So they walked around and they were speaking their own language. This was interesting, because I could understand them. What they asked everyone was, "Did anyone touch that thing that fell out of the sky?" And everyone pointed at me and said, "He did." Of course, I hadn't, but they came over and started hitting me all over my body with the tops of the young trees. Then they did the same to everyone else that was on top of the hill. It was still dark and they continued the ritual. They seemed sort of hyper as they finished, then they went to the west, back over the hill, and disappeared.

As soon as they disappeared, a man appeared on the right side, from the north. He had a cape on, and a long staff, and I know he had braids. The yucca was still on the ground, smoldering, and the fire wasn't that big. But the man grabbed the burning yucca and put it in his cape. Then he left and went back in the same direction he came from.

As I was standing around and thinking this was kind of strange, all of a sudden I could hear this lady's voice screaming behind me, which was a little to the northwest, "Help me!"

I turned around and walked a little way down the hill, and there was this cage sitting on the side of one of the kivas. Inside of it was a woman, so I walked over there. I could hear people yelling and screaming behind me, and could hear them saying, "Don't let her out! She's crazy! Don't let her out!" I didn't really listen to them and before I realized what I was doing, I opened the cage. As soon as I did that, the sun rose and the sky cleared. Then I woke up from my dream.

## INTRODUCTION

During recent years there have been many attempts to understand domestic violence in our society. Many intervention and research projects have been launched that would shed some light on the problem. It is well known that violence continues to grow, and many people fear that they may become a victim of violence. Although there has been an attempt to examine domestic violence in—this—society, it is remarkable that very few studies have been conducted in Indian country. Presently, we do not know the extent of domestic violence in Indian communities since no comprehensive epidemiological studies exist.

Through the collective clinical and community work that the authors have been doing over the past 20 years, it is safe to say that there is at least as much domestic violence in Indian country as there is in the rest of society. At any rate, there are no data to disprove the authors' findings. The fact that the problem is almost completely ignored by researchers and funders of research is an indictment of a social science system that chooses to further the violence by ignoring it.

Many of the models for treatment are based on Western interventions. Imposing these models of intervention on Indian people would merely perpetuate another form of violence and further colonization on our community. Epistemic violence[1] of this sort may be one of the contributing factors to the high rate of violence in Indian country. Therefore, the authors will take a different road in the analysis of and treatment recommendations for domestic violence in Indian country.

Theories that have emerged on domestic violence do not exist in a vacuum, and they may be laden with attempts at social control of Indian peoples.

> Recent philosophical and scientific advances counsel us that theories do not mirror or correspond to reality; at best they are tools. This realization opens up space for investigation into not what is but what works. . . . These approaches, however useful, are not neutral insights and assessments of native drinking patterns but rather venture to explain and predict behavior based on a very historically and culturally specific mode of representation—realism—which erroneously assumes unity between the sensible and intelligible. Embedded within this Eurocentric mode of representation is a biased assessment of non-Western cultures. Behavioral theories decontextualize and individualize social problems and many sociocultural theories continue European representations of native peoples that have origins in the politics of the colonial and early American era. Insofar as these approaches are cultural products—a form of literature—we can say that they are hegemonic. By this we mean that they partake in ideological/cultural domination by the assertion of universality and neutrality and by the disavowal of all other cultural forms or interpretations. (Duran & Duran, 1995, p. 110)

---

[1] Epistemic violence occurs when production of meaning and knowledge fails to capture the truth of Native and tribal lives. For a further discussion, refer to Spivak (1988).

Academics and clinicians believe that alcohol may be the most significant contributing factor to domestic violence. This type of thinking is simplistic and fails to place the problem in the proper context. Alcohol may be closely related to the problems underlying domestic violence, thus being more parallel than hierarchical in relationship. "A review of the existing literature on the subject of Native Americans and alcohol contains gross inconsistencies between what is considered by many to be the genesis of the problem and suggestions for its amelioration. In addition, all but a few authors maintain a definition of the problem that masks the issues of domination and subjugation, issues which must be considered given the historical context of this problem" (Duran & Duran, 1995, p. 106).

Hegemonic discourse through the propagation of psychological literature posing as neutral because of its Eurocentric scientism has been violent toward Indian people, and presently this violence has targeted Indian men. Many of the approaches that pretend to heal the pain of domestic violence instead seek someone to victimize and blame. Workshops and other methods of disseminating information on the topic single out men in the community and label them pathological without any consideration for historical context. The most simplistic empirical question may be "How much domestic violence was there before White contact?" From all the oral accounts that we have, it is safe to say that the Indian males in precolonial times had a much more nurturing and respected role in the community.

We are not advocating romanticized remembering of the past. Even without the devastation of colonialism, there would have been changes within Native American structures and systems over time. However, those changes would have taken place within the context of cultural change and development. In addition, in the pre-Columbian world there were systemic structures to deal with family and community problems. These healing systems were systematically destroyed throughout the colonization process. We discuss here some of the subjugated knowledge of the events that led to the present world of Native Americans and their families. In the process we hope to provide space for reimagining the present. This reimagining is also an important component of the treatment process.

We realize that not all tribes or all Native American people were subjected to the same amount of trauma. The discussion here is to illustrate the effects of trauma on the tribes and people who suffered as colonization occurred. The problems that our communities face today are a result, at least in part, of not being given the time and resources to resolve the trauma. A belief by some that present symptoms exist merely because the Native American community is deficient in one way or another is a form of epistemic violence that only exacerbates the problem. It is especially sad to see that epistemic violence is being utilized by some Indian people working within institutions that supposedly are there to help Indian people.

## RELEVANT DATA

Unfortunately very little data is available on Native Americans and domestic violence. A study was done that presents some data on violence in Indian country. Bachman (1992) found that there are an estimated 37,000 assaults on Indians per year. Violent incidents between husband and wife occur at the rate of 15.5% versus 14.8% for White couples. Severe violence by husbands occurs at the rate of 12.2% versus 11.0% for White couples. The authors find that

> it can be seen that the American Indian rate of couple violence is 5 percent higher than the White rate. When this is limited to severe violence, American Indian families experience nearly 36 percent more assaultive behaviors than do White families. Similarly, when husband-to-wife violence is compared, any violence perpetrated by husbands is about 10 percent higher in American Indian families, and severe violence by American Indian husbands is 6 percent higher. (Bachman, 1992, p. 104)

The authors caution that these rates are "lower bound" estimates due to sampling problems when researching American Indians.

Results from the study are tentative. Understanding about Indian families continues to be fragmented, anecdotal, descriptive, and overpowered by poor understanding and inadequate research methodologies. Bachman recommended:

> With regard to domestic violence, future research should focus on exploring such violence within more homogeneous units, such as specific tribal and reservation communities. Urban and rural differences also need to be considered. American Indian intrafamily violence is a complex and multifaceted issue. (Bachman, 1992, p. 107).

## THEORETICAL BACKGROUND

It is unreasonable to begin understanding health related problems in Indian country without first realizing that the geneses of many of the factors related to the problems are historical in nature. Central to the historical contribution to the problem of domestic violence is the factor of historical trauma. In addition to historical trauma being a critical variable, we must then examine how internalized oppression contributes to the suffering of Indian families.

Recent literature clearly demonstrates how historical trauma continues to manifest itself in all types of unhealthy behavior patterns across Indian country (Braveheart-Jordan & DeBruyn, 1995; Duran & Duran, 1995). Briefly stated, historical trauma is unresolved trauma and grief that continue to adversely affect the lives of survivors of such trauma. It is remarkable that historical trauma is passed from one generation to the next and is also cumulative. Therefore, the pain and suffering inflicted on Indian people several generations ago can contribute to the suffering that occurs today.

Internalized oppression is a factor because it is pain that is not resolved and instead is projected onto someone close to the person who has suffered personal or historical trauma. The notion of internalized oppression illustrates how pain that the person carries, if not resolved, may be imposed on someone else. The incidence of domestic violence provides evidence indicating that there is significant unresolved trauma in the Indian community.

Within the internalized oppression paradigm, male dynamics have a specific expression:

> The Lakota wicasa, or man, was robbed of his traditional role as hunter, protector (warrior) and provider. He lost status and honor. This negatively impacted his relationship with Lakota women and children. A further assault on the Lakota and all Indian peoples was the prohibition against indigenous spiritual practices in 1883. (Braveheart-Jordan & DeBruyn, 1995, p. 351)

The removal of roles for men affected the societal system, thus paving the way for unhealthy family patterns of behavior. Without access to spiritual ceremony, Indian people were susceptible to other forms of spiritual colonization and hegemony. The emptiness caused by cultural genocide left the people open to a foreign cosmological way of being.

European cosmology has been heavily influenced by Judeo-Christian thought. Core to this cosmology is the concept that everything is in opposition or in an antagonistic relationship. This antagonistic relationship is further compounded by the fact that there has been a subject-object split in the Western psyche. Western thinking is therefore prone to seeing the world as separate and something to be dominated (in Genesis, God tells Adam that everything is in His charge and He is dominant over the earth). This perspective has been responsible for the colonization of native peoples.

Thinking based on antagonism plays a significant part in human relationships. In Western thinking, feminine and masculine naturally are in opposition rather than existing harmoniously. If feminine and masculine are in opposition to each other, it makes sense that strife rather than peace and harmony is a more predictable way of relating. Antagonistic psychology is not the only way of being in the lifeworld, and there are many indigenous peoples who perceive the world in a completely different fashion.

We will be using a framework that is part of the Dine' (Navajo) traditional worldview to describe harmonious relationships. We will demonstrate how domestic violence may have some of its deep roots in a cosmology of antagonism. We will discuss how the clinical process can facilitate understanding in the client that will in turn enable the client to lead a more harmonious life with people from the other gender (this sentence was difficult to write because the usual way of saying this would be "lead a more harmonious life with the opposite sex").

## SLAYERS OF MONSTERS AND CHILD BORN OF WATER

One must be careful and respectful when introducing oral teaching related to lifeways of the native peoples. At times it is difficult presenting native words using the English language, therefore, graphic representations have been provided to reinforce theoretical discussions.

The oral teachings of the Navajo people accompanied by parallel concepts of their Athapaskan cousins, the Apaches, will be used to illustrate knowledge that can help young men and women learn to respect self-growth, marriage, family, tribe, and community. In setting the stage for teaching purposes, it must be made clear that there are many versions of the cosmic/mystical/soulful/spiritual relationship between man and woman. Life-giving forces as taught by the Navajo, Apache, and other

**Figure 6.1** Gender and power cosmology.

indigenous peoples are complex and require an immersion into that life-world. What follows can be described as a mere paraphrasing of sacred knowledge to bring about what Western psychology describes as a cognitive shift in understanding accompanied by discourse, hopefully leading to new paradigms. These new insights can help a human being see other perspectives and understand how self-hate (the spirit of internalized oppression) can be controlling his or her life and causing imbalance. It is hoped that this ancient model of knowledge will help our brothers and sisters explore paths of self-healing practiced for centuries by our predecessors. Some believe that this knowledge has been forgotten. We believe it is still alive, just as our mother earth continues to provide us with gifts of growth as she relates with father sky.

Figure 6.1 depicts the universal concept of duality between male and female. In the Dine[2] (Navajo) cosmology, the soul (psyche) of the male and female lies within each person regardless of sex. The female side is called Tobajishchini (Child Born of Water), and the male side is Naayeeneizghani (Slayer of Monsters). The paternal father for both of these children is Johonaaei (Sun or Fire), and the maternal mother is Asdaanadleei (Changing Woman) for Slayer of Monsters and Yoolgaiasdzaa

---

[2] By using Dine' cosmology we do not intend to say that this is the only way to understand the dynamics. Other tribes can analyze the dynamics through a similar process utilizing their own tribally specific stories. What we attempt to offer is a method of analysis, i.e. process instead of content.

(White Shell Woman) for Child Born of Water. Changing Woman is identified as White Painted Woman by the Jicarilla Apache (Opler, 1938). Changing Woman/White Painted Woman is related to the earth. White Shell Woman is related to water. The last god or spirit is Nilchi (Wind or Air), who blew the breath of life into Slayer of Monsters and Child Born of Water. One could interpret this story as a description of the birth of the human soul (this is closely related to the Judeo-Christian story of the creation of man, in which God blew the air of life into the molded clay). In the Navajo puberty ceremony the young female represents both Changing Woman and White Shell Woman. In the Jicarilla Apache puberty rite the female represents White Shell Woman and Child Born of Water, and the young brave also represents Child Born of Water (Opler, 1938). In the Navajo tradition the male appears to play a lesser role, and the female represents mother earth and all creation. Earth, air, fire, and water are a common theme among indigenous peoples and are glorified through worship.

Changing Woman literally is changing constantly through the generations of people. In other words, since our physical mother is made of earth and we are brought into life by the female, we are part of the female energy. The changes occur through our changing across the life cycle. At any one time there are old people and young people alive, representing all phases of the life cycle. Therefore, Changing Woman lives perpetually in all forms, changing yet constant. The myth is alive in-every-moment, with ancestors— and unborn—also being an integral part of the present moment.

*Saa,ah'naagei* can be described as sky/sun/moon/stars and beyond, and *Beeke,hoozoon* can be described as ground/earth/water, with the wind/air acting as mediator. What is not described is the interaction between earth and sky and how this relates to harmonious life and balance between and within men and women, as seen from the teachings of the Dine' culture. The interaction between the life force or center of sky, earth, and the four directions taken as a whole is the soul of man and woman which must be kept in balance by constant self-evaluation, prayer, and offerings to all life forces including the seventh sacred direction, which is the human being. This postcolonial[3] concept appears to run counter to the Western view of the relationship between the different genders.

---

[3] Postcolonial can also be thinking that existed in precolonial times. In essence it is a way of being in the world that attempts to understand the effects of colonization and through this reflection allows the person to free themselves from the problems imposed by colonization. In-depth analysis has been done in this area by Duran and Duran (1995) and Braveheart-Jordan and DeBruyn (1995).

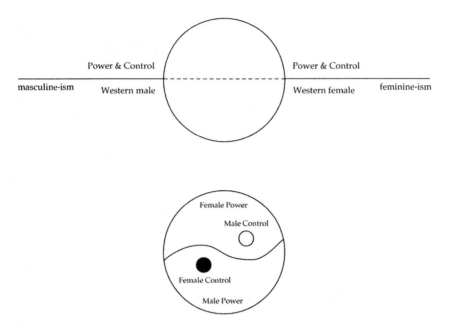

**Figure 6.2** Gender and power in Western and Chinese cosmology.

Figure 6.2 (top) illustrates the western view of the relationship between man and woman. There appears to be a linear "tug of war" between the two sexes. The image depicting the yin and yang in Figure 6.2 (bottom) represents the interrelationship of energies. Within this paradigm and cosmology the energies are not in antagonism; instead they coexist within each other. In Figure 6.2 (top) it is apparent that Western male masculinism versus Western female femininism[4] creates tension between the sexes, leading to struggles for power and control. Figure 6.2 (bottom) represents masculine and feminine existing within and through each other. The antagonism that exists in Figure 6.2 (top) is no longer there.[5] Historically, the indigenous peoples of North and South America were forced to conform to the ideals and teachings of their colonizers.

---

[4] The terms masculinism and femininism are used here to depict the undifferentiated sides of the respective energies. Masculinism is an energy that can be destructive and is a force that interplays in domestic violence. Femininism is the undifferentiated destructive side of the female energy that also interplays in domestic violence relationships. In Jungian jargon, these would be the shadow side of the anima or animus.

[5] We use the Chinese image representing the tao to make this more accessible to our readers. The understanding of male and female forces in the Taoist teachings are for all practical purposes the same as the teachings we are offering. The only difference is the types of metaphors and images used to carry the same archetypal idea.

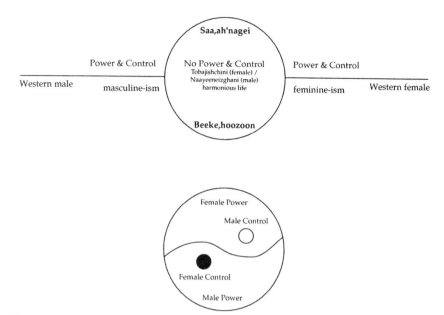

**Figure 6.3** Model illustrating antagonistic relationships.

During the colonizing process, the harmonious cosmology was wounded. The wound and pain continue to cloud the previous state of psychological balance and ability to see the world as a harmonious place.

Figure 6.3 (top) consists of a combination of Figures 6.1 and 6.2. One postcolonial view of human beings as holistic is distorted by the Western view of human beings. The current body of knowledge being written about American Indians demonstrates how disease, captivity, violent death, starvation, forced relocation, and forced Western religious/academic education were the historical norm. Education of indigenous native children was carried out by rounding up children and moving them as far away as possible from family, community, and land. This was done to ensure cultural hegemony over these children and their subsequent generations.

Even though many other attempts to acculturate and assimilate the indigenous natives of North America were made; traditional teachings survived. Most indigenous peoples have similar cosmologies about the relationship between male and female. These teachings may have been lost from consciousness but have remained as part of the personality and continue to emerge in dreams. Postcolonial psychology makes the case for indigenous knowledge having legitimacy and not allowing any other epistemology to be privileged over another. Indigenous healing ways

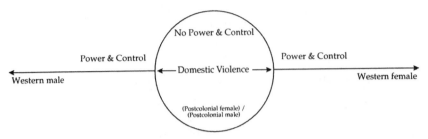

**Figure 6.4** Linear relationship between genders.

continue to exist even at a time when "misoneism"—meaning fear, intolerance, and an oppressive hatred of new and innovative knowledge and an attitude of keeping these ancient healing teachings in the realm of a few—predominates among contemporary Western psychological thought.

Figure 6.4 depicts the "spirit of the time" as related to issues of violence, specifically domestic violence. Western programming has forced indigenous people to follow the linear relationship between genders. The circle remains but is bypassed for a more Western form of domination. Postcolonial work begins by recognizing that both the circle and the line must become integrated or the violence will continue. A hybrid way of being in a bicultural lifeworld needs to develop in order to begin intervening in domestic violence issues. Relating to the figure above, the line must be moved into the circle, but the circle cannot be moved into the line (see Figure 6.5). This process on the surface appears simple, but it is complex.

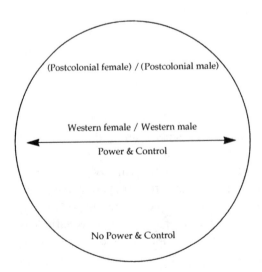

**Figure 6.5** Healing of gender antagonism: transitional phase.

In essence, the problem becomes one of being able to conceptualize the world in a completely different way. This process cannot be forced, that is, the circle cannot be forced into the line (not without destroying its essence of circleness). We find that it is this very forceful process that is used in Western systems to make sense of different worldviews that do not fit a linear approach to the world.

For the integration process to begin, current literature about indigenous people must be reevaluated through postcolonial analysis. This examination must be carried out by people with a vision of truly accepting indigenous knowledge as is. The attitude of the Western "A not B" versus the postcolonial "A:B" as presented by Duran and Duran (1995) should be integrated.[6] Briefly stated, this notion asserts that Indian identity should not be realized by comparing Indian people to what they are not, that is, by categorizing them as non-White. Instead there should be distinct categories of identity that need no legitimization by another group.

Literature continues to romanticize the indigenous American Indian experience of the past 500 years. Articles discuss the many different periods in history of subjugation of the natives, then immediately jump to blaming the victim, systematically overlooking the obvious. This form of epistemic violence is rarely discussed or acknowledged in most academic discussions and literature dealing with the psychology of indigenous peoples. Furthermore, many public health, social, and clinical programs continue to go to battle in hopes of alleviating the indigenous psychosocial problems. Some of our own people have joined in this battle as well. Many of these programs are superficial in nature and powered by a Western frame of reference using monetary and academic tools of persuasion.

Integrating the linear thinkers of power and control with the circular cosmologies of indigenous peoples will serve to neutralize and reveal this power and control spirit (archetype). But first the historical dichotomy created within the indigenous psyche must be revealed. The dichotomy is this: I am a native man or woman who rides on this linear chair fueled by "power and control," and I have incorporated this line into my experience. Yet I am not fulfilled because this is not me, so I repress and dissociate these thoughts and feelings. At this point, respect between

---

[6] In many Western systems, people are identified by what they are not. We suggest that subjectivity be determined by what the person is. In other words, do not identify women as non-men. Instead, women should be identified as women.

genders is forgotten and is replaced by Western ideas of power. I am an independent female who is discriminated against; therefore I must create a movement against my oppressor, who is the male. On the other hand, the native Indian male simply accepts his stereotypical dominant role but has no power in the dominant or Western society.

In prayer, the Jicarilla Apache or Dine' will first sprinkle corn pollen on top of his or her head before it is sprinkled in the mouth and out to the external life forces as a gesture of respect and participation in any activity that serves to continue the legacy of the people and the person. The significance of this is that prayers include "the person who stands inside me." If you are male, a female stands inside you; if you are female, a male stands inside you. In offering pollen in prayer in this manner, a balance in soul and a balance in nature are attained and maintained. This balancing ritual between the two life forces of male and female serves to remind both sides of the interrelationship and respect due each other.

The indigenous male finds himself attempting to be what he is not. In addition, his role is constantly being defined for him. According to Western thought he is a warrior, a shaman, and represents nature. He is a protector of our planet. If he does not meet these criteria, either he is assimilated and acculturated and has lost all remnants of his culture or he is a social problem who needs to be treated or locked up. It is understandable that one of the symptoms suffered by our men and women is that they try to destroy each other. The choices are limited, and what remains is an individual who is forced to accept and live out either a romantic or tragic fantasy.

Postcolonial concepts of intervention bring to the surface these current definitions of what an Indian male should be. The use of interventions discussed in Duran and Duran (1995) can begin to provide clues to violence problems among native males without placing blame or forcing upon another teachings inconsistent with his or her worldview.

## CLINICAL INTERVENTIONS

Some of the clinical interventions suggested in this section should be part of a full array of services offered to the individual or family. The strategies that we discuss focus on the cultural aspect of the intervention, and we assume that the providers have training and experience working in the area of domestic violence. The authors want to avoid the presentation of a therapy that may not be effective. At times clinicians who are not culturally competent take suggested approaches in a vacuum and neglect treating the case as a complete case.

A typical treatment protocol should address areas described in the following sections.

## Assessment Phase

The client must have a full assessment that will shed light on his overall functioning. Western-based assessment as well as assessment of cultural functioning must be performed. At this point, we will not elaborate on the Western functioning since such an assessment is well known and is described in other sections of this book.

Cultural assessment should follow a process that will yield cosmological information that is tribal specific. The analysis that we present here provides an example of how this may be done. By having the client understand his traditional cosmology, a template of health can be established. In other words, the client will know that violence and dysfunction are not a tribal way of life and that there is a different standard of behavior than the one he is accustomed to. Many times we have found that dysfunctional behavior has been in the family for so many generations that the client assumes that this is a traditional, culturally sanctioned way to live.

## Therapeutic/Healing Phase

Once the client realizes that the dysfunction is a way of life imposed on a healthy traditional lifeworld, the therapy can begin to focus on the soul wound or historical trauma. It is our experience that by having the client understand the sociohistorical context, it becomes easier for him to let go of the guilt and anxiety that continue to grip him in the cycle of violence. The client can begin to understand how through the internalizing of trauma and the oppressor, he has acted out self-destructive energy on his loved ones.

Therapy during this phase must take on a didactic approach. The therapist must be knowledgeable of the historical trauma and the effects that these events had on the Native American family structure. The clients must be made aware that much of the rage that he feels is internalized oppression and the violence a manifestation of that intergenerational spiritual injury.

At this point in the therapy the transference can move in two directions if the therapist is a Native American. If the therapist persists in working within the Western model, he or she will reinforce the internal oppressor that the client brings into treatment. Basically what the therapist is doing is disallowing, either through ignorance or blind spot, the historical reality that has brought the client into the session. It is highly recommended that these therapists undergo supervision or therapy so that they can resolve their *own* historical trauma. If therapy continues in this type of transference relationship, it is merely recapitulating the dynamics of historical trauma. This will make for iatrogenic harm[7] to both therapist and client. If the Native American therapist integrates the process of therapy through the reification of cultural ceremonial norms, the transference will develop toward the ceremony itself. At this point, it is the therapy or healing that is actually the object of projection.

With a Caucasian therapist, a different type of transference will be elicited. The client will project historical contents into the therapeutic ceremony. Caucasian therapists that we have worked or trained with usually have great difficulty with historical trauma issues. The guilt that is elicited by historical truth makes the guilt turn into anger; this anger in the therapeutic circle will result in failure and iatrogenic harm. Through acknowledgment of historical truth that validates the client's pain, therapy can become more successful. The therapist must take scrutiny and ownership of his or her history in order to have a more honest therapeutic encounter. In addition, the therapist must take responsibility for the way history has afforded him or her privilege in our current society. Without this honesty the therapy is bound to fail. Prevailing literature illustrates that most current Western therapeutic modalities with Native Americans are not very successful (Duran & Duran, 1995).

If the therapist understands historical trauma and brings this knowledge into the therapeutic ceremony, the transference becomes one of liberation. The client can see that the traditional cosmology is valid and is being lived out by one of the role models of the community in a bicultural, healthy manner. Through understanding and teaching of similar cosmology as presented here, the client can free himself of the internal oppressor and start to resolve some of the personal issues that brought him into the healing circle in the first place. At this point,

---

[7] Literally this means that the doctor is making the patient sick. For an in-depth study on this topic, read *The Iatrogenics Handbook* (Morgan, 1983).

Western interventions can be made and the client can deal with the domestic violence that afflicts the family.

## Hybrid Therapy Brought to Life

A typical case would involve the therapist going through the teaching that is outlined in this chapter. The client would be made aware of the universality of the concept of male and female energy existing in everyone. The ideas of Child Born of Water and Slayer of Monsters would be discussed in such a way that the client will integrate the teaching into his present life. (Notions of anima and animus as described by Jung may be helpful for training therapists and helping them make sense of the traditional teaching.)

The client should also be encouraged to record his dreams and to work on these images through a medium with which he is comfortable (i.e., painting, poetry, sandtray).

The clients can then be taught about the harmonious relationship that has existed between female and male energy throughout time. The tension between the energies is caused by a foreign interpretation of the relationship and the incorporation of a mythology that views relationships in cosmology as antagonistic. Once the antagonistic way of seeing the world is integrated, the personal myth is thrown into a chaotic unbalance. The anxiety created by the unbalance creates a power and control struggle between the male and female energy.

Historical trauma further complicates the overall picture through the internalizing of the oppressive energy; this energy has been mostly masculine energy.[8] This logocentric masculine energy is attracted to the masculine energy of the indigenous male. It is as if the logocentric energy is seeking a different form of balance that is more earth-related. Because of historical trauma the indigenous male cannot assimilate the logocentric energy in a healthy, balanced way, and it becomes undifferentiated within his psyche. It is this undifferentiated energy that seeks to control and overpower the female energy and is manifested in violence.

The indigenous female has an energy that is qualitatively different in mythological makeup from the European energy. This energy cannot

---

[8] It is well known that Western mythology is based on the logocentric masculine principle. The logocentric energy has been behind much of the devastation of indigenous peoples as described in the historical trauma paradigm. These notions are discussed at length by Duran and Duran (1995).

harmonize with the undifferentiated logocentric energy that has taken over the male. Her balance and harmony are also placed in a chaotic situation, thus making her react in a manner that seeks to control in an antagonistic way. This chaotic unbalance provides the raw materials for antagonism and violence. Healing can occur only through a proper understanding of the dynamics that occur at a deep psychological and spiritual level.

There are times when the therapy can only go so far, even if the dynamics of this brief chapter are implemented. At this time, it is imperative that the therapy incorporate ceremony through the consultation of traditional indigenous healers.[9] Within traditional ceremony it is possible to bring the spiritual energy back into balance. The ceremony must be used within a model that employs some form of psychotherapy in order to help the client assimilate the healing in a way that makes some cognitive sense. Most of the medicine people we have worked with agree that the ceremony will take care of the spiritual component. Psychotherapy can help the client assimilate the process of the ceremony. Traditional healers prescribe methods of living that will help clients maintain the harmony achieved through ceremony, and the client has the responsibility to live and behave in a prescribed manner that will not create the chaos that afflicted him in the first place. At this point the therapist must be skilled and knowledgeable in traditional practices. The client can then be helped to bridge the continuum between ceremony and the daily lifeworld.

The reason it is so critical that the client be able to bridge between ceremony and lifeworld is that colonization has inflicted a wound in this area also. Western cosmology allows for the compartmentalization of the different aspects of the personality. Indian people have internalized the shadow side of compartmentalization, and some (the ones who are dysfunctional) find no connection between ceremony and daily life. Clients in this situation are searching for magical cures out of the ceremony and feel that they do not have responsibilities to live in a certain prescribed fashion outside of the ceremony proper. The compartmentalization has become so deep that many of our relatives have adopted the ceremony of chemical abuse and incorporated it into the daily lifeworld.

---

[9]Ceremonies are process-oriented, as the reader well knows. Therefore, it is not appropriate to give particulars on the type of ceremony used in the therapy, since every healer has her or his own way of doing so. Therapists who need to incorporate this type of intervention must call qualified providers of such services in order to provide for the Native clients' needs.

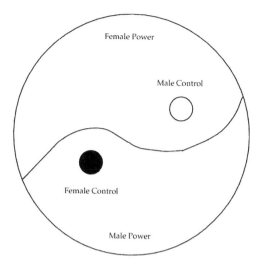

**Figure 6.6** Healing of gender antagonism: balanced power.

Figures 6.5 and 6.6 represent the restoration of the harmony between the different energies. The male and female who overcome the effects of colonialism have moved into a postcolonial lifeworld. Figure 6.5 is the transitional phase where power and control enter into the circular paradigm. Through both traditional and Western intervention the energy becomes harmonious as in Figure 6.6. Figure 6.6 represents aspects of both power and control from both male and female energy. Since the energy is in balance, there is no antagonism that can be acted out, as is seen in cases of domestic violence. At this point, the ceremony is complete.

Sacred is restored in beauty
Sacred is restored in beauty
Sacred is restored in beauty
Sacred is restored in beauty

## REFERENCES

Bachman, R. (1992). *Death and violence on the reservation.* New York: Auburn House.

Beck, P. V., & Walters, A. L. (1977). *The sacred, ways of knowledge sources of life.* Tsailee, AZ: Navajo Community College Press.

Braveheart-Jordan, M., & DeBruyn, L. (1995). So she may walk in balance: Integrating the impact of historical trauma in the treatment of Native American Indian women. In J. Adleman & G. Enguidanos (Eds), *Racism in the lives of women* (pp. 123–153). New York: Hawthorne Press.

Duran, E. F., & Duran, B. M. (1995). *Native American post colonial psychology*. New York: SUNY Press.

Matthews, W. (1994). *Navajo legends*. Salt Lake City: University of Utah Press.

Morgan, R. (1983). *The iatrogenics handbook*. Toronto: IPI Press.

Opler, M. E. (1938). *Myths and tales of the Jicarilla Apache Indians*. Lincoln: University of Nebraska Press.

Spivak, G. (1988). Can the subaltern speak? In C. Grossberg & N. L. Grossberg (Eds.), *Marxism and the interpretation of culture*. Urbana: University of Illinois Press.

Zolbrod, P. G. (1984). *Dine bahane, The Navajo creation story*. Albuquerque, NM: University of New Mexico Press.

# 7

# He Waka Tapu: Working Together for the Well-being of Family

DARYL GREGORY

## INTRODUCTION

New Zealand lies in the South Pacific Ocean, east of Australia. It is made up of the North and South Islands and a number of smaller islands, with a total land area of 268,000 square kilometers. New Zealand is the most geographically isolated of all countries. Its closest neighbor, Australia, is 2,000 kilometers to the northwest of the main islands across the Tasman Sea. The only land mass to the south is Antarctica, and to the north are New Caledonia, Fiji, and Tonga.

New Zealand became a British colony in 1840 with the Treaty of Waitangi, which recognized "complete chieftainship" (*tino rangati-ratanga*) of the Māori tribes of New Zealand. To this day, the exact meaning of the Treaty is still under dispute, and it remains a source of division and resentment. Since 1840, New Zealand has developed into a fully independent parliamentary democracy under the British monarch.

The Māori people, who are of Polynesian origin, are the indigenous inhabitants of New Zealand. As of 2006, they numbered over 565,329, which is about 14.6% of New Zealand's population (Statistics New Zealand, 2006). Over 95% of Māori live on the North Island.

Māori immigrated to New Zealand from around 800 A.D. onward. They arrived from the Cook Islands, Society Islands, and Marquesas

Islands in the Pacific Ocean. Before the arrival of Europeans in the mid-eighteenth century, Māori had settled throughout New Zealand.

Prior to European contact and the signing of the Treaty of Waitangi in 1840, the indigenous people of New Zealand had spent a thousand years establishing themselves in this land, which they had named *Aotearoa* (Land of the Long White Cloud). A number of different tribes had established themselves, their boundaries, and the traditions that governed how they lived and interacted. Knowledge of genealogy and tribal links was an important way of maintaining identity and history.

Today the Māori, like other indigenous groups who have been colonized, suffer from many social ills. Māori make up less than 15% of New Zealand's total population, but account for almost half of the prison population. One in every 47 Māori males aged between 15 and 40 is currently in prison. Māori are more than twice as likely as New Zealand Europeans to be victims of violent crime. By 1997 Māori were entering prison at 8 times the rate of non-Māori. Sentenced Māori males are generally younger (61% under 30 years) than their European counterparts (44% under 30 years). Commonly, they leave high school without qualifications and are highly represented in the mental health, unemployment, alcohol and drug, and teenage pregnancy statistics (Department of Corrections New Zealand, 2000).

## THE IMPORTANCE OF *TIKANGA* IN MĀORI LIFE

*Tikanga* (the correct way of doing things) is what governs the Māori way of life. It incorporates concepts of *wairuatanga* (spiritual belief) including *tapu* (the sacred), *karakia* (prayer or incantations), *manaakitanga* (hospitality), and *whanaungatanga* (family bonds), to name a few. These formed the basis of everyday life for the traditional Māori, and many aspects of *tikanga* continue today.

For example, when a group from one tribe visits the home base of another tribe, the correct *tikanga* must be adhered to. The welcoming ritual, known as a *pōwhiri*, is the means of welcoming people onto your home *marae* or home territory. Within the process, both groups have certain responsibilities. When engaging with another group, it is important to consider both the natural and the spiritual realms. The process of *pōwhiri* starts with the visitors gathering outside the gates of the village. Warriors from the home side will approach the visitors with a *wero* (challenge), to determine whether they come with good intentions or not. Once the home people are satisfied with the motives of the approaching group, they are happy to call the visitors on. This ritual call is carried out by at least one woman and is answered by at least one woman from the approaching group. In the calling, information is exchanged and the way is opened spiritually for the visitors to approach. There are several stages to the *pōwhiri*, which must be followed before the two groups can be joined and can relate in a relaxed and united way.

In this chapter I will describe how He Waka Tapu staff use this model as a best practice when engaging with clients. The need to connect on all levels is very important for us, and it must happen before any work around the issues of domestic violence can happen successfully.

## HE WAKA TAPU

He Waka Tapu (which literally translated means "a sacred vessel") is the name of a Māori-based, charitable, nongovernment organization comprising different *iwi* (tribes) and operating in the tribal area of *Ngai Tahu kei Ōtautahi me Te Wai Pounamuin* (the city of Christchurch in the South Island). I established the agency in 1996 in response to the expressed need of the community, and of government agencies such as Community Corrections, for a program that dealt specifically with issues of violence by Māori men against women and children.

## Origins of the He Waka Tapu Program

Initially, the local probation service contracted me to provide group programs for up to 12 men once a week for three-hour sessions. The service sent me referrals, and I followed up by going to people's homes to conduct a brief assessment and give them the necessary details of the program times and venue. I ran these programs in the community, separate from probation service locations, so that He Waka Tapu could begin to build its own identity. There were many issues to consider, such as safety of all concerned and confidentiality when visiting people's homes. However, we wanted to establish a way of working with our own people that was based on our cultural norms, so we felt that seeing people face to face and allowing them to make some decisions about inviting us in was much more respectful than the usual process. Our method also gave us more insight into people's relationships and home lives.

Our success rate over the first 12 months in terms of engagement was about 80%. Initially I did all of the assessments; eventually, I contracted another experienced facilitator to help run the groups. Community probation paid about $4,500 per 12-week program (40 hours), which covered the costs of interviewing, group work, hiring a venue, writing reports, and following up with clients who missed sessions or dropped out.

At first, our program was no different from other mainstream programs concerning family violence. (At that time in New Zealand, most offender and victim interventions were based around models of power and control, primarily the Duluth model, which features a strong feminist perspective.) However, having spent a number of years working in the local community and men's prisons, I had come to see that what we needed to do was to focus on the healing of men, their relationships, and their families. This required working with the whole family; not just the perpetrators of violence, but their victims as well. At the time, this sort of thinking contradicted what was considered best practice.

I also wanted to shift the debate from just focusing on male violence to including other facets of abuse that occur within family dynamics, such as the abuse of alcohol by both partners and historical sexual abuse. The issues of female abuse, especially against children and (for some) against their male partners, also needed to be addressed, without colluding with or minimizing male violence or the patriarchal system. I wished also to highlight the effects of colonization and facilitate understanding of how mainstream cultural approaches suppress the indigenous voice in many aspects of New Zealand society.

> *Rurea, taitea, kia toitu, ko taikaka anake*
> *Strip away the bark. Expose the heartwood.*
> *Get to the heart of the matter.*

## Establishing the Program

The first step in establishing a practice was to approach the local tribal leaders for their permission and blessing. My colleagues and I met with the tribal elders (*kaumatua*) to explain what we wanted to do, and that we wanted to work from a Māori framework. We asked whether they would be willing to contribute their own tribal customs. They gave us their blessing and the assurance that if we were challenged by anyone about setting up this program, they would be willing to stand with us.

Then we set about establishing a group that would deal mainly with men who were in the Corrections system. These were men who had been sentenced to attend programs and were monitored by their probation officers. This quickly gained momentum, and the Department of Courts also wanted us to receive Māori men through their system. However, we first had to become certified under the Domestic Violence Act 1995 (DVA) of New Zealand, which meant we had to complete application forms that met the criteria of the regional panel for the courts. This was a difficult process: we had to answer a lot of questions and submit the application to a panel that sat every two months. The application kept being returned for further information; in particular, the panel wanted to see more of the philosophy of the DVA clarified in our practice. For example, we needed to show that the group facilitators would be of mixed gender.

After about eight months of sending information back and forth, we withdrew our application and informed the panel that if they wanted a Māori provider to work with Māori men, then they needed to stop dictating how this would happen. We also suggested that it would be more appropriate culturally to meet with us face to face (*kanohi ki te kanohi*). The panel eventually invited us to meet with them. We took along a local tribal elder to show we had the blessing of the local tribe to do this work according to Māori *tikanga*. Eventually, we became certified to work with men from the courts who were under protection orders served by their partners. This story illustrates how a dominant culture can dictate to the minority culture how it should work.

The Southern Regional Domestic Violence Programme Approval Panel approved the content and structure of the He Waka Tapu program. This approval indicates that the panel considers the agency and programs to have met the requirements of all relevant regulations under the Domestic Violence (Programmes) Regulations 1996. The regulations specify content areas that must be covered within each program type, for example, "Increasing understanding about the impact of domestic violence on the victim, including its effects on children" (New Zealand Domestic Violence Act, 1995, Reg. 32(2)(d)).

It should be noted that He Waka Tapu is approved to offer a Regulation 27 program:

> Every programme that is designed for Māori or that will be provided in circumstances where the persons attending the programme are primarily Māori, must take into account Tikanga Māori, including (without limitation) the following Māori values and concepts:

(a) Mana wāhine (the prestige attributed to women)
(b) Mana tāne (the prestige attributed to men)
(c) Tiaki tamariki (the importance of the safeguarding and rearing of children)
(d) Whanaungatanga (family relationships and their importance)
(e) Taha wairua (the spiritual dimension of a healthy person)
(f) Taha hinengaro (the psychological dimension of a healthy person)
(g) Taha tīnana (the physical dimension of a healthy person) (New Zealand Domestic Violence Act, 1995, Reg. 27)

The naming of the trust and ongoing development of the organization reflected a process of thinking about the sort of program that would meet the needs within a Māori framework. An understanding of the image of the *waka* (canoe) is pivotal to understanding the work of the agency.

## COMPONENTS OF THE HE WAKA TAPU PROGRAM

He Waka Tapu is designed as a closed program with up to 16 participants. As many men attending have ongoing court matters, it is not uncommon for some to exit the program because they have been sentenced to imprisonment. There are also other men who self-refer, or who are referred by other agencies, who are accepted outside of the normal start time. This process is managed on a case-by-case basis, balancing individual and group needs, and in consultation with any referring agent.

### Engagement and Assessment

Our workers ensure that sufficient time is given to the process of relationship building. Making tribal connections, talking through the process of what is involved, and exploring the motivational levels of participants are vital to ensure that all participants are ready to embark on what can be a very challenging journey. It also allows our *kaimahi* (workers) to begin modeling the skills of relationship building.

Much energy goes into a thorough assessment process. Māori believe that the aspect of connecting with each other, *whanaungatanga* (relationship building through tribal connections), is important. The *pōwhiri* process, as already mentioned, is about moving people from a state of *tapu* (separateness) to a state of *noa* (oneness). We are no longer two groups but one. Within this process both groups have responsibilities, and must monitor each other both physically and spiritually. It is only when we reach that place of *noa* that we can begin to do the work that has brought us together. This takes time and it means many other people need to be involved, not just the perpetrator and victims but significant others within those social structures. This gives accountability and safety for all involved; it is a team effort.

The *pōwhiri* process sits nicely with models, such as the "stages of change" model by Prochaska and Di-Clemente, as it is about moving through a clear process. We also tend to favor approaches such as the use of motivational skills and a naïve inquiry approach to assessment, which is a good way for us to open up the place for conversation and explore the participant's readiness to make changes. Also, as in a traditional *pōwhiri* process, people are weighing up the costs and benefits for them in regards to the topic (*kaupapa*) of discussion.

## Program Structure

The core program has 12 sessions. Each session utilizes a key *whakatauakī* (proverb) as well as *karakia* (prayer or incantations), *waiata* (folk songs), or *hīmene* (hymns) as appropriate. Each session has clearly defined aims, with a progressive introduction of concepts. A skill development component is built into each session. Sessions are three hours long (with the exception of the assessment). Group participants enjoy the range of activities and the opportunity to listen, speak, and reflect. Regular breaks are scheduled to maintain participant ability to engage.

## Resources and Activities

A mix of large-group and small-group activities are used throughout the sessions. Literacy barriers limit the number of paper-based activities that can be carried out, so video is a preferred medium for many participants. In addition to the Family Court videos, program facilitators make use of video clips from relevant documentaries. Media coverage of domestic violence incidents can also provide a basis for discussion relevant to a session theme.

*Haka* (dance and chant, originally performed before battle), *mau rakau* (martial arts exercises), *hīmene*, and *waiata* are used during sessions, and have a number of functions including:

■ Increasing cultural competence and cultural safety of group members

- Providing opportunities for physical movement and transition between session components
- Use of cultural material that reinforces stopping violence and other positive messages
- Meeting learning style needs of participants
- Development of the group working environment
- Facilitating awareness of *taha wairua* and *taha tinana*

The use of *haka, waiata, mau rakau,* and *hīmene* is consistent with the requirements of Regulation 27.

## Skill Building

The following skills are progressively developed throughout the program:

- Communication—especially listening and speaking
- Problem solving—especially alternative strategies to the use of violence in situations of conflict
- Goal setting—especially in relation to developing respectful relationships
- Conflict resolution—especially in partner relationships

## Services for Women and Children

A range of support services is available to the partners and children of men in our programs. These services are offered to ensure the accountability of men attending groups, to ensure that women and children have access to services, and to ensure that women have safety plans in place.

A female *whānau* support worker has primary responsibility for working with women and their children. Most of the women she comes into contact with are not initially interested in attending programs because they have so many issues going on in their lives. She goes to their homes (with appropriate safety established). Her work with women includes:

- Provision of safety information
- Assessment of current violence, needs assessment
- Development of individual plans
- Provision of information about available services
- Referral to other agencies or programs as required
- Counseling

- Women's Group—small open group
- Co-facilitation of *whānau hui* (family meeting)

Women who wish to access these services become clients in their own right. Separate files are maintained for them, and our worker is able to coordinate with the facilitators of the men's groups in order to discuss safety and accountability issues. Her role in working with the partners of men in the group program is strengthened by her ongoing contact with program participants. This includes a clear explanation of her role in providing support for their partners.

He Waka Tapu workers are thoroughly trained concerning safety issues for women and children, and they put considerable energy into promoting safety. This commitment to the safety of women and children is the strength of the agency and occurs in a context where *whānau* dynamics are also recognized.

In addition to the 12 group sessions, a further two discretionary sessions are available to access *whānau, hapu* (subtribe), and *iwi* resources in order to ensure the maximum safety for partners and children. The building of culturally appropriate support networks to reduce the likelihood of further violence is a key part of the agency work. Women may request a *whānau hui* (family meeting) to be facilitated by He Waka Tapu within this provision. A safety assessment is carried out prior to *whānau hui*, and the *whānau* support worker is able to provide follow-up for women afterwards.

## THE IMAGERY OF HE WAKA TAPU

As mentioned earlier, the name He Waka Tapu, literally translated, means "a sacred vessel." *Whānau* (families) are invited to come on a journey of exploration, to discover new pathways, and to reach for horizons that have only been a far-off dream. The *wero*, or challenge, laid before men and their *whānau* is to consider what our *tūpuna* (ancestors) had to do in preparing to cross the vast Pacific Ocean, *Te Moana nui a Kiwa*, and reach Aotearoa safely, equipped to begin a new life.

We invite participants to consider that the *waka* that will carry them and their *tamariki* (children) into the future is the *whānau*. To ensure that they will reach that far-off horizon, to ensure that the dreams and visions of *tūpuna* for their *mokopuna* (grandchildren) are realized, *whānau* must ensure that the *waka* they build are seaworthy enough to face the challenges that lie before them.

They must consider who is going with them and what skills they have to ensure success. Do they know how to get there? What navigation instruments or knowledge do they possess? This is an invitation to men and their partners to consider what it means to begin the most important journey of their lives—establishing a family—and to consider what their ancestors must have gone through when they left the comfort of the familiar to journey where all was fluid, where no pathway existed, trusting to the *ara whetū* (star paths) above and to their knowledge of the sea.

Program participants at He Waka Tapu are encouraged to look at their dreams, aspirations, and beliefs and to acknowledge that violent behavior blocks them and their family from achieving their goals. Workers need to confidently facilitate a process that motivates people to want to reach their *Taumata Whakakitenga* (the term we use to encapsulate our vision). This will help them go after and realize their dreams.

One way of facilitating this within the group sessions is by using stories, such as this one written by my wife from her book of short stories called *Don's Waka* (Gregory, 2007). This particular story looks at how our ancestors would have gone about preparing themselves for a major journey, so it is a good one for getting people to focus on the sorts of disciplines that were very much part of our traditional practices.

## STORY: ONE MORNING

> Soon, the sky in the east would begin to lighten but it was still dark. The night sky was brilliant with stars and the air still. Lagoon water moved gently on pale sand. Out on the reef, a thin line of white water gleamed in the dark where ocean waves met the coral barrier curved in protection right around the island home.
>
> Rama was almost sick with excitement. He had given up trying to sleep. Now he sat, here on the sand waiting, remembering and praying. This was to be the day; the day long-expected; the day long-planned for and hoped for. This was the day the family had worked for over many moons. This day, they would set sail for Aotearoa.
>
> Rama's father had been there before, years ago, as a young man and the lure of that long, bright land had never left him. The longing of his heart had grown with his children.

He had told them, 'It is a strange and glorious place, a huge land, lying wide and open, so big you cannot see the end of it. Its mountains are mighty, its forests deep and abundant, its seas filled with food and its air clear and light. Yes, it is cold and we must clothe our bodies like birds. But there is space there, and freedom—room for us—and many more—to live in peace and prosperity.'

It was agreed. They would go.

At first, Rama's father had spent much time alone. He would rise before dawn, at just such a time as this and sit remembering, planning, praying to the great creator god, Io Matua Kore. Sometimes, he could be heard singing. Rama had looked out of the sleeping hut to see his dark silhouette standing by the moon-shiny lagoon or walking slowly in the shallows.

Then, there was much talk. There were those who were doubtful, of course, those who were fearful and others who had no desire to leave the home island. Some were too old; others just didn't see the sense in it.

Among those wishing to join in this great adventure was Toroa, a tohunga kaihautu (navigator) of considerable reputation. He was, however, without wife or children since a terrible storm some years earlier. His grieving, deep and terrible itself, had rendered him silent and withdrawn for long periods. He had become a shadow, drifting about the island, almost unseen. Now, with the hope of this great journey before him, his eye had regained its light. His smile had returned, not so broad as before perhaps, but tender and true. His skills would be needed and the knowledge he carried of star paths and other navigational devices, knowledge which had been passed down from generation to generation, would be invaluable.

Suitable trees had been found and the work was begun. It was patient, slow work, carving out the hulls. It was not done quickly but there was a sense of destiny, as cousins, brothers and friends sat working together, shaping the wood. Minds were open. Questions and answers flew. There was often laughter. Sometimes, there was concern. Someone would say, stroking the sides of the vessel, 'This must be strong for such a voyage out there beyond the reefs' or 'Such a small craft in such a large ocean!'

But always, hands were moving. That is the way this enormous task was completed: little by little by little by little. By many hands that kept moving, working, adzing, smoothing, drilling, lashing and weaving.

Pina was an old woman, a very old woman, who used to totter down from her house and sit with the workers. They liked having her there because of her age and because she was a seer. She encouraged them and made them laugh. She would grasp the muscled arm of one of the young men and say, 'Put this one at the steering paddle—his arm's as strong as a tree trunk' or she would squint with her failing eyes and feel for drill holes that had been missed when the lashings of coconut sennit rope were threaded through.

'Yes—I knew it!' she'd say. 'Here's one—and another—do you want to sink out there in the great ocean of Kiwa?'

One day she arrived earlier than usual, holding the hand of a young girl, her great grandchild, who led her carefully along the uneven track. Her wrinkled face was stretched, smiling. She would not sit down, but raised her arm high and said, 'I dreamed of this beautiful boat last night. It was floating up into a big bay with forest right to the water's edge. And I could hear many voices—the voices of birds—shouting and singing. This is a good dream. It shows that you will arrive safely and that you'll be welcome.'

This pleased everyone and comforted many hearts, for such a journey is not without danger and the human heart is not immune to fear and worry.

Nevertheless, the preparation went on.

Most of the work did not seem like sacrifice, although it was. All the effort, time and energy spent often left the workers exhausted with blistered hands and aching backs. But still, they fell asleep to dreams of the great land to which their hearts had already flown and awoke refreshed in vision, ready to toil on again.

Some sacrifices were not easy. Mahina had to choose whether to stay with her child or to go with her husband. Her little daughter, just two years of age, was being raised by Mahina's parents, the child's grandparents. This was natural and right. After all, the child was a joy and comfort to her old people and their house was only a short distance from the one in which her parents lived. The old people refused to let her go. It was enough sorrow to be losing their daughter.

'Leave her with us,' they wept. 'You will have more children to people the new land where you go.'

So Mahina reluctantly agreed and turned her thoughts to the unborn child in her womb. She began to gather stores of kumara, taro, ta'rua, dried fruit and fish, coconuts and wild honey. Some of the roots would be for planting too and there would be precious cuttings and seeds to cultivate in the new land. Gourds would be needed for the water they must carry with them in plentiful supply. All must be prepared and carried safely. In this way, Mahina's sorrow was turned to strength, was turned to the greater good.

The ocean moved like a living being, full and dark except for the bright stream of moonlight on its surface. Rama, sitting on the shore watching, knew these skies, knew the vessel that would carry them all to places unknown. The months of trials and testings, both inside and outside the lagoon, had familiarized them all with the boat. This was no craft with which to creep around the islands, or paddle slowly to fishing grounds and back. This boat leaped eagerly when wind filled its sails, ready to fly into the distance.

He heard stirring and turned to see his father whose eyes gleamed though his face was in shadow. Resting a hand on his son's shoulder, Huihui i te Rangi sighed deeply with happiness.

'We are now ready, my son, to commit ourselves to the journey—to the leaving and to the arriving. We are well-prepared. We have done all that is needed. Our provisions are loaded, the sea is calm and the wind will soon rise. Look, the people are gathering for karakia. This is it! It is time to leave this place and sail into the hands of the God who shapes our destiny.'

Using the story as a basis for group discussion, we explore the main themes and consider how they can be applied to our personal lives. The following are some of the things men will take from such a story and discuss:

- The Vision—*Te Whakakitenga*: In the story, the father had explored distant lands before and had always wanted to return. (What is your dream?) How did the father go about sharing his vision with others?
- The Decision—*Te Whakataunga*: What were the group's reasons for going? Once the decision was made, others joined the committed group. There was sharing of information about what lay ahead, what experiences and skills would help. It was a group effort.
- The Preparation—*Te Whakatikanga:* The group's preparation was physical, spiritual, emotional and relational. A holistic approach ensured that all elements were addressed. Who else was needed? What skills did each person bring? Was there agreement?
- The Work—*Te Mahi*: In the story, they worked hard to make the trip happen. There was sacrifice. It took time. They worked alongside others to ensure the task was completed. They encouraged each other.
- The Leaving—*Te Wehenga Atu*: They let go of the old and stepped out into the new and somewhat unknown. However, as much as possible, the group ensured that they took the right provisions and left behind those things that would hinder them. Because there was limited space, they needed to choose wisely.
- The Journey—*Te Haerenga*: They followed the pathway of their ancestors, using knowledge that had been passed down. Because they knew the signs, they had the ability to navigate through an ever-moving sea of change. Their course was not visible to the naked eye. They needed faith, skill, trust, communication, teamwork, responsibility. They couldn't change their minds!

Although the story does not go further than the departure, it can also be helpful to discuss how the sailing canoes used refuges and islands of refreshment along the way in order to rest and replenish supplies. Arriving in a new place would require the adaptation of knowledge or the acquisition of new skills for new circumstances. For example, the climate in Aotearoa was much colder than in the tropical islands and some of the crops brought did not grow well here. Tasks, roles, and responsibilities may have needed adjustment in order to survive.

As these discussions take place, many men will comment that they never even thought of building a relationship or laying any sort of foundation. They just set out on the journey. Some will say they just grabbed a piece of driftwood and started paddling. Many men very quickly begin to see why their life and their relationships feel as if they are adrift in a constantly changing sea.

The task for us, as workers in the field of family violence, is not to continually challenge men about their violence but to facilitate a process that enables them to discover what is going wrong in the journey of their life and how they can help themselves and their women and children from drowning, drifting apart, and getting lost. Using our culture to facilitate this process and creating an environment to support it is a much more effective way of addressing violence within intimate relationships. It helps men and their families to get a greater sense of where they stand and how they arrived at this point.

Once men are engaged with us, the important aspect for us to focus on is healing. For instance, decolonizing oneself is a very necessary step that, in turn, helps to heal any issues around identity, connecting a man to his tribal affiliations, the history of New Zealand, and his belief systems. The anger carried within can be seen differently against this backdrop.

> This is a Māori style—for Māori by Māori—it's heart to heart—not mouth to mouth.
>
> Programme Participant

*Tikanga*-based programs do, however, want men to be accountable for their actions of violence and abuse. The promotion of *tikanga* (correct processes), *te reo Māori* (Māori language), and acknowledgment of *te taha wairua* (the spiritual dimension) as means of addressing violent behavior is grounded in acknowledgment of the *mana* (dignity) and *tapu* (sacredness) of each person. To enhance the health of a perpetrator of violence by strengthening his four cornerstones of well-being (spiritual, mental, physical, and family) is not to deny the impact of the violence on others or to deny the accountability of perpetrators of violence.

He Waka Tapu–based interventions do not necessarily use a modulated program for facilitators to deliver each time a group comes together, but they need to be able to move in the aspect of *wairua*. They need to have the knowledge and skills to go with the current, steering the talk in the right direction while ensuring that others do the work. They also need to maintain the *kapakapa manawa*, the heartbeat, or rhythm of the group, which makes for an exciting journey. The art is to make the subject come alive, to take people on a journey of discovery so that they will not want to stop, to light a flame that will pass from one to the other, to give hope and vision to people who have felt as if they are drowning, and to *tautoko* (support) them through the challenges. It is a process that aims to ensure that all our *mokopuna* will travel within a *waka tapu*.

## BEST-PRACTICE MODELS

There is increasing attention paid to defining and developing best-practice models in this field. This includes examination of the development of indigenous practice models that meet the needs of Māori and contribute to the safety of Māori women and *tamariki* (Te Puni Kokiri, 1997).

A growing recognition of the effectiveness of "of Māori for Māori" service delivery has frequently resulted in the creation of new program providers, including mainstream providers who seek to add "cultural components" to their existing program models. There is also thinly disguised unease among some mainstream providers that Māori models, which emphasize *whanaungatanga*, or working holistically with perpetrators of violence, may compromise safety or result in collusive practices. It is also true to say that in some instances there is a belief that exposure to *Tikanga Māori* or *Te Reo* is in itself a cure for violent behavior. There is a diversity of ways of being a Māori, encompassing differences such as *iwi* affiliation, age, gender, rural or urban location, connectedness to *whānau/hapu/iwi*, and the *mana ake* (uniqueness) of each person.

Given the risks—the well-being of our *whānau*, our women, our *tamariki*, and our men, and the *mamae* (pain) that we see—it is crucial that Māori models of service delivery be evaluated and that critical best-practice factors be identified.

The following are best-practice factors that are features of He Waka Tapu program delivery.

- Clear and consistent focus on challenging men to take responsibility for their violence
- Ability to challenge while demonstrating respect for *te tapu i te tangata*, the *mana* and *tapu* of each group participant
- Development and use of an integrated conceptual framework based in *waka* imagery, and *Te Whare Tapa Whā*—or the cornerstones of well-being: *te taha wairua* (spiritual well-being), *te taha hinengaro* (mental well-being), *te taha tinana* (physical well-being), and *te taha whānau* (family well-being)
- Integration of recognized stopping-violence concepts and tools, such as power and control analysis
- Comprehensive assessment processes
- Emphasis on engagement, understanding of learning styles, and conscious reflection about group dynamic with participants
- Use of experienced and well-trained Māori staff who undergo rigorous accreditation processes
- Willingness to engage with other practitioners in the field, and a positive commitment to ongoing staff and program development
- Network of links to other agencies for referring clients as required
- Ability to provide services that meet other needs of men on the program
- Commitment of resources to identifying needs of partners and children of men on the program, and developing strategies for meeting those needs
- Effective and well managed administrative systems

## FUTURE DIRECTIONS

The ongoing struggle for us as an agency is that we have clients who are referred through the courts and community probation services and our contracts outline how we have to meet the regulations of the Domestic Violence Act, including the number of sessions and the gender of facilitators. We also have about 60% of our male clients attending programs who are not mandated. We are currently evaluating ourselves and looking at a research and development model as a way forward.

The Department of Corrections in Canterbury has had a long standing and very positive relationship with He Waka Tapu. They provide, under contract, a Tikanga Māori based stopping violence service. This service has proven itself to be invaluable to us as it forms an extremely important part of our attempts to address Māori re-offending in our community. He Waka Tapu is well respected across the region for the work they do and the quality of the service they provide.

Nick Scott<br>
Area Manager<br>
Community Probation Service<br>
Christchurch

## REFERENCES

Department of Corrections New Zealand. (2000). *Census of Prison Inmates 1999.* Retrieved from http://www.corrections.govt.nz/.

Gregory, R. (2007). *Don's waka.* Christchurch: Wilson Scott Publishing Ltd.

New Zealand Domestic Violence Act. (1995).

Statistics New Zealand. (2006). *QuickStats About Culture and Identity.* Retrieved on April 21, 2008, from http://www.stats.govt.nz/.

Te Puni Kokiri (1997). *Maori family violence in Aotearoa.* Te Puni Kokiri 1997.

# 8

# Asian-American Domestic Violence: A Critical Pyschohistorical Perspective

BENJAMIN R. TONG

There is hardly anything resembling an extensive and informative literature on who abuses whom in Asian American households, and how often
and, most important of all, why. If such a body of work actually exists,
I myself have not seen it, save for a scant number of published articles.
Yet if people on the clinical frontlines know what they have witnessed,
domestic violence does indeed go on. Only in recent years have we witnessed the emergence of a few suggestive and promising research-based
writings (Chan, 1988; Tsui, 1985; Huisman, 1996; Kim & Sung, 2000;
Yick & Berthold, 2005; Yoshioka, DiNoia, & Ullah, 2001), pointing to
a factual basis for the phenomenon, but with limited demographic or
empirical documentation. There continues to be a glaring paucity of
substantial hard data with respect to prevalence and incidence (see also
Chan, 1988; Christensen, 1988; Hirata, 1979; Ho, 1990; Ocampo, 1989;
Root, 1985; Tsui, 1985).

Because the present chapter is necessarily of limited scope (as
opposed to a much more comprehensive, multivolume book–length discussion), I will select one Asian American group—Chinese Americans—
as a focus for observations on the psychohistorical roots of domestic
violence. The reader is invited to consider the proposition that in certain

respects related experiences of other Asian Americans might well be compellingly similar if not entirely identical.

There are, by most estimates, some nineteen ethnoculturally distinct Asian American communities.[1] It would certainly not do for me to couch my comments in general "Asian American" terms and, in the process, imply that experiences presumably common to all nineteen are somehow more significant than the differences between those groups. Such is not the case. The very same observers who would insist on the obvious convenience of such overgeneralizations would, in another instance, be appalled at the notion that all European cultures are necessarily identical or more similar than different; that is, that growing up in Luxembourg is no different from a childhood in London.

Restricting my attention to Chinese Americans, I invite the reader to decide, if he or she is able to, the extent to which my remarks might have wider relevance vis-à-vis other Americans of Asian descent. For the balance of this discussion, I will argue that the etiological roots of domestic abuse—whether physical, emotional, or sexual—are to be found in four interrelated phenomena: problems of adaptation, cross-cultural clashes, racist oppression, and repressive heritage.

## ADAPTATIONAL PROBLEMS

The phenomenal growth of the Asian American population over the period of 1965–2002 has received a great deal of attention as of late. Many conclude, quite accurately, that Asian America consists of a substantial number of so-called recent newcomers.[2] Hence, the understandable media, scholarly, and social service priority given to adaptational problems of immigrants, Asian and otherwise. According to federal Census Bureau surveys for the years 1975 to 1985, for example, almost half of the 4.7 million Asian, Hispanic, and Black people who moved to the United States from abroad in that period settled in suburban and

---

[1] Chinese, Japanese, Korean, Pilipino, Burmese, Vietnamese, Laotian, Kampuchian (Cambodian), Mien, Miao, Asian Indian, Malaysian, Thai, Indonesian, Hawaiian, Fijian, Samoan, Guamanian, Okinawan. Note: the terms "Asian American Pacific American" and "Asian American Pacific Islander Americans" attempt to be more inclusive.

[2] Of the 570,000 immigrants who entered this country legally in the year 1985, 46% were Asian, while 37% were Latin American, 11% European, 3% African, and 2% Canadian (Herbers, 1986). From 1965 to 2002, "approximately 8.3 million Asians were admitted to permanent residency, making up about 34% of total immigrants" (Pyong, 2006, p. 26).

non-metropolitan areas, obviously making for adaptational struggles of an unprecedented nature (Herbers, 1986). When Chinese as well as other Asian newcomers encounter the demands of everyday life in the United States, values, beliefs, and norms are "compared," or "shaken," or "broken up," or "tried on for size," or "imposed," depending on one's way of understanding such experiences.

Regardless of interpretation, discerning observers have noted that domestic stress, which often enough leads to conflict and abuse, is frequently traceable to such newcomer issues as language difficulties, status anxieties, money hassles, pressures to perform well at school and work, abrupt and unprecedented shifts in traditional family roles, and separation or loss of significant others (Huang & Ying, 1989; Lee, 1982; Shon & Ja, 1982; Wong, 1988; Ching-Louie, 1992; Toji & Johnson, 1992; Zeng & Xie, 2004).

> The Lee family came from Hong Kong about 4 years ago. Neither parent has had the opportunity to learn English, as between the father and mother there are a total of four part-time blue-collar jobs. The children are now of middle and high school age. They, too, work, when not keeping school hours, to help supplement the family income. Whenever strangers appear at the front door (e.g., police, mail deliveries, solicitors, survey searchers), the children assume responsibility for being interpreters and translators. Sometimes they even make major decisions for the entire family as a result of this special role of spokespersons with representatives of the outside world. Lately, Mr. Lee has been unusually cranky, irritable, and emotionally abusive of both spouse and children. A neighbor recently reported seeing Mr. Lee slap his oldest child during a heated argument in front of their house, "something which seemed unusual for him to do."

In his deliberations on the nature of myth and identity, Bruner (1979) offered a psychohistorical paradigm that might well serve to account for a significant volume of symptomatic behavior—including domestic violence—related to the stresses of the migration experience. A people's deepest beliefs and worldviews, or mythos, provide for a coherent narrative to address three fundamental concerns that cut across collective existence as well as individual lives: (1) history, a sense of the past, or "who we have always been"; (2) identity, a sense of the present, or "who we are, or should be, right now"; and (3) destiny, a sense of the future, or "who we are meant to be." Events such as war, economic chaos, and natural disasters disrupt the substance and continuity of all three. Furthermore, migration aimed at escaping the consequences of such catastrophic events exacerbates that very same disruption. Sluski's (1979) rather eloquent "stage" theory of migratory adjustments suggests something of the impact on family structure and dynamics.

> Some families manage to mourn what has been left behind and integrate it constructively into a blend of old and new rules, models, and habits that constitute their new reality. . . . In other families, whatever has been left behind in the country of origin, may become increasingly idealized (making adaptation more difficult) or denigrated (making mourning and working through of the loss more difficult). (Sluski, 1979, p. 386)

## THE CLASH OF CULTURES AND CULTURAL DOMINATION

Scholars and clinicians alike have observed, if we may stay with Sluski's (1979) perspective, that modern Western psychotherapists tend to be positively oriented toward such White middle-class values as differentiation and independence of family members, but "in families of other cultures, however—Southern Italians, Arabs, Chinese, among others— mutual dependence may be equated with loyalty, and any attempt at increasing the independence of members will be considered an attack on basic family values" (p. 388).

In many, if not most, Asian American homes, whether newly arrived or otherwise, children, particularly females, are expected to perform all manner of chores and tasks with precision and thoroughness. Whereas failure to comply in a White middle-class family might mean loss of television viewing privileges for a time, Asian American children "falling down on the job" are frequently told, as Wong-Fillmore and Cheong's (1976) research on the early socialization of Asian American female offspring has documented, that they are basically worthless as human beings.

> To do well on a task, on the other hand, does not bring praise or reward. Instead, the parent is likely to say nothing at all. Praise is considered emotional excess and in bad taste, and to be avoided, especially where girls are concerned. Thus, the female (child) can hope only for silence, which might be taken as a sign of non-disapproval—or the next best thing to approval. (p. 8)

From the vantage point of contemporary mental health standards, this kind of parenting smacks of that brand of domestic violence known as emotional abuse. I for one could not agree more, which, I would argue, does not necessarily make me culturally insensitive or biased. In the view of this Asian American health practitioner, the devastating psychological consequences of certain child-rearing customs, however longstanding, mitigate against according respect and honor to such practices.

If viewed in terms of a continuum of disciplinary behaviors, procedures like severe physical beatings resulting in broken limbs and profuse bleeding are almost universally defined across "normal" American ethnic and cultural groups as truly abusive. A few notches up from that polar extreme, however, we encounter a definitional gray zone. Sending a child to bed without supper may seem, to White middle-class parents, quite appropriate for misbehavior, while Asian Americans might very well judge that very same procedure ("starving a child") to be inhumanly deprivational. Similarly, many Asian Americans regard whacking a child on the buttocks or behind the thighs as appropriate, all the while educated White middle-class parents remain vehement about any and all forms of corporal punishment as physically abusive.

My own stance here is that given such quandaries, parents and health professionals alike cannot avoid certain inescapable existential decisions as to what is right and wrong. To be sure, it is not a simple matter of taking cultural "sides." In my mind, whatever leads to psychological injury or impairment is abuse, no matter how "traditional" the practice. Despite the risk of cultural imperialism, culture is not to be exalted in every instance as sacred and beyond question. It should be borne in mind that, more often than not, people emigrate from other shores in order to escape cultural traditions experienced as oppressive. I shall have more to say about this complex and delicate issue in the section on "Repressive Heritage."

The clash of cultures also results in identity problems, both fake and real. This is a phenomenon that, I would argue, results in many instances of domestic violence. According to Frank Chin and Jeffrey Paul Chan (1972), in their famous essay, "Racist Love," White America dominates Yellow America by defining the content and parameters of our existence. Asian Americans learn, early on, that we are supposedly caught in the vise of a unique identity problem, namely, the problem of having only two options for answering the question "Who am I?"

Asian Americans must necessarily see themselves as either "Asians," meaning perpetual aliens on these shores, or "Americans," meaning "imitation Whites." According to this either-or or "dual personality" mindset, we are to assume that (1) Asian Americans, being foreigners, do not belong in the United States, and (2) the word *American* applies exclusively to Whites, the alleged "real" Americans. Moreover, Asian America as a unique, vital, self-generating way of life unto itself must be assumed to not exist. We are seen as having no history, literature, language, mythology, or sensibility all our own.

Asian Americans are frequently singled out as the "model minority," the ideal racial pets of White America. So long as our behavior is aligned with the "racist love" stereotype of passive, industrious, non-complaining, meek and mild servants, the White power structure rewards us. Assertive, aggressive, outspoken, confident, sensuous behavior invites White "racist hate," the kind meted out to people of color in America who dare challenge White authority. Whether forever foreigner or fake white, Asian Americans are expected to be hardworking, inexpressive, compliant, and generally invisible, all the while euphemizing constricted personality as the legacy of an exotic, effeminate, little-understood ancestral "Oriental" culture (see also Tong, 1971, 1974, 1978, 1983b, 1990). The end result is a well-behaved, self-monitoring "model minority" caught in the jaws of such cruel disparities as that between high educational achievements (as measured by acquisition of degrees and credentials) on the one hand, and low income level and workplace status (when compared with Whites) on the other (Cabezas, 1990; Hong, 1988).

Mr. Wong, 39, a senior accounting clerk of many years at City Hall, was reportedly distraught over a blocked promotion, an experience apparently not new to him or Asian American coworkers in his department and throughout the civil service system. For an entire week, he drank rather heavily at the end of the work day. One evening, his wife was treated at County Hospital's emergency services for facial bruises, the result of what was initially described as an unfortunate "home accident" ("I tripped and fell on a couple of boxes that were near the bottom of the basement stairs," Mrs. Wong explained.) Later, Mrs. Wong confided to a sympathetic female paramedic that her husband had actually struck her when he "lost control of himself" in the course of venting rage about yet another frustrated attempt at a deserved promotion.

When he finally agreed to try couples counseling with a culturally competent therapist, Mr. Wong said, "I do as I'm told, y'know, I do good work. I'm always reliable. And I'm not like other people who make a lot of noise, do a lot of fancydan office politics to get what they want. I've just done my job, as best as I know how. Never complained, not even when I felt like it. And, boy, there were plenty of times when I felt like it! I'd always hoped, always expected, my supervisor would notice that I deserved a promotion to middle manager. I mean, I am fully qualified. Some of my coworkers would even say more than fully qualified. So what do I get? Nothing! The word is that they say my accent is too heavy, and that I just don't look or act or sound like a management type. They say that a manager or executive type has to be an 'American.' So what does that make me? Hell, I've never left this country! Am I some alien from outer space with an incurably thick foreign accent? After all these years, I'm insulted by being asked to train a new guy, a white man, who's supposed to get the management position I deserved. What the hell, I mean, that was really the last straw. I can't take it anymore."

## RACIST OPPRESSION

When dealing with the question of domestic violence, we must address, as standard clinical practice usually dictates, the need to "take a history." If we were to take a history of perpetrators of Asian American domestic violence, we would find an abundance of evidence for "early experiences" of abuse. Victimizers, more often than not, were themselves victims at one time. This, as we know only too well, is a well-established truism in clinical work. The compelling "psychohistorical" studies of eminent scholars such as Robert Jay Lifton have made it abundantly clear that human beings overwhelmed by successive, multiple experiences of uncontrollable brutality will themselves become, in short order, monstrous perpetrators of heinous violence, as we have come to learn in such wartime atrocities as the infamous My Lai Massacre (Lifton, 1983, especially chapter 12).

Long before an Asian American abuses spouse or children, he has already suffered flagrant and wholesale abuse. This preceding history is not simply traceable to troubles in that universe of experience known as "family of origin": it is at the same time bound up with nothing less than the entire fabric of Asian American history and culture itself. Put another way, the full range of violence experienced by Asian Americans must first be acknowledged and situated in proper context (Tang, 1997; Xie & Goyette, 2004).

For example, I have long held the position that the life of virtually every Asian American group has been marked by at least one major episode of what might be called "collective racist trauma," an experience of White violence so thoroughly inundating that it functions up to the present day as a central point of reference for making sense of themselves in America (Tong, 1971, 1974, 1978, 1983b). It is the ground from which arises the raw material for language, myth, and metaphor that an entire people struggle to forge in order to codify and deal with that trauma.

For Filipino America, it was the brutal colonial subjugation of the Philippine Islands at the turn of the century (Takaki, 1989); for Japanese America, the concentration camps of World War II (tenBroek, Barnhart, & Matson, 1954; Weglyn, 1976; Tong, 1983a; Nagata, 1988; Kuwabara, 1992). For Korean wives of White American servicemen, it was the alienation and abuse of dysfunctional post–Korean War interracial marriages (Kim, 1980). For Vietnamese America, it was the intervention of the United States in a civil war between the Vietnamese (Owan, Bliatout, Lin, Nguyen, & Wong, 1985; Lawson, 1989). And for Chinese America, it was the infamous Anti-Chinese Movement (1785–1943) (tenBroek et al, 1954; Nee & Nee, 1973; Weglyn, 1976; Takaki, 1989; Pfaelzer, 2007).

In recent years, it might be noted, anti–Asian American sentiment and violence have been on the rise throughout the United States (Chin, 1992; Hing, 1990). Presently, hate-motivated crimes against Asian Americans break down into four recurrent types, according to John Hayakawa Torok of the New York City–based Committee Against Anti-Asian Violence (Cacas, 1992, p. 26):

- Police misconduct: police use racial slurs or other offensive language.
- Neighborhood-based aggression: Asians moving into a neighborhood are made to feel uncomfortable as a result of acts such as throwing garbage on the front lawn or offensive language.
- Random attacks by civilians on buses or in the street: verbal assaults through the use of racial slurs or threatened physical harm and actual attacks.
- Abusive behavior in schools: classmates react to teachers' labeling Asians as "model" students by verbally harassing, physically attacking, or robbing Asian students.

Following the September 11, 2001, terrorist attacks, South Asian Americans suffered from hate crimes, vandalism, arson, public place harassment, threatening phone calls, and bodily injury (including murder). According to Min (2005), "South Asians have been targets . . . partly because Muslims compose a large proportion of them and partly because they share physical characteristics of Arabs . . . Sikhs in particular have been targets . . . because their turbans and beards make them look like Osama Bin Laden" (p. 99). Furthermore, the USA PATRIOT

Act, passed by the United States Congress in October 2001, resulted in detentions and deportations of many innocent Muslim immigrants and American citizens of color, including those of South Asian descent (Bozorgmehr & Bakalian, 2005).

## REPRESSIVE HERITAGE

If one would take a truly comprehensive "clinical history" of domestic violence in the Chinese American as well as other Asian American communities, it would be necessary to attend not only to Asian American but also Asian "roots" with a critical eye. The long record of the Chinese experience is replete with countless instances of the violence of a cruel patriarchal social order (Fairbank, 1974), ostensibly attributable to Confucius, the greatest and most revered of China's ancient sages. Power, influence, and authority resided exclusively in adult males, beginning with fathers and teachers and, finally, government officials and the emperor. "Negative" emotions were to be impounded in public, particularly in the presence of male authority figures. Respect for authority was equated with unconditional obedience. Moreover, the family came first, and everything and everyone else was insignificant or not even real. Women were allowed a modicum of power, provided they lived long enough to become mothers-in-law and grandmothers. Then the abused became abusers (Stacey, 1983).

By the time of the last dynasty, the Ch'ing (A.D. 1644–1911), monarchic and scholar-official politics had reshaped the classical Confucian concept of *pao-tia*, "taking care of one's own," into an insidious device for social control. It was an officially imposed but unofficial arm of the state, through which the government and local ruling class used the family system for political purposes (Fairbank & Reischauer, 1960). Under the *pao-tia* system, redefined as "local order through mutual responsibility," the family was the basic unit of political control and kept the individual in line with such psychological devices as fear of punishment and moral exhortation.

A group of households was accountable collectively for an individual within any household. "This allotment of responsibility by groups of neighboring farms was particularly suited to a static society rooted in the land . . . Mutual responsibility, as totalitarian systems have . . . demonstrated, is a powerful device, especially when combined with a paternalistic morality sanctioned by a long cultural tradition" (Fairbank &

Reischauer, 1960, pp. 374–375). In other words, the ruling elites controlled the peasantry and commoner populace by having people in villages continually turn on one another. Resentment or rage toward the government was "safely" deflected or projected onto less powerful family members and neighbors.

The constant distrust, intimidation, jealousies, isolation, and control maneuvers made for what psychotherapists today would call a kind of classic "abuse dynamic." It is against this psychohistorical backdrop that Chinese and even Chinese American domestic violence is to be understood. Many a Chinese American has suffered massive emotional ambivalence about whether such a repressive, and most certainly violent, "heritage" deserves to be preserved.

It bears noting that Chinese Americans (and countless Chinese as well) have been operating on the highly questionable assumption that this "traditional" autocratic, quasi-military family system, dating back some two thousand years to the early dynasties of the Han emperors, is somehow continuous with the original ("classic") humanistic teachings and vision of Confucius. The historical record indicates, however, that nothing could be further from the truth.

The Confucius of antiquity is not the Sage of the scholar-official ruling elite, who, centuries following his death, reworked his ideas for purposes of social control. Sinologists are in general agreement that the ruling groups of imperial China exploited Confucian philosophy as a potent device for controlling a numerically overwhelming commoner population. Balaz (1964), for one, observed that "[t]he scholar-officials and their state found in Confucianist doctrine an ideology that suited them perfectly . . . in Han times, shortly after the formation of the empire, it became a state doctrine. The virtues preached by Confucianism were exactly suited to the new hierarchical state: respect, humility, docility, obedience, submission, and subordination to elders and betters" (p. 18).

In Arthur Wright's (1960) authoritative work, we learn of convincing documentation, much like that produced by Balaz (1964) and others, that:

[a]s a consequence of major social and political changes beginning in the late T'ang and continuing through the Sung, the content of one of the Confucian moral norms, "loyalty," was radically altered. From its earlier meaning as an obligation tempered by moral judgment, it was redefined as a blind and unquestioning allegiance to a superior. This shift and others related to it occurred under the pressure of an increasingly centralized and despotic monarchy. (p. 5)

This refashioned Confucianism eventually became the official religion of the Chinese state and the ideological framework within which the government operated. This was the moral order imposed on the Southern Chinese during the T'ang era, when the previously unconquered Yueh people, aboriginal ancestors of the Cantonese and today's Cantonese Americans,[3] were subdued. Miyakawa probably has the last word on the phenomenon in his essay "The Confucianization of South China": "It cannot be said, however, that Confucianism confucianized the southern peoples solely by functioning as a religion. Its religious function was supported by military and political power of Chinese dynasties, and by local officials and literati." (Wright, 1960, p. 41)

In contrast to the familiar autocratic patriarch of the typical Chinese and Cantonese family, the Ideal Adult as envisioned by Confucius had only the "ambition" of becoming a "true" or "authentic" person (*jun yun*) (Waley, 1958). The eminent Confucian scholar Tu Wei-Ming (1976) wrote that such an individual, "wishing to establish his own character, also establishes the character of others":

> His learning is "for the sake of himself . . . and he does not regard himself an 'instrument' . . . , for his mode of existence is to be an end rather than a tool for any external purpose. . . . In fact, no matter how hard he works and how much distance he covers, a true man is, as it were, all the time on the Way (toward enlightened personal development). (Ming, 1976, p. 115; see also Cleary, 1992)

In closing, we can say that the dark side of the Chinese American experience and, by implication, the larger Asian American experience, contains unresolved trauma and internalized violence in response to the legacy of the autocratic nightmare of imperial Confucianism, on the one hand, and White racist oppression, on the other. Coupled with the adaptational demands of migration (particularly for recent newcomers) and the conflicts resulting from the clash of cultures and White cultural domination, these powerful forces have shaped the special arena within which Asian American domestic violence, in all its forms, is played out.

---

[3] The earliest Chinese to appear in significant numbers in this country were those of Cantonese (Southern Chinese) descent, a seafaring, highly adventurous people known to come and go continually from the Chinese Empire, establishing "Chinatowns" wherever they settled outside of China, despite imperial edicts (which were seldom enforced) that warned of dire legal consequences. The majority of Chinese Americans today are still those of Cantonese background.

## REFERENCES

Balaz, E. (1964). *Chinese civilization and bureaucracy: Variations on a theme* (H. M. Wright, Trans.). New Haven, CT: Yale University Press.

Bozorgmehr, M., & Bakalian, A. (2005). Violent and discriminatory reactions to September 11 terrorism. In P. G. Min (Ed.)., *Encyclopedia of racism in the United States* (pp. 213–231). Westport, CT: Greenwood Press.

Bruner, J. (1979). *On knowing: Essays for the left hand* (2nd ed). Cambridge, MA: Harvard University Press.

Cabezas, A. (1990). The Asian American today as an economic success model: Some myths and realities. In Chinese for Affirmative Action (Ed.), *Breaking the silence*. San Francisco.

Cacas, S. R. (1992, April 3). Recognizing and responding to hate, violence and bigotry: A survival guide for Asian Pacific Americans. *Asian Week*.

Chan, C. S. (1988). Asian American women: Psychological responses to sexual exploitation and cultural stereotypes. In L. Fulani (Ed.), *The psychopathology of everyday racism and sexism*. New York: Harrington Press.

Chin, F., & Chan, J. P. (1972). Racist love. In R. Kostelanetz (Ed.), *Seeing through Shuck*. New York: Ballantine.

Chin, S. A. (1992, February 28). U.S. study finds wide anti-Asian prejudice. *San Francisco Examiner*.

Ching-Louie, M. (1992). Immigrant Asian women in Bay Area garment sweatshops. *Amerasia Journal, 18*(1), 1–26.

Christensen, C. P. (1988). Issues in sex therapy with ethnic and racial minority women. *Women and Therapy, 7*(2/3), 187–205.

Cleary, T. (1992). *The essential Confucius: The heart of Confucius' teachings in authentic I-Ching order*. San Francisco: HarperCollins.

Fairbank, J. K. (1974). *The United States and China* (3rd ed). Cambridge, MA: Harvard University Press.

Fairbank, J. K., & Reischauer, E. (1960). *East Asia: The great tradition*. Boston: Houghton Mifflin.

Herbers, J. (1986, December 14). Many immigrants now bypass cities for suburbs. *New York Times*.

Hing, B. O. (1990). Current factors in the re-emergence of anti-Asian violence. In Chinese for Affirmative Action (Ed.), *Break the silence*. San Francisco.

Hirata, L. C. (1979). Free, indentured, enslaved: Chinese prostitutes in nineteenth-century America. *Signs: Journal of Women in Culture and Society, 5*(1), 3–29.

Ho, C. K. (1990). An analysis of domestic violence in Asian American communities: A multicultural approach to counseling. *Women and Therapy, 9*(1/2), 129–150.

Hong, F. (1988, May). Barriers at the top: What invisible barriers keep Asian American executives from climbing the corporate ladder to the top? *ASIAM*.

Huang, L. N., & Ying, Y. W. (1989). Chinese American children and adolescents. In J. T. Gibbs et al. (Eds.), *Children of color: Psychological interventions with minority youth*. San Francisco: Jossey-Bass.

Huisman, K. A. (1996). Wife battering in Asian American communities. *Violence Against Women, 2*(3), 260–283.

Kim, B. K. L. (1980). Asian wives of U.S. servicemen: Women in shadows. In R. Endo et al. (Eds.), *Asian Americans: Social and Psychological Perspectives* (Vol. 2). Palo Alto, CA: Science and Behavior Books.

Kim, J. Y., & Sung, K.-T. (2000). Conjugal violence in Korean American families: A residue of the cultural tradition. *Journal of Family Violence, 15*(4), 331–345.

Kuwabara, L. (1992, April 15). No denying: R. A. Shiomi's "Uncle Tadao" struggles to sort through the emotional and psychological aftershocks of internment. *San Francisco Bay Guardian.*

Lawson, J. E. (1989). "She's a pretty woman . . . for a gook": The misogyny of the Vietnam War. *Journal of American Culture, 12*(3), 55–63.

Lee, E. (1982). A social systems approach to assessment and treatment for Chinese American families. In M. McGoldrick, J. K. Pearce, & J. Giordano (Eds.), *Ethnicity and family therapy.* New York: Guilford Press.

Lifton, R. J. (1983). *The broken connection: On death and the continuity of life.* New York: Basic Books.

Min, P. G. (Ed.). (2005). *Encyclopedia of racism in the United States.* Westport, CT: Greenwood Press.

Miyakawa, H. (1960). The Confucianization of South China. In A. F. Wright (Ed.), *The Confucian Persuasion.* Palo Alto, CA: Stanford University Press.

Nagata, D. K. (1988, August). The long-term effects of victimization: Present-day effects of the Japanese American internment. In D. Nagata (Chair), *Varied forms of victimization during World War II.* Symposium conducted at the meeting of the American Psychological Association, Atlanta.

Nee, V., & Nee, B. D. (1973). *Longtime Californ': A documentary study of an American Chinatown.* New York: Pantheon.

Ocampo, B. (1989, August 25). Some battered wives suffer "cycle of abuse." *Asian Week.*

Owan, T. C., Bliatout, B., Lin, K. M., Nguyen, T., & Wong, H. Z. (Eds.). (1985). *Southeast Asian mental health: Treatment, prevention, services, training, and research* (DHHS Publication No. ADM 85–1399). Rockville, MD: National Institute of Mental Health.

Pfaelzer, J. (2007). *Driven out: The forgotten war against Chinese Americans.* New York: Random House.

Pyong, G. M. (2006). *Asian Americans: Contemporary trends and issues* (2nd ed). Thousand Oaks, CA: Pine Forge Press.

Root, M. P. P. (1985). Guidelines for facilitating therapy with Asian American clients. *Psychotherapy, 22*(2 S), 349–356.

Shon, S. P., & Ja, D. Y. (1982). Asian (American) families. In M. McGoldrick, J. K. Pearce, & J. Giordano (Eds.), *Ethnicity and family therapy.* New York: Guilford Press.

Sluski, C. E. (1979). Migration and family conflict. *Family process, 18*(4), 379–390.

Stacey, J. (1983). *Patriarchy and social revolution in China.* Berkeley: University of California Press.

Takaki, R. (1989). *Strangers from a different shore: A history of Asian Americans.* Boston: Little, Brown.

Tang, J. (1997). The glass ceiling in science and engineering. *J. Socio-Economics, 26,* 383–406.

tenBroek, J., Barnhart, E. W., & Matson, F. W. (1954). *Prejudice, war and the Constitution.* Berkeley and Los Angeles: University of California.

Toji, D. S., & Johnson, J. H. (1992). Asian & Pacific Islander American poverty: The working poor & the jobless poor. *Amerasia Journal, 18*(1), 83–91.

Tong, B. R. (1971). The ghetto of the mind: Notes on the historical psychology of Chinese America. *Amerasia Journal, 1*(2), 1–31.

Tong, B. R. (1974). A living death defended as the legacy of a superior culture. *Amerasia Journal, 2*(2), 178–202.

Tong, B. R. (1978). Warriors and victims: Chinese American sensibility and learning styles. In L. Morris et al. (Eds.), *Extracting learning styles from social/cultural diversity: Studies of five American minorities.* Norman: Southwest Teacher Corps Network, University of Oklahoma.

Tong, B. R. (1983a). Long-term consequences of the Nikkei internment. *East Wind* (Fall/Winter), 51–53.

Tong, B. R. (1983b). On the confusion of psychopathology with culture: Iatrogenesis in the treatment of Chinese Americans. In R. F. Morgan (Ed.), *The iatrogenics handbook: A critical look at research and practice in-the helping professions.* Toronto: IPI Publishing.

Tong, B. R. (1990). "Ornamental Orientals" and others: Ethnic labels in review. *Focus, 4*(2), 8–9.

Tsui, A. M. (1985). Psychotherapeutic considerations in sexual counseling for Asian immigrants. *Psychotherapy, 22*(2 S), 357–362.

Tu Wei-Ming. (1976). The Confucian perception of adulthood. *Daedalus,* 105(2), 109–123.

Waley, A. (1958). *The analects of Confucius.* New York: Grove Press.

Weglyn, M. (1976). *Years of infamy.* New York: William Morrow.

Wong, M. G. (1988). The Chinese American family. In C. H. Mindel, R. W. Haberstein, & R. Wright Jr. (Eds.), *Ethnic families in America: Patterns and variations* (3rd ed.). New York: Elsevier.

Wong-Fillmore, L., & Cheong, J. L. (1976). *The early socialization of Asian American female children.* Paper presented at the Conference on Educational and Occupational Needs of Asian-Pacific American Women, San Francisco.

Wright, A. F. (Ed.). (1960). *The Confucian persuasion.* Palo Alto, CA: Stanford University Press.

Xie, Y., & Goyette, K. (2004). Asian Americans' earnings disadvantage reexamined: The role of place of education. *Amerasia Journal, 109,* 1075–1108.

Yick, A. & Berthold, M. (2005). Conducting research on violence in Asian American communities: Methodological issues. *Violence and Victims, 20*(6), 661–677.

Yoshioka, M., DiNoia, J., & Ullah, K. (2001). Attitudes toward marital violence: An examination of four Asian communities. *Violence Against Women, 7*(8), 900–926.

# 9

# Asian Men and Violence

### LEE MUN WAH

I think that the hardest part of writing about one's life experiences is trying to convey the *feeling* of what happened—at best, we can only describe it, reflect on it, circle the place where our pain began. What I remember of what has taken me to this place where I am right now is only easier to talk about because something greater has come out of it. But the memory of that day never leaves me, and writing about it only refreshes the terror and the difficulty in finding the words for my grief and the depth of my aloneness when it happened. For anyone who has ever been harmed, physically or emotionally, there is no cure, no complete recovery. We remain survivors who are emotionally disabled and, like the terminally ill, appreciate more tenderly how close death is to life. What we share is not so much what happened to us, but how it changed our lives and how we struggle daily to cope with the many constant reminders of that moment. An old Buddhist story relates that we all experience pain. Some of us remain bitter and continue to be suspicious of all life, while others decide to be prepared and to accept that pain is also part of life along with joy and birth. I think that both experiences are a part of our journey through any crisis—bitterness that it happened to us, and eventually acceptance. The remembrance of our anguish and our hurt can help us remain vulnerable and hopefully more compassionate toward others. Since my own experience with death, every time I hear

**195**

about someone dying or murdered, I hold my breath for a moment in honor of their death and of my own someday.

In a way, when I look back to that moment in 1985, there were two deaths, my mother's and my own. She lost her life, and I lost a way of living that would never be mine again. I wrote about that year in my diary:

"In the winter of '85, my mother was murdered. She was shot four times in the head. It was a warm Tuesday afternoon." Those are the facts of how she died. In the beginning, whenever I was asked what happened, those were the kinds of answers I would give. It was easier and simpler that way, for me and the person asking. I don't remember a whole lot from that first year, only that I kept crying all the time, on warm days and when something good happened to me. There are so many "ifs" that I have given up trying to visualize what might have been. What happened changed my whole life and everyone in our family. Even our friends were moved and frightened by the way our mom died. They seemed, like ourselves, to sense the frailty of the moment and strong bond of a mother to her children.

It is so hard for me to let go of her and not to have had the chance to say goodbye and to let her know how much I loved her.

I can only hope she can hear me now. I whisper it every day.

> I thought of you, today
>> falling behind into time
>> Trying to find your way out of the ground
>> a seed afire beneath the earth.
>> And what I realized is that there is no bed
>> that can hold back the pain of moving on.
>> When night falls, it matters not who leaves
>> or who chooses to stay.
>> A great silence comes
>> to sleep in every room.

What happened during the first year after my mom's death seemed a lot like being frozen and slowly thawing out, as I scratched and crawled my way through the terror of living again inch by inch. Toward the end of the year, on the suggestion of a friend, I joined a men's group. I remember how scared I was being in a room filled with men and just being left to talk about my feelings. Deep down I knew I was in this group because my mother's death brought up how much I was afraid of other men emotionally, spiritually, and physically. I also realized that I had a great deal of anger inside of me toward the man who killed my mom, at myself for not being there to protect her when she died, and at my mother for dying so soon before she had a chance to hold my son in her arms.

In the years that passed I learned a lot about how to trust and to let other men into my life without being afraid or defensive. One day, I got really mad at one of the men in the group. One of the other men said that he thought I wasn't being angry enough. I was furious; I told him that for an Asian man I was really angry. At that moment, I realized that he wanted me to get angry the way a White man got angry. I had never seen an Asian man get angry in public, on television, or in the movies. All my life, the only models I had for getting angry were White men. But somewhere deep inside of me I always knew I could never live up to John Wayne's fury or rage. Too much of my culture held me back as my anger and my rage circled inside of me, longing to scream and to be heard.

Months later, I started an Asian Men's Group to help other Asian American men like myself find a place where they could explore and be supported in expressing their anger and their passion without feeling inadequate or inferior to other cultures. What I learned was that working through anger is not something that can be taught in isolation or without the recognition of one's cultural background. Dealing with anger is a personal and developmental journey that needs to be nurtured and acknowledged for each personal story and struggle. A. S. Neill once observed that children at his Summerhill school cut his classes in proportion to the amount of time they were angry in their previous schools. The children returned when their anger was spent and when they felt they could "choose" to return. I think that somewhere from my own experiences I sensed that these Asian American men in the group needed to feel comfortable and accepted for who they were. They needed to choose to work through their anger at their own pace and in their own way without feeling they needed to be like someone else or sound a certain way. They could also say no when they didn't want to go any further without being judged as passive or being seen as mysterious.

In the months that followed, what I discovered were some of the roots of their anger as well as some of the results of not having their anger expressed or understood. None of the men in the group had ever witnessed anger being resolved in their families. Most of them felt that they would not be heard or would lose control or hurt someone if they really let their anger out. All of them learned about anger from their parents, particularly from their fathers. Each of them wanted and needed to be acknowledged and accepted by his parents for who he was and for what he was doing with his life.

I came to realize after a few weeks that men in the group needed something from myself and the rest of the group that they weren't getting from their families or their communities: acknowledgment and support to explore their fears, their anger, their relationships, their hurt, their dreams, and their desires. So what I did was to create a "container" that would enable each man in the group to feel listened to and acknowledged. I did this by creating a number of exercises on how to deal with conflict so that the men in the group would feel safe with each other and also feel that there was a way they could express their anger without hurting anyone physically. We then explored the relationships that the men had with their fathers and how their fathers affected how they related to others today. We also dealt with the issue of racism and the effect it had on the men in the group. Essentially, we covered three important areas: their individual lives, their family histories, and the effects of the community on their development. Finally, I had the men invite their families and friends to an acknowledgment ceremony. This ceremony was to enable the men in the group to hear from their loved ones how much they cared for them and what they best remembered about them.

We have been meeting since 1985, one night a week for three hours. In that time, we have grown and we have changed. We have shared our lives with each other, and we have become a family. One man in the group described it perfectly: "This group is like my family. Maybe even better than my family because, here, I can start all over fresh. I can say things here that I wouldn't anywhere else, and still be accepted week after week. No one will leave me because I said something or did something wrong. In some ways, you guys are a lot closer to me than my own family. You are the family I always wanted."

## CONFLICT RESOLUTION

"If you don't like what I'm saying, you can step outside later and I'll show you what I'm *not* saying!" When one of the men said this to another man in a violence workshop I was facilitating, I realized that he was angry and hurt because he didn't feel seen or heard (a recurrent theme in his marriage and family of origin). The only means he knew of for expressing his anger was to use violence. So often anger is not the primary emotion; rather it is the feeling of being hurt that comes first, hurt at not being listened to or acknowledged. And so the anger is about not having one's hurt be seen or validated. Men who are violent are often unable or don't know how to state clearly that they are hurt, and so they resort to violence.

Before any of the men begin to work on a conflict, I ask them whether or not they want to resolve this conflict or simply to win. I do this so that their intentions are clear and so is the desired outcome. So often we enter into a battle without any vision, except that we're angry, not knowing where we want to go or where we want to end up. In the battle of trying to win, there is always a loser, and if that is their intention, it is important to be sure that each person involved is willing to be the loser or the winner.

In the Japanese culture, when one enters into a conflict, the relationship is held to be what is most important, to be preserved, not the individual. The role of the Japanese community is to help those involved to keep this as their focus and goal. When the community order is honored, the culture remains intact and protected. The American approach often emphasizes the individual interest as the most important goal, even if it means sacrificing the relationship. In many ways there is a lot to be said for the Japanese perspective of not humiliating someone to the point that the other feels isolated or in danger of having his or her integrity questioned in public. The term "losing face" is about humiliation and disgrace.

Once in the group, one of the men yelled back at me when I asked him what he was willing to give up to resolve a conflict. He said, "I'm tired of always having to give up something! People of color always have to give up something, and I'm tired of it!" And so I asked him what it was he wanted to keep. And he replied, "I want to keep my integrity. I want the other person to honor my integrity." The essential message here is that when someone feels he is going to lose something or have something he holds dear be destroyed or diminished, he will become defensive and attack.

Before anyone can share how "hurt" he feels, he often needs to release the anguish first. To do so, the environment needs to feel safe. In our group, I work with both men on first deciding whether the space between them is comfortable and safe. To Asians and to many other men of color, feeling physically too far away or too close has a lot to do with trust and whether or not they feel threatened. In addition, Asians, like other men of color, often aren't asked what they *need* to feel comfortable. They are usually *told* how to accommodate, or they are simply left to react, and that is usually defensively. So, given an opportunity to decide what is the best distance is a beginning in the conflict where each man feels listened to and in control of his life.

After the men have shared what is a comfortable distance (and that may require some negotiating), they are asked to have a moment of silence to "observe" how they are feeling and how the other person is feeling. I also ask them to notice where they feel closed or hurt. To Asians, so much is said nonverbally, that a lot can be learned.

In our group, there are four steps that lead to conflict resolution: stating why you are angry, how and why you were hurt, what you need from the other person to heal, and what you are willing to offer to the other person to begin the healing process. To begin the negotiation process, one agrees to begin while the other person listens without interruption. When the man speaking is finished, the listener must repeat back what he as heard and ask whether there is anything he has left out. If he has, the speaker will let him know what is missing, and the listener repeats it back until everything is accurately stated.

This process is essential to any kind of conflict resolution—accurately acknowledging what is said. Acknowledgment is the first step in feeling validated. So often when we hear why someone is mad at us, we selectively shut out what we don't want to hear or we change what we decide to hear. I know that when I get involved in a conflict, I sometimes stop hearing what's being said and start preparing how I'm going to defend myself. Repeating back what we have heard gives both persons a chance to know that they are being heard. This doesn't mean that both persons have to agree with what they hear, but that they are open to listening to the other's concerns. The Buddhist would call this honoring another person's heart.

So often I have seen the men's fears calmed when they both agreed that they wanted to resolve their conflict. I remember a professor in college who asked his classes every year whether or not they had ever witnessed a conflict resolved in their families. No one had raised their hands in all those years. It seemed so sad to recognize that we all came from families where conflicts weren't resolved, but it also brought up a sense of compassion and understanding why so many conflicts are left unresolved. We all go as far as the extent of our experiences. As a Chinese philosopher once said, "To go in a new direction, we have to take a different path."

So how does the Asian American man express his anger? How does he reconcile the Asian culture with his American counterpart? These are not easy questions to answer or to recognize. I remember the words of the Asian men when they walked into the room for their first meeting.

They all said, "This is like coming home to all your brothers, knowing that you'll be understood and you won't have to explain certain things all the time. Everyone will just understand because they went through the same thing and they know how it feels." But the world outside our group is not the same ethnicity, and so we all have to cope with that difference and our uniqueness.

Being an Asian American is a special culture in itself because it carries the seeds of two worlds. One man in our group described it perfectly. He said, "Here, in America, I'm always faced with never being fully accepted because I'm Japanese and not White. I went back to Japan to reclaim my roots, but once I got there I felt odd and out of place. They saw me as an American. I'm proud of my Japanese heritage, but I didn't fit there either. So who am I?"

There are useful tools and lessons to be learned from both cultures and also tremendous contradictions that have to be dealt with to survive. I remember working for the Shanti Project as a facilitator and being purposely interrupted to see how I would deal with the situation. I remember stopping each time I was interrupted and waiting for the other person to finish talking. No matter how hard I tried I just couldn't interrupt him. There were so many levels of emotions that I felt at that moment. I couldn't interrupt him because, to me, that would be disrespectful. At the same time, I felt that he was being disrespectful to me and that my silence would be seen by him as a sign of how hurt I felt. He didn't notice my silence or he chose to ignore me, which made me feel unseen by a White man once again and also how different I was to other White men. Their persistence of the director to have me "break through something" made me feel like I was not good enough and surely not as bold as White men are. In retrospect, I remember feeling angry at the humiliation and at myself for not meeting their expectations. I felt that I had somehow failed an important ritual of "becoming an American," which most often means not being like a White American man.

My nonacceptance by the White culture also brought up my not feeling accepted by the Chinese community, because I wasn't born in China and I didn't speak my native language. I remembered being called a "banana" (white on the inside and yellow on the outside) and later as "empty bamboo" (Chinese on the outside but empty of tradition and language on the inside). Both terms made me feel isolated and alone.

I remember sharing with an all-White therapists' group that I felt reluctant to talk because even though I would raise my hand to speak next, someone else would interrupt me without being recognized by the facilitator. What was worse was that nobody noticed that I hadn't had a chance to speak. There always seemed to be this sense of urgency in this group that if someone didn't get to speak immediately, he would lose any chance of ever speaking again. I told them of a story I heard about a group of Hawaiian teachers who were asked by their White colleagues why they never spoke and they replied, "Because you never stop talking!"

What I learned from sharing this with my White colleagues was that there was a need to educate and to inform them about Asian ways of listening and sharing that could allow for more dialogue and greater participation from everyone. Most of them agreed and were willing to try things differently. They also really appreciated my saying something. Deep down I would have liked it if they had noticed my pain and spoken up, but perhaps that will happen in the future. For now, it seems that my work is in sharing how I feel unseen and unheard as it happens, just as this chapter and the book as a whole may serve the same purpose. Speaking out may not be safe, but it is necessary.

What I believe that I offer, and the purpose of the Asian Men's Group, is to say that we, as Asians, don't have to imitate the White culture or to be ashamed of our Asian ancestry. There are valuable traits of the Asian culture that are useful and beautiful and that can add and enhance the American culture. What I see is the need for the American culture to respect and not to judge that other cultures that are different are automatically inferior. What is needed is a community of ideas and a welcoming of a diversity of perspectives. Being different can be a thing of beauty and not an obstacle. How we choose to see the world determines how the world perceives us.

Creating as an individual, speaking up for individual rights, and standing up when we experience unjust institutions or corrupt politicians is only a part of the beauty of being born in America. Just as the usefulness in the Asian culture of noticing the words spoken by the face and body, waiting and watching to be sure that everyone had a chance to speak, not interrupting until someone has finished speaking, honoring our communities and our family is important.

## FATHER ISSUE

One of the more intense workshops was about our fathers. So much of how the men in the group viewed themselves was defined by how they felt about their fathers. They were looking for a male mentor who would give them all the things that their fathers couldn't. The most common need was for acceptance. More specifically, they wanted assurances from their fathers that they were proud of their sons and felt good about what they were doing with their lives.

Recently, I had the men write down five failures that they had experienced and to come back in a week to share their list with the entire group. I did this exercise on failure because one of the men shared how difficult it was for him to tell the group about why he was fired from a previous job. He was afraid that the group would somehow look down on him or think less of him. I felt that this failure exercise could somehow take away some of the shame as well as foster support and acceptance among the men that failure was an important and natural part of life.

When the whole group did this failure exercise as homework, they discovered that they were more attuned to their failures and less able to get in touch with their successes. Often the men in the group felt that they weren't doing enough and had they been better prepared they wouldn't have failed. The Asian American men talked about feeling family pressures from their fathers and mothers to always act responsibly and to be prepared—to watch out for failure. There was always this sense that relatives and the community were watching and judging their actions. One of the men pointed out that his father never talked about his failures, but he also never talked about his successes.

The men in the group weren't sure why their fathers didn't share their failures or successes with them, but they did feel that when their fathers talked about being oppressed and being put down by society they felt unprotected and open to the same kinds of racism that their fathers had experienced. Somewhere there was this inadvertent message from their fathers not to let their guard down or they would be harmed and humiliated by the White man. When I continually heard this from my father about Whites, I kept wondering to myself, how could I trust that Whites would honor my efforts or accept my shortcomings if they didn't accept my father, who was more powerful and experienced than I was? I think that at that moment of my recognition about racism towards Asians, I was angry at the world at being so untrustworthy. I was also feeling betrayed by my father, who I had always thought was invincible and protective. I was left with this anger and sense of helplessness that I couldn't express or share with my father. I've often wondered whether my father felt that way too, as a young man. Maybe the only way he knew how to express his anger as he became a father was to warn me about the dangers of trusting anyone outside the family.

So often the men's movement, as described by Robert Bly and others, ignores that men of color aren't just dealing with relationships with their fathers, but also with the impact that White America has had on their fathers, which affected how they dealt with their sons. My father taught me that the world was not a safe place to compete with the White man or to show him anger. Standing up to the White man could mean your job, your chances of promotion, and, in many cases, even your life. He told me never to offend White people or to share any family secrets with them because Whites could not be trusted and might someday use that information against me or our family.

My father also told me to use my education and my wealth as a way of telling Whites that I was better than they were. What he was indirectly saying to me was that I should keep my anger and my hurt to myself. My wealth and my position in life and not my words would be my revenge and my sword. What I learned from my father was that my survival was dependent on my silence and my ability to blend in and to support the White society's values and rules. After all, this was America, and being American meant imitating the White man's ways. We were Chinese, the White man was "American."

It isn't surprising, then, that Asian men have a difficult time expressing their successes and their failures. What they need are assurances from others that their disclosures can be expressed safety, with acceptance and—with honor. The kind of safety that I am speaking about requires that there be trust and compassion on the part of the listener. The listener needs to be supportive and acknowledging and not to interrupt with his or her stories or judgments.

## FATHER WORKSHOP

The Asian men dress up like their fathers and come to the group. We spend a few prior meetings discussing how it feels to ask their fathers for something, as well as how it feels to reveal to their fathers why they need their clothing. Very often, exercises like these bring up old issues of how to communicate with their fathers as well as fears of bringing up old feelings that haven't been resolved. What was interesting was that some of the men communicated through their mothers instead of their fathers to get their fathers' clothing. They seemed to feel safer asking their mothers instead of their fathers, for fear their fathers would laugh at them or not understand.

The men whose fathers had passed away were asked to find clothing that most looked like the type their fathers wore. Having the men play their fathers who had passed away was healthy for the group for several reasons. One, it allowed the other men whose fathers were still alive to deal with their fears of their fathers' dying before they had a chance to reconcile with them. Two, it gave the men whose fathers had passed away an opportunity to deal with some of their grief and anguish at not having their fathers here when they needed them.

Each man who played his "father" was asked to talk about his son (which was himself) and how he experienced their relationship. The "fathers" were also asked to reveal what it was like for them in their families when they were growing up. In the end, each "father" was asked to share with us some wise words that maybe he had wished his father had said to him. When the "fathers" shared their wise words with their sons, it was the kind of acceptance and acknowledgment the men in the group had always dreamed that their fathers would give them. For others, it gave them an opportunity to reveal what they had always felt too vulnerable to ask from their fathers for fear of rejection or abandonment.

This father exercise is important because it affords an opportunity to return to a place where the men in the group felt stuck or good about their fathers, and from there they would perhaps gain some insight into how their relationship with their fathers affects how they are with others today. It also gave the Asian men in the group a chance to receive acceptance and acknowledgment from their "fathers" so they didn't have to go around looking for a father substitute. Too often, we as men carry a "hidden expectation" that a particular man in our lives will heal our father wounds, only to be disappointed and angry again when that man fails us or doesn't give us exactly what we need.

In learning about their fathers' past as well as how they perceived their sons, the Asian men gained some compassion for their fathers' struggle through his perception of their relationship. The men in the group were surprised at how much they knew about their fathers' family histories. When the men in the group came to understand that their fathers were only coming from their own experiences, there was an opportunity for acceptance. Sometimes accepting our fathers means accepting them for who they are without any changes. I remember that when I did this father exercise, I was surprised to recognize how much I wanted my father to "accept" me without any changes, but I insisted on him changing before I could accept him. It was a humbling acknowledgment about the part I played in our relationship.

## ACKNOWLEDGMENT CEREMONY

The acknowledgment ceremony is an opportunity for the group to invite their parents and friends to come and acknowledge them and to share any memorable stories about their relationship together. I found it to be especially important for Asian men and for men of color because it centers on the need for community support and acknowledges the importance of the family.

The ceremony requires a consensus, because each man is needed to participate and to be willing to let it be known in the community that he is a member of this group. Some of the men felt apprehensive about sharing such an intimate experience with their parents. Since 1986, the group has had an acknowledgment ceremony every year. One of the Asian men expressed it quite well. He said, "It's scary to invite your parents here because this has been a special place I come to every Monday night. It's like we're being intruded on and I don't want strangers to come into my home. And yet I know what we've been doing here has been really revolutionary and breaking new ground for Asian men. It's just hard to share that with my friends. I'm afraid they might not understand what I'm doing here, and I'll be embarrassed. What if they don't want to come?"

At first, I had a lot of apprehension about how this ceremony could change the group and all the many ways it could fail and perhaps be very painful for the parents and for them. And yet, deep down, I knew that this opportunity to be acknowledged and accepted publicly by our parents and friends is something each of the men longed for and that I, too, needed.

There is a Japanese term, called "death by overwork," which I believe has a lot to do with the need of Asian men to overachieve because they are starving for acknowledgment and don't know how to ask for it. In so many ways, White society and the Asian culture don't make it easy or safe to ask for acknowledgment. Asian men are often seen as insecure or self-centered if they express what they need emotionally, such as wanting to be listened to, needing to be told they are doing well, or being acknowledged publicly.

Often, the only time we honor someone's achievements is when he or she is dead or retiring. There is really only one time in our lives that we are totally accepted, and that is when we are babies. We don't have to do anything or be anything to be loved—just be ourselves. What a great beginning, and what a tremendous letdown it must be never to have that kind of acceptance and acknowledgment again. I believe this hunger and loss of acceptance are the roots of a lot of anger and violence. Often men who are violent have poor self-esteem and feel powerless and unaccepted in their relationships.

As a way of involving them, the parents and friends are asked to bring something to eat or to drink. The reason for this is because, in the Asian culture, bringing food to someone's house is considered a way of thanking the host and honoring the invitation. We encourage some of the guests who were a bit shy to begin opening up by sharing with someone else what they had made and maybe swap some recipes. Food is such a universal bridge for creating friendships and understanding.

Another exchange we do is pairing folks up with someone they haven't met before and asking them to introduce each other. Sometimes they're asked to share with the group the origin of their names. More recently, they were asked to talk about something they've never shared with anyone. We do this to illustrate the art and gift of listening as well as to create a situation for each person to relate with someone new safely and equally.

## ACKNOWLEDGMENT CEREMONY STORIES

During the ceremony, one of the Asian men who had been divorced for many years had his 8-year-old son turn to him and say, "Dad, I don't want you to go away again. I want you to stay home and play with me while I grow up. I love you, Daddy." They both hugged and cried. The father later shared that he never knew that this decision to leave the area reminded his son of the time he left his family when they divorced. He also didn't know how important it was for his son that his father be there while he grew up. For a long time the father had lived with the shame of having left his family for another woman. He had never quite forgiven himself. His major issue in the group was with commitment and shame. The ceremony was the first step in a renewed relationship with his family and his children, as well as an important beginning in feeling good about himself as a father and as a man.

Another father shared that he wished he had a group like this when he was growing up because he might have been a better father. He also shared that his father never really talked to him and that he wanted it to be different between him and his son. At the end he hugged his son and told him how much he loved him.

There was a Japanese father who stood up and shared that ever since he came to this country he had never used his Japanese name in public. On this night, he shared with us his Japanese name, and there were tears of pride in his eyes as we cried in happiness with him.

These are only a few of the many touching stories that have been told over the past five years that have opened our hearts and moved everyone who came. The acknowledgment ceremony has created a space and an opportunity for the parents to give to their sons what they might have longed for from their parents. As for the Asian men, the ceremony has been a chance to hear from their friends and parents the gift of acceptance and acknowledgment, so that they can feel empowered and good about themselves.

## ISSUES OF RACISM

The issue of racism has a tremendous impact on the Asian American community. Racism in America toward Asians is on the rise and continues to cause a great deal of anguish and pain, even death. To deal with the issue of violence and anger, one must always include racism as a major cause.

When I started the Asian Men's Group in 1985, I attempted to begin with the issue of racism, but I found that the men quickly turned to issues affecting their personal lives, such as girlfriends and family pressures. Why was that? Were they afraid of confronting their ethnicities? Were there too much anger and pain?

As the months progressed, I realized that they were asking me to take them to a different place, one that they hadn't shared with anyone else—a journey through their personal history. What they were asking for was for everyone to share their most intimate secrets and relationships, including me. To them, this was a way of testing the safety and trustworthiness of the group. Over the years, each man realized that this group had become his second family, in many ways, more accepting and more intimate than any family he had ever experienced; that week after week, no matter how difficult it got in the group, no one would leave or abandon him.

When we finally dealt with the issue of racism, we were faced with a great deal of internalized racism. "Internalized racism" is a term that is used to describe the perpetuation by an individual of stereotypes that have been developed about his or her particular ethnic group. For example, when an Asian American woman won't date Asian American men because she has heard that they are wimps, lacking in passion, sexist, and passive, she has "internalized" White society's stereotypes of Asian American men. To break this internalized racism, psychodrama and self-disclosure exercises were used in the group, as well as validation and acknowledgment.

## Racism Workshop

Psychodrama is a powerful tool in reliving a racist experience. If the environment is safe and honest enough, the experience can be used to reenact the pain and anguish. The men in the group created a role play in which a Japanese man is double-parked and a White man drives up and gets out of his car, swearing and using racial epithets.

What came out of the role play was both painful and enlightening. The Japanese man responded to the White man with logic and explanation, trying to appeal to the rational side of the White man. When the Japanese man's explanations failed, he tried to walk away. After the play, the Japanese man explained that, if he had stayed, he probably would have killed the White man.

So often, Asian men and men of color share this fear of "killing" the White man if they were to reveal their anger to them. The Asian men in the group expressed that they had never felt safe enough to believe that their anger would be well received or acknowledged by White men, and so they kept their anger inside themselves. In my experience, not once on television or in the movies have I witnessed a White man listening to the anguish and pain of an Asian American man, let alone a White man acknowledging the validity of an Asian American man's anger. What I have seen is White men rescuing Asians, as if they were too weak, emotionally and physically, to help themselves without the powerful, handsome, articulate White American man. My father's childhood stories of winning in a situation were only of how a White man came to his rescue, but never of himself winning the day and never of another Chinese man coming to his aid.

Many of the men in the group deeply identified with the Japanese man in the role play. They shared how humiliated they felt in a similar situation and how they also feared for their lives. The men told about how they felt angry and ashamed of themselves for not having "stood up" and defended themselves, verbally and physically. Racism causes self-hatred and self-mutilation: a mutilation of the Asian American man's image as a powerful and articulate father, warrior, and lover. When that kind of emotional destruction is passed on from one generation to another in the form of warnings from our fathers to watch out for the White man and limitations on the type of careers we can pursue, then it degrades and diminishes the community and its potential to develop powerful leaders.

The Asian men in the group related how their fathers told them to plan for the future, to postpone any kind of anger they were feeling now. They were told to go to college and to get a good-paying job. My father used to say, "When you have a good home and a good job, then the White men will have to look up at you. For now, let them call you names. How can that hurt you? They are only stupid. You know who you are." The trouble I had with my father's statement was that, at 12 years old, I *didn't* know who I was. I think my father was afraid and unsure of himself at my age too, but later pride and shame kept him from revealing that part of himself to his sons. I also think that Asian fathers warn their children to be careful and to avoid trouble, because they want to protect them from disappointment and racist responses. However, the problem with this type of postponement is that if you don't get the great education or the great home in the suburbs, does that mean that you're not as good as the White man? Or if you do get a good education and have a good house, does that mean you won't experience racism?

The man who played the part of the White man was ecstatic at the amount of rage and racism he could express. Yelling at the top of his voice without the fear of reprisal and being able to threaten bodily harm were just two of the new emotions he felt. He was exhilarated and overwhelmed at the extent of power being a White man encompassed. The use of the White mask was helpful because he felt like a "new person" removed from his usual cultural restraints of honor and modesty. Also, the mask hid his emotions, so he could just rely on his voice and body gestures. The mask was appropriate because the men in the group often talked about how "unfeeling and invulnerable" Whites looked when they called them racist names. With the mask, this man could hide his uncertainty—he could be cruel and outrageous without any emotional limitation. There are ample models of White men reacting out of control and full of rage on television and at the movies that the Asian man could imitate but, as usual, very few Asian models with the same kind of emotions.

To heal the pain of feeling humiliated, the Japanese man who played the victim in the role play was encouraged to talk about what he had "lost" in this experience and the grief he felt at not being able to fully express the rage and humiliation. What came up for the other men in the group were feelings of being unsupported and invalidated in their own lives when they told their White friends about what had happened to them during a racist experience. Some of the reasons their White friends gave for racist remarks were that the White man was probably having a "bad day at work," the Asian man probably misunderstood what the White person said, or the incident didn't really happen. The men in the group also told of other cases, where the White person who was listening related about worst cases of racism he had heard of, thereby diminishing the Asian American man's experience. I remember when I told a White counselor about a painful racist experience, she started to tell me about a similar experience she had gone through. When she finished, I felt somehow obligated to take care of her. In any case, I felt that my story was not as important as hers, even though somehow her experience was supposed to make me feel better.

The dilemma facing Asian men is that if they tell someone else what happened to them, they are often invalidated. If the Asian men don't say anything, they are left to "swallow their anger" and to feel ashamed. No wonder our fathers protected us. An Asian man to express his anger was often in a no-win situation. The purpose of the Asian Men's Group is to support each man in "reclaiming" his power and rightful place in American society by listening and validating his experience. Notice that I use *reclaim*, not the word *empower*. To reclaim means that Asian Americans always had what they were told was missing in them; they need only reclaim their power. For example, White America portrays Asian Americans as passive and inarticulate, while in fact they may be merely listening and waiting for an opportunity to speak. This differs from *empower*, which connotes that power needs to be given.

Recently, the Asian men talked about what they had lost because of racism. They talked about losing their sense of pride, safety, and powerfulness. They also shared a loss of seeing people as individuals. Now they viewed people as "ethnic groups," not as individuals. One of the men said, "Not only did I lose my trust of other people, but I also lost trust in myself. I no longer felt as self-assured and confident. I felt more guarded and watchful." Another Asian man related, "I lost my sense of commonness with other people, that we were all alike. I realized I couldn't walk into North Carolina without feeling defensive and isolated." A Chinese American man in the group said, "What I lost was this sense that my dreams had no boundaries. I lost my feeling of being accepted and having pride in myself. Now I felt I was in competition with other groups for acceptance by Whites."

What the Asian Men's Group offers a survivor of racism is a chance to grieve about his loss and his betrayal, his anguish and his shame. This is important, because the group validates that indeed something did happen, something horrible and unjust was done. These "reality statements" are necessary to help with the giving process because when an act of betrayal occurs, being able to trust someone else to hear your story and to believe you is essential to feeling safe again. So often as American men, we are told to avoid grief and to keep a "stiff upper lip" and to "hold up our end." But the grieving process is necessary to the anger process. Often anger is not our first emotion. Many times we get angry because our hurt is not seen or validated. When our hurt is acknowledged, so is our anger. However, I think that in the case of Asian American men, when their anger is not validated or safe to express, they feel sure that their hurt will not be, either.

In our group, after the grieving process has started, the survivor of racism has the opportunity to "reclaim" what he has lost. He does this by declaring in front of the whole group what he wants back. He can also choose to reenter the role play and act out what he wanted to say and do the first time. When he finishes what he needs to say, he is then acknowledged and validated by the White man in the role play. Having a second try at something we have failed at or feel ashamed about is very rare in life. So what the group offers the men is a chance to reframe their past, to complete their anger, to feel validated and acknowledged, to "reclaim" their power.

In 1991 I wrote a poem that best describes my "reclaiming" of my birth name and all the other things that I felt that White America had me feel that I was missing. I dedicated the poem to my father and my grandfather whose courage and perseverance inspired me to reclaim my birthright to be honored and respected for who I am.

**Bok Fan**

> I never knew that my eyes were not as opened as yours
> that the color of my skin was yellow
> that these words I spoke were harsh and foreign.
> I always thought that this land of my birth
> this place were I took my first breath
> was the same as yours.
> When I was young, I thought we both ate horn yeur ging gee yook,
> bok fan see you guy and lop cheung

The same as any family coming home from work.
I did not know that my foods were strange or smelled
Just as I never knew my quietness would be seen as weak
My waiting, a sign that I was empty and without fire.
I was taught that waiting was a sign of virtue and an honor
And that the eyes and heart were more direct than words.
But I have learned; you do not follow the path of my hands
or hear the words of my eyes.
You do not smell the sweet fire of the blackbean
or lower your eyes to honor the old ones.
Instead, you speak over my words
Call me "little" as if I were a child
Decide that I cannot sing the sweet songs of love
or hold a woman with my tenderness alone.
You have stolen the dragon's fire from my father's lips
And now you seek to rob me of a warrior's life.
Do you not see the blood that you have spilled
or the children you have shamed?
*See me now.*
My name is Lee Mun Wah. My name is Lee Mun Wah.


## CONCLUSION

How to deal with anger in the Asian American community is not only complex but also difficult to understand, because there is so little information available or groups working on this issue. The Asian Men's Group that I founded in 1985 is a 6-year study about six men, of whom four are from the original group. What I have written is only a small glimpse of some of the many issues and feelings that Asian American men are experiencing today. Nonetheless, the work in this group is important because it represents a way of working with Asian American men that has helped create choices in the ways that they can express their anger and feel validated and powerful. It has also shown how their families have affected how they dealt with anger and how racism creates and reinforces self hatred and distrust of others.

One of the challenges for Asian Americans is the issue of assimilation to decide for ourselves what part of the American culture works for us and which part is demeaning and insulting to our heritage. As Asian Americans, we need to also sift through our Asian culture and embrace what is meaningful, useful, and necessary for our self-esteem and identity without feeling compromised or ashamed. The difficult work that lies ahead is how to bring our "blended selves" into mainstream America to be seen and accepted as passionate, powerful, and articulate Asian Americans. Until that time comes, there needs to be places and ways in which Asian Americans can safely express their anger and hurt in safe and validating environments.

# Epilogue

JERRY TELLO AND RICARDO CARRILLO

It is the belief of indigenous people of all roots that we are part of a larger story and that each of us has a role to play and a lesson to teach. Life is a duality and carries with it both the beautiful and the painful lessons. The painful part of the lesson that we have focused on is that of family violence and the men that struggle with this imbalance. It is the responsibility of all of us because we know it not only hurts the victim but the offender and the interconnected web of people who make up the family and human circle.

In truth, the task of presenting a reflection of this issue and its implications was no easy journey, but one that needed to be traveled and explored. Not that the knowledge and experience was not present, but attempting to find "the way" to convey the necessary teachings in a respectful and honorable manner was a lesson in itself. It took a total of *seven* years to complete this circle, a number that is held sacred in many traditions. Along the path there were many obstacles, lessons, and blessings that accompanied us. The authors attempted to share their knowledge and experience in a respectful way with an eye toward balancing the traditional indigenous teachings and that of Western contemporary theory and practice. The result is a reflection of teachings and challenges for all of us to discuss while searching for the interconnected healing for all involved.

In this volume Etiony Aldorondo set the foundation by reminding us that family violence is an international epidemic and that research indicates that comprehensive and varied approaches are more effective. More significantly in this context, the issue of race is a significant factor, and that a social justice approach is necessary for the cessation of all violence and support of human rights.

Research has begun to suggest that some studies reveal that marital violence may be partially due to these historical experiences of institutional racism, integrated oppression, and colonialism. Finally, the findings substantiate the lack of culturally competent literature, research, and treatment models in the areas of family violence and men of color.

In the subsequent chapters, which focus on the Latino population, Ricardo Carrillo and Jerry Tello demonstrate the significance of culturally syntonic aspects of theory and intervention processes. Through the discussion and use of narrative processing (storytelling), cultural indigenous teachings, ceremony; ritual, and traditional healing, they stress the significance of identity and culture and the integrated impact of colonialism and multi generational oppression. Through the utilization of a story, Tello lays the groundwork for seeing family violence within the context of young men lost on the journey to manhood. He further reveals in "The Bridge Story" the multigenerational lessons that are never learned by some while attempting to cross the bridge to maturity, thus leading to wounded men with false lessons. He then challenges us to consider the re-traumatization that occurs daily to victims and offenders by stating:

> We see how it becomes necessary not only to address the imbalanced, violent behavior that is a symptom of a deeper, self-denigrating spiritual identity violation but to address it in the context of the total past and present-day social-historical oppression.

Carrillo and Zarza present an integrated model of substance abuse, domestic violence, and trauma. The authors begin the next chapter by stressing the importance of family in the treatment of domestic violence. Carrillo states, "The end result of the present day system appears to have essentially taken the 'family' out of family violence." He offers a culturally based treatment process that combines clinical treatment with indigenous, culturally sensitive healing practices. Then, as echoed by all the other authors, Carrillo speaks to the impact of European colonialization on Latino men.

Latino men are traditionally socialized to protect their family and the paradox is that after several periods of colonialization they have become the oppressor in their own home.

It is his premise that domestic violence in the Latino male population has its roots in European colonialization. Dr. Carrillo gives specific examples of the significance and the use of ceremony, spirituality, symbols, music, and metaphors. "The use of these cultural processes allows for the unfreezing of the dysfunctional thoughts and behaviors that contribute to the violence." Finally he speaks to the importance for lifelong healing in the need for a culturally based support group of men (compadres) who are not afraid to reject violence in their communities. The model is summarized by addressing personal learning of intimate partner violence, historical colonial violence, the impact of trauma on continued IPV and community violence, and the healing of the impact of the violence. Social justice, accountability, and providing a model (National Compadres Network) for developing safe communities are what all the groups advocate in this book.

Dr. Oliver Williams begins the next chapter with an allegory depicting the African American male as an endangered species. The healthy individual "tend(s) to flourish in environments that match their capabilities."

In this chapter Dr. Williams examines the inordinate amount of stressors that African American men have historically faced and continue to face just to maintain their purpose or "rhythm" in life. Williams, in this chapter, challenges the conventional explanation of domestic violence as merely based in gender inequality and man's attempt to maintain control. He states

> The intersection of race, social status, social context, and violence creates a set of issues that have typically not been discussed in the literature on domestic violence. . . . before we can truly understand violence perpetrated by African American males there must be a critique of the African American man's experience in the United States.

Truly this view would dictate a much larger scope of training, understanding, and development for anyone wanting to treat African American offenders. Williams goes on to outline his philosophy and the basis for addressing effectively the issue of domestic violence and the African American male.

An enriched perspective retains the beliefs presently held in the field of partner abuse, but it differs because African American male perspectives are included as ingredients that shape the treatment content and design. For example, there is no justification for partner abuse; men who batter must take responsibility and be held accountable for their behavior; violent men must learn alternatives to violence and controlling, sexist attitudes and behaviors. Accordingly, culturally competent programs will also include traditional and alternative explanations for violence among African American men who batter in approaches to treatment. Treatment interventions must incorporate these explanations and make the link between these explanations and the man's behavior. Violent African American men must learn how to negotiate life challenges arising from social context and environment. In domestic violence treatment groups and in the African American community, it is essential to address healing, identity, and community responsibility.

In this updated revision Williams articulates the historical development of research, social structural change, and modifications and adaptations of progress in the field. A new generation of young African American men are now struggling with IPV.

Ulester Douglas, Sulaiman Nuriddin, and Phyllis Alesia Perry explain in detail a very radical and innovative approach to working with African American men in BIP. Race matters to them, and they skillfully portray ways of integrating sexist, racist, and ecologically political ideology that explains how oppressive intimate partner violence is learned. They also share historical antecedents for family violence from the post-slavery and civil rights periods of time. Men Stoppping Violence is a model of cultural and political conciousness that needs to be studied and learned to successfully engage and re-educate men about their violence.

In the Chapter 6, Eduardo Duran, Bonnie Duran, and others guide us through an in-depth understanding of a postcolonial perspective on domestic violence in Indian country. Wilbur and Pamela Woodis begin by sharing a dream narrative that extends the view that domestic violence is reflective of "caging" the spirit of the Indian culture. In a field that has virtually ignored the Indian population in research and treatment, the authors offer insightful and relevant knowledge and experience. They urge the additional focus needed for the Indian population by stating:

> Through the collective clinical and community work that the authors have been doing over the past 20 years, it is safe to say that there is at least as much domestic violence in Indian country as there is in the rest of society.

On the same note they emphasize the need for culturally relevant models.

> Many of the models for treatment are based on Western interventions. Imposing these models of intervention on Indian people would merely perpetuate another form of violence and further colonization on our community. . . . By this we mean that they partake in ideological/cultural domination by the assertion of universality and neutrality and by the disavowal of all other cultural forms or interpretations.

In a continued criticism of conventional interventions, the authors share:

> Many of the approaches that pretend to heal the pain of domestic violence instead seek someone to victimize and blame.

They too concur with other authors in this book as they speak to the effects of oppression.

> Recent literature clearly demonstrates how historical trauma continues to manifest itself in all types of unhealthy behavior patterns across Indian country. . . . Within the internalized oppression paradigm, male dynamics have a specific expression:
> The Lakota wicasa, or man, was robbed of his traditional role as hunter, protector, and provider. He lost status and honor. This negatively impacted his relationship with Lakota women and children. A further assault on the Lakota and all Indian peoples was the prohibition against indigenous spiritual practices in 1883 (quoting Braveheart-Jordan and DeBruyn).

Later in this chapter Duran and coworkers offer an indigenous based framework to view and treat domestic violence. This profound insight allows us to expand our perception of domestic violence from an indigenous perspective.

> If you are male, a female stands inside you; if you are female, a male stands inside you. In offering pollen in prayer in this manner, a balance in soul and a balance in nature are attained and maintained. This balancing ritual between the two life forces of male and female serves to remind both sides of the interrelationship and respect due each other.

In Chapter 7, Daryl Gregory fleshes out the move from colonialization to rebuilding a nation through ceremony, behavioral practices, song, poetry, and metaphor in the life of Māori men. Together they build their future for their families, symbolized by He Waka Tapu (the sacred canoe), just as their forefathers prepared to cross the wide ocean to New Zealand.

In the final chapters, Benjamin Tong and Lee Mun Wah look into Asian men and domestic violence. Dr. Tong begins by summarizing the political, historical, social, and psychological context in which violence is supported and condoned. Tong continues by offering his perspective that

> The etiological roots of domestic abuse—whether physical, emotional, or sexual—are to be found in four interrelated phenomena: problems of adaptation, cross-cultural clashes, racist oppression, and repressive heritage.

He goes on to stress the importance of culture in one's view and behavior in the world.

> A people's deepest beliefs and worldviews, or mythos, provide for a coherent narrative to address three fundamental concerns that cut across collective existence as well as individual lives: (1) history, a sense of the past, or "who we have always been"; (2) identity, a sense of the present, or who we are, or should be, right now"; and (3) destiny, a sense of the future, or "who we are meant to be." Events such as war, economic chaos, and natural disasters disrupt the substance and continuity of all three. . . . Long before an Asian American abuses spouse or children, he has already suffered flagrant and wholesale abuse.

Finally, Tong leaves us with the importance of considering migration and its effects.

> Coupled with the adaptational demands of migration (particularly for recent newcomers) and the conflicts resulting from the clash of cultures and White cultural domination, these powerful forces have shaped the special arena within which Asian American domestic violence, in all its forms, is played out.

The second author in this section, Lee Mun Wah, continues the discussion of these issues utilizing a narrative flow to reveal the personal nature of domestic violence and healing. In a personal reflection he offers,

> One day I got really mad at one of the men in the group. One of the other men said he thought I wasn't being angry enough. I was furious; I told him that for an Asian man I was really angry. . . . What I learned was that

working through anger is not something that can be taught in isolation or without the recognition of one's cultural background.

Mun Wah gives us insight not only into anger and Asian men but how important the cultural influences are. "None of the [Asian] men in the group had ever witnessed anger being resolved in their families." He continues by reflecting the needs of Asian men in dealing with domestic violence.

> I came to realize after a few weeks that each of the men in the group needed something from myself and the rest of the group that they weren't getting from their families or their communities: acknowledgment and support to explore their fears, their anger, their relationships, their hurt, their dreams, and their desires.

From here on he guides the process and the thinking behind working with Asian men and domestic violence. He concludes,

> What I see is the need for the American culture to respect and not to judge that other cultures that are different are automatically inferior. . . . How we choose to see the world determines how the world perceives us.

## CONCLUSION

This writing was more than an exercise in theoretical formulation—it was a journey of dialogue, prayer, ceremony, and healing. Authors from various roots concurred on several important points.

1. *Race matters.*
2. The field is sorely lacking in research and treatment models to assist in the healing of men of color and domestic violence; however, there have been strides to overcome the paucity of research and treatment.
3. The present models not only are not adequate but, many times, mirror the violence and control that we are attempting to address. Humanistic, holistic, approaches with an emphasis on social justice are promising.
4. A major root cause of domestic violence and men of color is in the historical oppression and violence that people of color have experienced and continue to experience today.

5.  Spirituality is a foundational element needed in the assessment and healing processes in working with men of color.
6.  The integrated inclusion of family/community as part of the healing and ongoing recovery process is essential.

In the traditional way, we end as we began: by acknowledging that we the authors are merely messengers (of the creator) of healing and learning. We attempted in no way to purport ourselves as the experts. We have offered not the final word but just another perspective to encourage the dialogue. With this in mind we apologize if, through this process, we have offended. In a consistent manner with the teachings we offer men in the healing process, we take full responsibility for what we have shared. Our hope is and has always been that what we have offered can contribute in a positive way toward the healing of all people so that the children and the subsequent generations can live in a world filled with peace, harmony, and an affirmed purpose in life.

The elders share that many of us have lived through seven generations of pain and it will take seven generations to heal, so we must start now.

Con Cariño Y Respeto

# Index